*To Christina for ... Christmas 2018*

*Love, Cynth*

# THE NEW FOLGER LIBRARY SHAKESPEARE

Designed to make Shakespeare's great plays available to all readers, the New Folger Library edition of Shakespeare's plays provides accurate texts in modern spelling and punctuation, as well as scene-by-scene action summaries, full explanatory notes, many pictures clarifying Shakespeare's language, and notes recording all significant departures from the early printed versions. Each play is prefaced by a brief introduction, by a guide to reading Shakespeare's language, and by accounts of his life and theater. Each play is followed by an annotated list of further readings and by a "Modern Perspective" written by an expert on that particular play.

Barbara A. Mowat is Director of Research *emerita* at the Folger Shakespeare Library, Consulting Editor of *Shakespeare Quarterly*, and author of *The Dramaturgy of Shakespeare's Romances* and of essays on Shakespeare's plays and their editing.

Paul Werstine is Professor of English in the Graduate School and at King's University College at Western University. He is a general editor of the New Variorum Shakespeare and author of *Early Modern Playhouse Manuscripts and the Editing of Shakespeare*, as well as many papers and essays on the printing and editing of Shakespeare's plays.

# Folger Shakespeare Library

The Folger Shakespeare Library in Washington, D.C., is a privately funded research library dedicated to Shakespeare and the civilization of early modern Europe. It was founded in 1932 by Henry Clay and Emily Jordan Folger, and incorporated as part of Amherst College in Amherst, Massachusetts, one of the nation's oldest liberal arts colleges, from which Henry Folger had graduated in 1879. In addition to its role as the world's preeminent Shakespeare collection and its emergence as a leading center for Renaissance studies, the Folger Shakespeare Library offers a wide array of cultural and educational programs and services for the general public.

EDITORS

### BARBARA A. MOWAT
*Director of Research emerita*
*Folger Shakespeare Library*

### PAUL WERSTINE
*Professor of English*
*King's University College at the University of Western Ontario, Canada*

FOLGER SHAKESPEARE LIBRARY

# Antony and Cleopatra

By

## WILLIAM SHAKESPEARE

EDITED BY BARBARA A. MOWAT
AND PAUL WERSTINE

SIMON & SCHUSTER PAPERBACKS
NEW YORK  LONDON  TORONTO  SYDNEY

Simon & Schuster Paperbacks
A Division of Simon & Schuster, Inc.
1230 Avenue of the Americas
New York, NY 10020

Copyright © 1999 by The Folger Shakespeare Library

Washington Square Press New Folger Edition October 1999
This Simon & Schuster paperback edition February 2010

SIMON & SCHUSTER PAPERBACKS and colophon are
registered trademarks of Simon & Schuster, Inc.

For information regarding special discounts for bulk purchases,
please contact Simon & Schuster Special Sales at
1-866-506-1949 or business@simonandschuster.com.

The Simon & Schuster Speakers Bureau can bring authors to your
live event. For more information or to book an event, contact the
Simon & Schuster Speakers Bureau at 1-866-248-3049 or visit our
website at www.simonspeakers.com.

Manufactured in the United States of America

20   19   18   17

ISBN 978-0-7434-8285-1

## From the Director of the Folger Shakespeare Library

It is hard to imagine a world without Shakespeare. Since their composition four hundred years ago, Shakespeare's plays and poems have traveled the globe, inviting those who see and read his works to make them their own.

Readers of the New Folger Editions are part of this on-going process of "taking up Shakespeare," finding our own thoughts and feelings in language that strikes us as old or unusual and, for that very reason, new. We still struggle to keep up with a writer who could think a mile a minute, whose words paint pictures that shift like clouds. These expertly edited texts, presented here with accompanying explanatory notes and up-to-date critical essays, are distinctive because of what they do: they allow readers not simply to keep up, but to engage deeply with a writer whose works invite us to think, and think again.

These New Folger Editions of Shakespeare's plays are also special because of where they come from. The Folger Shakespeare Library in Washington, DC, where the Editions are produced, is the single greatest documentary source of Shakespeare's works. An unparalleled collection of early modern books, manuscripts, and artwork connected to Shakespeare, the Folger's holdings have been consulted extensively in the preparation of these texts. The Editions also reflect the expertise gained through the regular performance of Shakespeare's works in the Folger's Elizabethan Theater.

I want to express my deep thanks to editors Barbara Mowat and Paul Werstine for creating these indispensable editions of Shakespeare's works, which incorporate the best of textual scholarship with a richness of commentary that is both inspired and engaging. Readers who want to know more about Shakespeare and his plays can follow the paths these distinguished scholars have tread by visiting the Folger itself, where a range of physical and digital resources (available online) exist to supplement the material in these texts. I commend to you these words, and hope that they inspire.

*Michael Witmore*
Director, Folger Shakespeare Library

# Contents

# Contents

# Editors' Preface

In recent years, ways of dealing with Shakespeare's texts and with the interpretation of his plays have been undergoing significant change. This edition, while retaining many of the features that have always made the Folger Shakespeare so attractive to the general reader, at the same time reflects these current ways of thinking about Shakespeare. For example, modern readers, actors, and teachers have become interested in the differences between, on the one hand, the early forms in which Shakespeare's plays were first published and, on the other hand, the forms in which editors through the centuries have presented them. In response to this interest, we have based our edition on what we consider the best early printed version of a particular play (explaining our rationale in a section called "An Introduction to This Text") and have marked our changes in the text—unobtrusively, we hope, but in such a way that the curious reader can be aware that a change has been made and can consult the "Textual Notes" to discover what appeared in the early printed version.

Current ways of looking at the plays are reflected in our brief prefaces, in many of the commentary notes, in the annotated lists of "Further Reading," and especially in each play's "Modern Perspective," an essay written by an outstanding scholar who brings to the reader his or her fresh assessment of the play in the light of today's interests and concerns.

As in the Folger Library General Reader's Shakespeare, which this edition replaces, we include explanatory notes designed to help make Shakespeare's language clearer to a modern reader, and we place the notes on the page facing the text that they explain. We also follow the earlier edition in including illustrations—of objects, of clothing, of mythological figures—from books and manuscripts in the Folger Library collection. We provide fresh accounts of the life of Shakespeare, of the publishing of his plays, and of the theaters in which his plays were performed, as well as an introduction to the text itself. We also include a section called "Reading Shakespeare's Language," in which we try to help readers learn to "break the code" of Elizabethan poetic language.

For each section of each volume, we are indebted to a host of generous experts and fellow scholars. The "Reading Shakespeare's Language" sections, for example, could not have been written had not Arthur King, of Brigham Young University, and Randall Robinson, author of *Unlocking Shakespeare's Language*, led the way in untangling Shakespearean language puzzles and shared their insights and methodologies generously with us. "Shakespeare's Life" profited by the careful reading given it by the late S. Schoenbaum, "Shakespeare's Theater" was read and strengthened by Andrew Gurr and John Astington, and "The Publication of Shakespeare's Plays" is indebted to the comments of Peter W. M. Blayney. We, as editors, take sole responsibility for any errors in our editions.

We are grateful to the authors of the "Modern Perspectives"; to Leeds Barroll and David Bevington for their generous encouragement; to the Huntington and Newberry Libraries for fellowship support; to King's College for the grants it has provided to Paul Werstine; to the Social Sciences and Humanities Research Council of Canada, which provided him with a Research Time Stipend for 1990–91; to R. J. Shroyer of the University of Western Ontario for essential computer support; to the Folger Institute's Center for Shakespeare Studies for its fortuitous sponsorship of a workshop on "Shakespeare's Texts for Students and Teachers" (funded by the National Endowment for the Humanities and led by Richard Knowles of the University of Wisconsin), a workshop from which we learned an enormous amount about what is wanted by college and high-school teachers of Shakespeare today; and especially to Steve Llano, our production editor at Pocket Books, whose expertise and attention to detail are essential to this project.

Our biggest debt is to the Folger Shakespeare Library—to Werner Gundersheimer, Director of the Library, who made possible our edition; to Deborah Curren-Aquino, who provides extensive editorial and production support; to Jean Miller, the Library's Art Curator, who combs the Library holdings for illustrations, and to Julie Ainsworth, Head of the Photography Department, who carefully photographs them; to Peggy O'Brien, former Director of Education at the Folger and now Director of Education Programs at the Corporation for Public Broadcasting, who gave us expert advice about the needs being expressed by Shakespeare teachers and students (and to Martha Christian and other "master teachers" who used our texts in manuscript in their classrooms); to Allan Shnerson and Kevin Madden for their expert computer support; to the staff of the Academic Programs Division, especially Rachel Kunkle, Mary Tonkinson, Kathleen Lynch, Keira Roberts, Carol Brobeck, Kelleen Zubick, Toni Krieger, and Martha Fay; and, finally, to the generously supportive staff of the Library's Reading Room.

Barbara A. Mowat and Paul Werstine

# THE LIVES

## OF THE NOBLE GRE-
### CIANS AND ROMANES, COMPARED

*together by that graue learned Philosopher and Historiogra-
pher, Plutarke of Chæronea:*

Tranſlated out of Greeke into French by I A M E S A M Y O T, Abbot of Bellozane,
Biſhop of Auxerre, one of the Kings priuy counſel, and great Amner
of Fraunce, and out of French into Engliſhe, by
*Thomas North.*

*A Clerrk to write*

Imprinted at London by Thomas Vautroullier dvvelling
in the Blacke Friers by Ludgate.
1 5 7 9.

Title page of the primary source for *Antony and Cleopatra*.

# Shakespeare's
## *Antony and Cleopatra*

In *Antony and Cleopatra*, Shakespeare dramatizes a major event in world history, the founding of the Roman Empire around 30 BCE. Rome's first emperor, Octavius Caesar (later to be called Augustus Caesar), has a prominent role in the play. In Shakespeare's presentation of Octavius Caesar's steady and, from our point of view, inevitable rise to supreme power, the future emperor controls much of the play's action by skillfully and cold-bloodedly manipulating the other characters. This control is matched in its relentlessness only by the iron control that he exercises over himself, banishing from his life both conviviality and emotion. When the play begins, Caesar, as a member of Republican Rome's second and last triumvirate, shares the governance of the city-state and its European, Asiatic, and African colonies. His fellow rulers are Mark Antony, Rome's preeminent military leader, and the much weaker Lepidus. As long as Caesar needs Antony's forces and military reputation in order to fend off other Roman strongmen, like Pompey, Caesar seeks to bind Antony to him. Caesar goes so far as to offer his widowed sister Octavia to Antony as a bride to cement the men's alliance against Pompey, even though Antony's notorious reputation as a libertine makes the success of such a marriage doubtful and even though the rivalry between the new brothers-in-law is of long standing and threatens to break out again whenever they may later disagree.

As soon as Caesar manages to defeat Pompey, the future emperor no longer needs allies. So he brings

charges against Lepidus and denies Antony a share in
the spoils acquired in Pompey's defeat. Once Octavia
returns to Caesar, he suddenly turns against Antony and
quickly seizes cities in the eastern Roman colonies that
Antony rules. Now Shakespeare's stage is set for the
final conflict between the soon-to-be-supreme Octavius
Caesar and the once-preeminent Antony.

Perhaps because the outcome of this conflict was so
familiar to Shakespeare's audience, the dramatist does
not give its representation much emphasis. Instead he
directs attention toward those whom Caesar defeats,
Antony and the Egyptian Queen Cleopatra, Antony's
wealthy ally who pays for a great part of their costly war
against Caesar. While Shakespeare in no way mitigates
either the flaws in Antony and Cleopatra that contribute
to their defeat or the bitterness of the loss, he also grants
his defeated heroes opportunities to best their conquer-
or Caesar. He first has them rise above the self-repressed
Caesar in their love for each other. Antony is the envy of
the Roman military caste because he has enjoyed the
woman whom earlier Roman great men, like Julius
Caesar, had loved. Cleopatra is an object of enduring
fascination to the Romans: "Age cannot wither her, nor
custom stale / Her infinite variety." The play does not
sugar over their famous love affair; instead Shakespeare
puts on stage Cleopatra's calculated attempts to seduce
Antony from his responsibilities in Rome, as well as
Antony's jealous rages and threats against Cleopatra's
life when he thinks she has betrayed him to Caesar.
Nonetheless, Antony and Cleopatra are represented as
finding together such sensual and emotional satisfaction
in their love for each other that each yearns for an
afterlife in which they may renew their union. Shakespeare lavishes such rich figurative language on his
heroes' recollection of their shared past and dreams of a
future together that Caesar's success in the business of

world conquest seems a smaller thing than what Antony and Cleopatra have found in each other.

Shakespeare also has Antony and Cleopatra rise above their conqueror in a second way as they attempt to frustrate his dearest wish. It is not enough for Caesar that he has beaten Antony and Cleopatra in war. He wants to capture for himself the fame of the defeated heroes by dragging them as captives at his chariot wheels through the streets of Rome in a triumphal procession that will be remembered forever because of their role in it. Much of what is presented in the concluding acts of Shakespeare's love tragedy concerns the struggle not over who will win the military contests but over which images of Antony and Cleopatra are going to be handed down throughout subsequent history—images of humiliated captives or of triumphant lovers.

After you have read the play, we invite you to turn to the essay printed after it, "*Antony and Cleopatra*: A Modern Perspective," written by Professor Cynthia Marshall of Rhodes College.

# Reading Shakespeare's Language:
## *Antony and Cleopatra*

For many people today, reading Shakespeare's language can be a problem—but it is a problem that can be solved. Those who have studied Latin (or even French or German or Spanish), and those who are used to reading poetry, will have little difficulty understanding the language of Shakespeare's poetic drama. Others, though, need to develop the skills of untangling unusual sen-

A map of the Roman Empire.

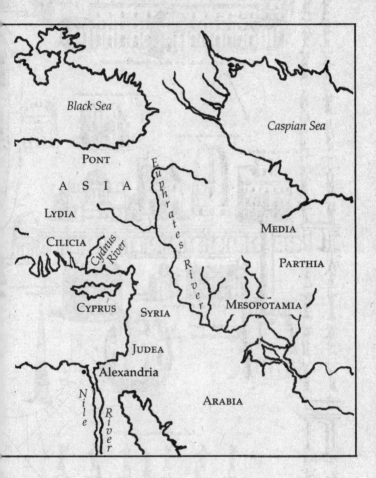

Stephen Llano; based on John Speed, *A prospect of the most famous parts of the world . . .* (1631).

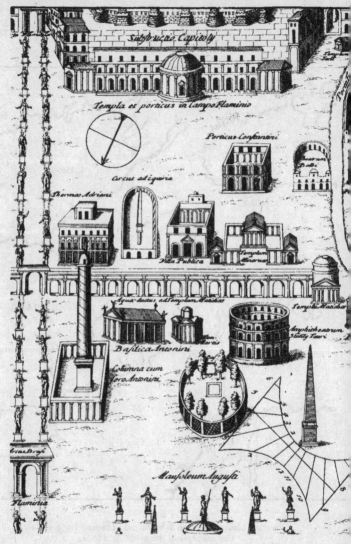

Rome, bounded on the right by the Tiber River.
From Alessandro Donati, *Roma* (1694).

Alexandria.

LAC MAREOTIS

COLONNE DE POMPEE

PORTADELPEPE

MO SAVEE

CHATEAV NEVP

CHATEAV VIEIE

PORTE DE LA MARINE

PORTO VECHIO

From Pierre Belon, *Les observations de plusieurs singularitez . . .* (1588).

tence structures and of recognizing and understanding poetic compressions, omissions, and wordplay. And even those skilled in reading unusual sentence structures may have occasional trouble with Shakespeare's words. Four hundred years of "static" intervene between his speaking and our hearing. Most of his immense vocabulary is still in use, but a few of his words are not, and, worse, some of his words now have meanings quite different from those they had in the sixteenth century. In the theater, most of these difficulties are solved for us by actors who study the language and articulate it for us so that the essential meaning is heard—or, when combined with stage action, is at least *felt*. When reading on one's own, one must do what each actor does: go over the lines (often with a dictionary close at hand) until the puzzles are solved and the lines yield up their poetry and the characters speak in words and phrases that are, suddenly, rewarding and wonderfully memorable.

## Shakespeare's Words

As you begin to read the opening scenes of a play by Shakespeare, you may notice occasional unfamiliar words. Some are unfamiliar simply because we no longer use them. In the opening scenes of *Antony and Cleopatra*, for example, you will find the words *dismission* (i.e., discharge), *homager* (i.e., tenant or vassal to a feudal lord), *belike* (i.e., perhaps), and *methinks* (i.e., it seems to me). Words of this kind are explained in notes to the text and will become familiar the more of Shakespeare's plays you read.

In *Antony and Cleopatra*, as in all of Shakespeare's writing, more problematic are the words that we still use but that we use with a different meaning. In the opening scene of *Antony and Cleopatra,* for example, the word *property* has the meaning of "distinctive quality," *full* is used where we would say "very," *ambassadors* is used where we would say "messengers," and *still* where we would say "always." Such words will be explained in the notes to the text, but they, too, will become familiar as you continue to read Shakespeare's language.

Some words are strange not because of the "static" introduced by changes in language over the past centuries but because these are words that Shakespeare is using to build dramatic worlds that have their own space, time, and history. In the first two acts of *Antony and Cleopatra,* for example, Shakespeare conjures up two such worlds. The first is Rome, which is vigorously engaged in empire building by "files and musters of the war" and whose god is "plated Mars." But Rome is also the site of political strife, "stirs" and "garboils," "contriving friends" and "scrupulous faction." In this strenuous exertion to extend Rome's empire and govern the state, Romans imagine that pleasure must lie in another world, "i' th' east," specifically in Egypt with Cleopatra, who can "make defect perfection" and whose "holy priests bless her when she is riggish." Yet this pleasure is never dramatized in the play. It is only remembered, anticipated, and imagined—even by Cleopatra and the Egyptians. The Romans remember how in Egypt they "did sleep day out of countenance and made the night light with drinking," but we never see them do so. Antony himself looks forward to an evening with Cleopatra in which they "wander through the streets and note the qualities of people," but such an evening never comes, for he must leave for Rome. Cleopatra calls for the narcotic "mandragora" to drink and speaks of listening to "an eunuch" sing, and her eunuch Mardian can "think what Venus did with Mars," but for both Cleopatra and Mardian these pleasures remain only imagined. Shakespeare relies wholly on brilliant language to present the Romans' and his play's fascination with the "east."

## Shakespeare's Sentences

In an English sentence, meaning is quite dependent on the place given each word. "The dog bit the boy" and "The boy bit the dog" mean very different things, even though the individual words are the same. Because English places such importance on the positions of words in sentences, on the way words are arranged, unusual arrangements can puzzle a reader. Shakespeare frequently shifts his sentences away from "normal" English arrangements—often to create the rhythm he seeks, sometimes to use a line's poetic rhythm to emphasize a particular word, sometimes to give a character his or her own speech patterns or to allow the character to speak in a special way. When we attend a good performance of the play, the actors will have worked out the sentence structures and will articulate the sentences so that the meaning is clear. In reading for yourself, do as the actor does. That is, when you become puzzled by a character's speech, check to see if words are being presented in an unusual sequence.

Shakespeare often, for example, rearranges subjects and verbs (i.e., instead of "He goes" we find "Goes he"). In *Antony and Cleopatra*, when Caesar says "to that end assemble we" (1.4.85–86), he is using such a construction. So is Menas when he says "so find we profit" (2.1.9). The "normal" order would be "We assemble to that end" and "So we find profit." Shakespeare also frequently places the object before the subject and verb (i.e., instead of "I hit him," we might find "Him I hit"). The Soothsayer's statement "A little I can read" (1.2.10) is an example of such an inversion, as is Charmian's "Our worser thoughts heavens mend" (1.2.64). The "normal" order would be "I can read a little" and "Heavens mend our worser thoughts."

Inversions are not the only unusual sentence structures in Shakespeare's language. Often in his sentences words that would normally appear together are separated from each other. Again, this is often done to create a particular rhythm or to stress a particular word. Take, for example, Philo's "Those his goodly eyes, that o'er the files and musters of the war have glowed like plated Mars, now bend" (1.1.2–4). Here, the clause "that o'er the files and musters of the war have glowed like plated Mars" and the adverb "now" separate subject ("Those his goodly eyes") from verb ("bend"). Or take Ventidius' lines to Silius:

> Sossius,
> One of my place in Syria, his lieutenant,
> For quick accumulation of renown,
> Which he achieved by th' minute, lost his favor.
>                                              (3.1.19–22)

Here, the subject and verb, "Sossius lost," are interrupted by the insertion of, first, the appositive "One of my place in Syria, his lieutenant"; second, the phrase "For quick accumulation of renown"; and third, the clause "Which he achieved by th' minute." In order to create for yourself sentences that seem more like the English of everyday speech, you may wish to rearrange the words, putting together the word clusters ("Those his goodly eyes bend" and "Sossius lost his favor"). You will usually find that the sentence will gain in clarity but will lose its rhythm or shift its emphasis.

Sometimes, although not often in *Antony and Cleopatra*, rather than separating basic sentence elements, Shakespeare simply holds them back, delaying them until other material to which he wants to give greater emphasis has been presented. Shakespeare puts this kind of construction in the mouth of Caesar early in the play when, desperately needing Antony's help against Pompey, Caesar comforts himself and his ally Lepidus by remembering in detail a retreat in which Antony showed the kind of soldiership that Caesar needs from him again. Caesar addresses the absent Antony:

> When thou once
> Was beaten from Modena, where thou slew'st
> Hirsius and Pansa, consuls, at thy heel
> Did famine follow, whom thou fought'st against,
> Though daintily brought up, with patience more
> Than savages could suffer.
>
> (1.4.65–70)

Holding back the essential sentence elements, the subject and the verb ("Did famine follow"—i.e., famine did follow), Caesar first establishes the authenticity of his report in a pair of clauses that specify the setting of his anecdote ("When thou once was beaten from Modena") and name the other participants in the engagement, their rank, and their fate ("where thou slew'st Hirsius and Pansa, consuls").

Finally, in many of Shakespeare's plays, sentences are sometimes complicated not because of unusual structures or interruptions but because Shakespeare omits words and parts of words that English sentences normally require. (In conversation, we, too, often omit words. We say, "Heard from him yet?" and our hearer supplies the missing "Have you.") Frequent reading of Shakespeare—and of other poets—trains us to supply such missing words. In the play's first two scenes, Antony often speaks in an elliptical way, leaving out words that we can easily guess at. Sometimes his omissions show him harsh with impatience, as when he orders a messenger "Grates me, the sum" (i.e., this *grates* [irritates] me; therefore give me only *the* briefest *sum*mary of your news), or when he asks another messenger "Well, what worst?" (i.e., *well, what*'s the *worst* of your news?). Yet the tone of his elliptical speeches to Cleopatra is altogether different. These are enticements to pleasure—"What sport [i.e., pleasure shall we indulge in] tonight?"—or they are declarations of devotion: "[I will listen to] No messenger but thine."

## Shakespearean Wordplay

Shakespeare plays with language so often and so variously that entire books are written on the topic. Here we will mention only two kinds of wordplay, puns and metaphors. These are crucial in *Antony and Cleopatra* to creating a fascination with Cleopatra and her court. The queen and her attendants are presented as attractively skillful at wordplay, and they also provide opportunities for the Romans to employ wordplay in an effort to describe how desirable Cleopatra can be.

Puns in *Antony and Cleopatra* sometimes play on the multiple meanings of a single word and sometimes on the different meanings of words that sound the same. When Antony rebukes Cleopatra, "But that your Royalty / Holds idleness your subject, I should take you / For idleness itself," Antony uses the word *idleness* in its sense of "foolishness" or "silliness." In deflecting his rebuke, Cleopatra not only uses another of the meanings of *idleness* (namely, "inactivity"), but also plays on multiple meanings of *labor* ("work" and "labor pains") and *bear* ("endure" and "give birth to"): " 'Tis sweating labor / To bear such idleness so near the heart / As Cleopatra this" (1.3.111–16). Cleopatra is also made engaging as a character because, when she is in the mood, she allows her attendants to give her punning answers:

CLEOPATRA    . . . Hast thou affections [i.e., erotic passions]?
MARDIAN [a eunuch]   Yes, gracious madam.
CLEOPATRA   Indeed?
MARDIAN
     Not in deed, madam, for I can do nothing. . . .
                                                   (1.5.15–18)

This pun depends on the similar sounds and different meanings of *indeed* (i.e., "Really?") and *in deed* (i.e., "in actual fact").

A metaphor is a play on words in which one object or idea is expressed as if it were something else, something with which it shares common features. For instance, when Antony says of his attraction to Cleopatra "These strong Egyptian fetters I must break" (1.2.128), he is using metaphorical language to describe Cleopatra's beauty and charm as "fetters" or chains and shackles that limit his movements. Enobarbus also uses metaphor when he says that Cleopatra "pursed up his [Antony's] heart upon the river of Cydnus" (2.2.223). In this case Enobarbus represents Antony's heart as an object valued by Cleopatra, who is said to keep it in the place where one preserves valuables (a purse), and, at the same time, Enobarbus expresses Cleopatra's enduring mastery of Antony's love in terms of her ability to keep the seat of his love, his heart, as her personal possession in her purse. Cleopatra is also the object of the most famous and lavish figurative language in the play, Enobarbus' description of her appearance when she pursed up Antony's heart:

> The barge she sat in like a burnished throne
> Burned on the water. The poop was beaten gold,
> Purple the sails, and so perfumed that
> The winds were lovesick with them. The oars were
>    silver,
> Which to the tune of flutes kept stroke, and made
> The water which they beat to follow faster,
> As amorous of their strokes. For her own person,
> It beggared all description: she did lie
> In her pavilion—cloth-of-gold, of tissue—
> O'erpicturing that Venus where we see
> The fancy outwork nature.
>
> (2.2.227–38)

This speech offers such a profusion of wordplay that a complete discussion of it would unduly extend this introduction to Shakespeare's language. Instead, we will here focus simply on the metaphors that compare the nonhuman to the human (personifications) and on the metaphor that compares Cleopatra to pictures of Venus. The first personification is "Purple the sails, and so perfumed that / The winds were lovesick with them." Here the perfume issuing from the sails is said to be so desirable that the winds become like lovers whose affections are so strong that they are sick with love ("lovesick"). Just as the winds are metaphorically transformed into lovers of the perfumed sails, so the water is figuratively turned into a lover of the oars: "The oars were silver, / Which to the tune of flutes kept stroke, and made / The water which they beat to follow faster, / As amorous of their strokes." Finally, in yet another metaphor, Cleopatra is compared to artists' representations of the Roman goddess of love, Venus; yet Cleopatra is said not simply to resemble such pictures but to surpass them in her resemblance to Venus, "O'erpicturing that Venus where we see / The fancy outwork nature."

## Implied Stage Action

Finally, in reading Shakespeare's plays we should always remember that what we are reading is a performance script. The dialogue is written to be spoken by actors who, at the same time, are moving, gesturing, picking up objects, weeping, shaking their fists. Some stage action is described in what are called "stage directions"; some is suggested within the dialogue itself. We should always try to be alert to such signals as we stage the play in our imaginations. Consider, for example, the stage action that is suggested by the following exchange between Enobarbus and Menas near the end of Pompey's drunken feast aboard his galley:

ENOBARBUS
　There's a strong fellow, Menas.
MENAS　　　　　　　　　　　Why?
ENOBARBUS　　　　　　　　　　　　　　He bears
　The third part of the world, man. Seest not?

　　　　　　　　　　　　　　　　　(2.7.103–6)

Here "the third part of the world" seems to refer to a ruler of a "third part of the world," or a triumvir. While all three triumvirs, Antony, Octavius Caesar, and Lepidus, are at the feast, only Lepidus' drunken state has been a topic of the dialogue for most of this scene, and he, unlike Antony and Caesar, has no more lines in the scene after the exchange quoted. Thus we may conclude that the dialogue signals that Lepidus has been carried offstage, and this edition therefore includes, after Enobarbus' first speech prefix, the stage direction "pointing to the Servant carrying Lepidus." This is one place, and there are others, where the dialogue allows us to be reasonably confident in adding, in brackets, a stage direction suggesting the action.

On other occasions in *Antony and Cleopatra* the signals for stage action are not so clear. Indeed the play seems sometimes to offer a unique challenge to readers' capacity to imagine the action that accompanies its dialogue. Take, for example, Antony's assertion to Cleopatra in the play's first scene that "The nobleness of life / Is to do thus" (1.1.41–42). His expression "to do thus" seems to demand that some action accompany it. Many editors include a stage direction indicating an embrace between Antony and Cleopatra, but Cleopatra's response to Antony, "Excellent falsehood," does not suggest her mood would necessarily allow for an embrace. We are therefore left to use our imaginations about what it is "to do thus."

The stiffest challenges to readers and directors alike come in the play's concluding scenes in which the fictional location is Cleopatra's "monument" (4.15, 5.2). In the first of these scenes the mortally wounded Antony is brought onstage by his Guard. When Cleopatra decides that Antony must be raised up to her in her monument, she seeks assistance in doing so: "Help me, my women! . . . Assist, good friends" (4.15.35–36). Several lines later the early printed text provides the bare stage direction *They heave Antony aloft to Cleopatra.* How Cleopatra's monument is to be represented onstage and how Antony is to be drawn up into it are left for the reader to imagine or for the director to devise. The same is true when, in 5.2, Cleopatra is captured by the Romans in her monument. Of her capture there is no doubt: a Roman comments "You see how easily she may be surprised"; and one of Cleopatra's ladies exclaims "O, Cleopatra, thou art taken, queen!" (5.2.40, 43). Therefore we have added in brackets a stage direction that indicates the capture: *"Gallus and Soldiers enter and seize Cleopatra."* Nonetheless, the early printed text and our edition leave entirely to the imagination of readers how the capture is to be staged.

It is immensely rewarding to work carefully with Shakespeare's language so that the words, the sentences, the wordplay, and the implied stage action all become clear—as readers for the past four centuries have discovered. It may be more pleasurable to attend a good performance of a play—though not everyone has thought so. But the joy of being able to stage one of Shakespeare's plays in one's imagination, to return to passages that continue to yield further meanings (or further questions) the more one reads them—these are pleasures that, for many, rival (or at least augment) those of the performed text, and certainly make it worth considerable effort to "break the code" of Elizabethan poetic drama and let free the remarkable language that makes up a Shakespeare text.

# Shakespeare's Life

Surviving documents that give us glimpses into the life of William Shakespeare show us a playwright, poet, and actor who grew up in the market town of Stratford-upon-Avon, spent his professional life in London, and returned to Stratford a wealthy landowner. He was born in April 1564, died in April 1616, and is buried inside the chancel of Holy Trinity Church in Stratford.

We wish we could know more about the life of the world's greatest dramatist. His plays and poems are testaments to his wide reading—especially to his knowledge of Virgil, Ovid, Plutarch, Holinshed's *Chronicles,* and the Bible—and to his mastery of the English language, but we can only speculate about his education. We know that the King's New School in Stratford-upon-Avon was considered excellent. The school was one of the English "grammar schools" established to educate young men, primarily in Latin grammar and literature. As in other schools of the time, students began their studies at the age of four or five in the attached "petty school," and there learned to read and write in English, studying primarily the catechism from the Book of Common Prayer. After two years in the petty school, students entered the lower form (grade) of the grammar school, where they began the serious study of Latin grammar and Latin texts that would occupy most of the remainder of their school days. (Several Latin texts that Shakespeare used repeatedly in writing his plays and poems were texts that schoolboys memorized and recited.) Latin comedies were introduced early in the lower form; in the upper form, which the boys entered at age ten or eleven, students wrote their own Latin orations and declamations, studied Latin historians and rhetoricians, and began the study of Greek using the Greek New Testament.

Since the records of the Stratford "grammar school" do not survive, we cannot prove that William Shakespeare attended the school; however, every indication (his father's position as an alderman and bailiff of Stratford, the playwright's own knowledge of the Latin classics, scenes in the plays that recall grammar-school experiences—for example, *The Merry Wives of Windsor*, 4.1) suggests that he did. We also lack generally accepted documentation about Shakespeare's life after his schooling ended and his professional life in London began. His marriage in 1582 (at age eighteen) to Anne Hathaway and the subsequent births of his daughter Susanna (1583) and the twins Judith and Hamnet (1585) are recorded, but how he supported himself and where he lived are not known. Nor do we know when and why he left Stratford for the London theatrical world, nor how he rose to be the important figure in that world that he had become by the early 1590s.

We do know that by 1592 he had achieved some prominence in London as both an actor and a playwright. In that year was published a book by the playwright Robert Greene attacking an actor who had the audacity to write blank-verse drama and who was "in his own conceit [i.e., opinion] the only Shake-scene in a country." Since Greene's attack includes a parody of a line from one of Shakespeare's early plays, there is little doubt that it is Shakespeare to whom he refers, a "Shake-scene" who had aroused Greene's fury by successfully competing with university-educated dramatists like Greene himself. It was in 1593 that Shakespeare became a published poet. In that year he published his long narrative poem *Venus and Adonis;* in 1594, he followed it with *The Rape of Lucrece.* Both poems were dedicated to the young earl of Southampton (Henry Wriothesley), who may have become Shakespeare's patron.

It seems no coincidence that Shakespeare wrote these narrative poems at a time when the theaters were closed because of the plague, a contagious epidemic disease that devastated the population of London. When the theaters reopened in 1594, Shakespeare apparently resumed his double career of actor and playwright

# CATECHISMVS

*paruus pueris primùm Latinè*
*qui ediscatur, proponendus*
*in Scholis.*

**LONDINI**
Apud Iohannem Dayum Typo-
graphum. An. 1573.

Cum Priuilegio Regiæ Maiestatis.

Title page of a 1573 Latin and Greek catechism
for children.

and began his long (and seemingly profitable) service as an acting-company shareholder. Records for December of 1594 show him to be a leading member of the Lord Chamberlain's Men. It was this company of actors, later named the King's Men, for whom he would be a principal actor, dramatist, and shareholder for the rest of his career.

So far as we can tell, that career spanned about twenty years. In the 1590s, he wrote his plays on English history as well as several comedies and at least two tragedies (*Titus Andronicus* and *Romeo and Juliet*). These histories, comedies, and tragedies are the plays credited to him in 1598 in a work, *Palladis Tamia*, that in one chapter compares English writers with "Greek, Latin, and Italian Poets." There the author, Francis Meres, claims that Shakespeare is comparable to the Latin dramatists Seneca for tragedy and Plautus for comedy, and calls him "the most excellent in both kinds for the stage." He also names him "Mellifluous and honey-tongued Shakespeare": "I say," writes Meres, "that the Muses would speak with Shakespeare's fine filed phrase, if they would speak English." Since Meres also mentions Shakespeare's "sugared sonnets among his private friends," it is assumed that many of Shakespeare's sonnets (not published until 1609) were also written in the 1590s.

In 1599, Shakespeare's company built a theater for themselves across the river from London, naming it the Globe. The plays that are considered by many to be Shakespeare's major tragedies (*Hamlet*, *Othello*, *King Lear*, and *Macbeth*) were written while the company was resident in this theater, as were such comedies as *Twelfth Night* and *Measure for Measure*. Many of Shakespeare's plays were performed at court (both for Queen Elizabeth I and, after her death in 1603, for King James I), some were presented at the Inns of

Court (the residences of London's legal societies), and some were doubtless performed in other towns, at the universities, and at great houses when the King's Men went on tour; otherwise, his plays from 1599 to 1608 were, so far as we know, performed only at the Globe. Between 1608 and 1612, Shakespeare wrote several plays—among them *The Winter's Tale* and *The Tempest*—presumably for the company's new indoor Blackfriars theater, though the plays seem to have been performed also at the Globe and at court. Surviving documents describe a performance of *The Winter's Tale* in 1611 at the Globe, for example, and performances of *The Tempest* in 1611 and 1613 at the royal palace of Whitehall.

Shakespeare wrote very little after 1612, the year in which he probably wrote *King Henry VIII*. (It was at a performance of *Henry VIII* in 1613 that the Globe caught fire and burned to the ground.) Sometime between 1610 and 1613 he seems to have returned to live in Stratford-upon-Avon, where he owned a large house and considerable property, and where his wife and his two daughters and their husbands lived. (His son Hamnet had died in 1596.) During his professional years in London, Shakespeare had presumably derived income from the acting company's profits as well as from his own career as an actor, from the sale of his play manuscripts to the acting company, and, after 1599, from his shares as an owner of the Globe. It was presumably that income, carefully invested in land and other property, which made him the wealthy man that surviving documents show him to have become. It is also assumed that William Shakespeare's growing wealth and reputation played some part in inclining the crown, in 1596, to grant John Shakespeare, William's father, the coat of arms that he had so long sought. William Shakespeare died in Stratford on April 23, 1616 (according to the epitaph carved

The Globe

A stylized representation of the Globe theater.
From Claes Jansz Visscher, *Londinum florentissima
Britanniae urbs . . .* [c. 1625].

under his bust in Holy Trinity Church) and was buried on April 25. Seven years after his death, his collected plays were published as *Mr. William Shakespeares Comedies, Histories, & Tragedies* (the work now known as the First Folio).

The years in which Shakespeare wrote were among the most exciting in English history. Intellectually, the discovery, translation, and printing of Greek and Roman classics were making available a set of works and worldviews that interacted complexly with Christian texts and beliefs. The result was a questioning, a vital intellectual ferment, that provided energy for the period's amazing dramatic and literary output and that fed directly into Shakespeare's plays. The Ghost in *Hamlet*, for example, is wonderfully complicated in part because he is a figure from Roman tragedy—the spirit of the dead returning to seek revenge—who at the same time inhabits a Christian hell (or purgatory); Hamlet's description of humankind reflects at one moment the Neoplatonic wonderment at mankind ("What a piece of work is a man!") and, at the next, the Christian disparagement of human sinners ("And yet, to me, what is this quintessence of dust?").

As intellectual horizons expanded, so also did geographical and cosmological horizons. New worlds—both North and South America—were explored, and in them were found human beings who lived and worshiped in ways radically different from those of Renaissance Europeans and Englishmen. The universe during these years also seemed to shift and expand. Copernicus had earlier theorized that the earth was not the center of the cosmos but revolved as a planet around the sun. Galileo's telescope, created in 1609, allowed scientists to see that Copernicus had been correct; the universe was not organized with the earth at the center, nor was it so nicely circumscribed as people had, until that time, thought. In terms of expanding horizons, the impact of these discoveries on people's beliefs—religious, scientific, and philosophical—cannot be overstated.

London, too, rapidly expanded and changed during the years (from the early 1590s to around 1610) that Shakespeare lived there. London—the center of England's government, its economy, its royal court, its overseas trade—was, during these years, becoming an exciting metropolis, drawing to it thousands of new citizens every year. Troubled by overcrowding, by poverty, by recurring epidemics of the plague, London was also a mecca for the wealthy and the aristocratic, and for those who sought advancement at court, or power in government or finance or trade. One hears in Shakespeare's plays the voices of London—the struggles for power, the fear of venereal disease, the language of buying and selling. One hears as well the voices of Stratford-upon-Avon—references to the nearby Forest of Arden, to sheep herding, to small-town gossip, to village fairs and markets. Part of the richness of Shakespeare's work is the influence felt there of the various worlds in which he lived: the world of metropolitan London, the world of small-town and rural England, the world of the theater, and the worlds of craftsmen and shepherds.

That Shakespeare inhabited such worlds we know from surviving London and Stratford documents, as well as from the evidence of the plays and poems themselves. From such records we can sketch the dramatist's life. We know from his works that he was a voracious reader. We know from legal and business documents that he was a multifaceted theater man who became a wealthy landowner. We know a bit about his family life and a fair amount about his legal and financial dealings. Most scholars today depend upon such evidence as they draw their picture of the world's

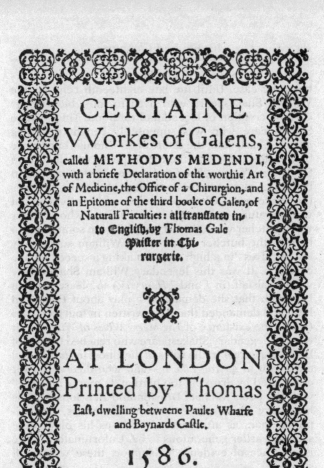

# CERTAINE

## VVorkes of Galens,

called METHODVS MEDENDI,
with a briefe Declaration of the worthie Art
of Medicine, the Office of a Chirurgion, and
an Epitome of the third booke of Galen, of
Naturall Faculties: all translated into English, by Thomas Gale
Maister in Chi-
rurgerie.

# AT LONDON

## Printed by Thomas

East, dwelling betweene Paules Wharfe
and Baynards Castle.

## 1586.

Title page of a medical treatise by Galen.
From Galen, *Certaine workes of Galens . . .* (1586).

greatest playwright. Such, however, has not always been the case. Until the late eighteenth century, the William Shakespeare who lived in most biographies was the creation of legend and tradition. This was the Shakespeare who was supposedly caught poaching deer at Charlecote, the estate of Sir Thomas Lucy close by Stratford; this was the Shakespeare who fled from Sir Thomas's vengeance and made his way in London by taking care of horses outside a playhouse; this was the Shakespeare who reportedly could barely read but whose natural gifts were extraordinary, whose father was a butcher who allowed his gifted son sometimes to help in the butcher shop, where William supposedly killed calves "in a high style," making a speech for the occasion. It was this legendary William Shakespeare whose Falstaff (in *1* and *2 Henry IV*) so pleased Queen Elizabeth that she demanded a play about Falstaff in love, and demanded that it be written in fourteen days (hence the existence of *The Merry Wives of Windsor*). It was this legendary Shakespeare who reached the top of his acting career in the roles of the Ghost in *Hamlet* and old Adam in *As You Like It*—and who died of a fever contracted by drinking too hard at "a merry meeting" with the poets Michael Drayton and Ben Jonson. This legendary Shakespeare is a rambunctious, undisciplined man, as attractively "wild" as his plays were seen by earlier generations to be. Unfortunately, there is no trace of evidence to support these wonderful stories.

Perhaps in response to the disreputable Shakespeare of legend—or perhaps in response to the fragmentary and, for some, all-too-ordinary Shakespeare documented by surviving records—some people since the mid–nineteenth century have argued that William Shakespeare could not have written the plays that bear his name. These persons have put forward some dozen names as more likely authors, among them Queen Elizabeth, Sir Francis Bacon, Edward de Vere (earl of Oxford), and Christopher Marlowe. Such attempts to find what for these people is a more believable author of the plays is a tribute to the regard in which the plays are held. Unfortunately for their claims, the documents that exist that provide evidence for the facts of Shakespeare's life tie him inextricably to the body of plays and poems that bear his name. Unlikely as it seems to those who want the works to have been written by an aristocrat, a university graduate, or an "important" person, the plays and poems seem clearly to have been produced by a man from Stratford-upon-Avon with a very good "grammar-school" education and a life of experience in London and in the world of the London theater. How this particular man produced the works that dominate the cultures of much of the world almost four hundred years after his death is one of life's mysteries—and one that will continue to tease our imaginations as we continue to delight in his plays and poems.

# Shakespeare's Theater

The actors of Shakespeare's time are known to have performed plays in a great variety of locations. They played at court (that is, in the great halls of such royal residences as Whitehall, Hampton Court, and Greenwich); they played in halls at the universities of Oxford and Cambridge, and at the Inns of Court (the residences in London of the legal societies); and they also played in the private houses of great lords and civic officials. Sometimes acting companies went on tour from London into the provinces, often (but not only) when outbreaks of bubonic plague in the capital forced the closing of theaters to reduce the possibility of contagion in crowded audiences. In the provinces the actors usually staged their plays in churches (until around 1600) or in guildhalls. While surviving records show only a handful of occasions when actors played at inns while on tour, London inns were important playing places up until the 1590s.

The building of theaters in London had begun only shortly before Shakespeare wrote his first plays in the 1590s. These theaters were of two kinds: outdoor or public playhouses that could accommodate large numbers of playgoers, and indoor or private theaters for much smaller audiences. What is usually regarded as the first London outdoor public playhouse was called simply the Theatre. James Burbage—the father of Richard Burbage, who was perhaps the most famous actor in Shakespeare's company—built it in 1576 in an area north of the city of London called Shoreditch. Among the more famous of the other public playhouses that capitalized on the new fashion were the Curtain and the Fortune (both also built north of the city), the Rose, the Swan, the Globe, and the Hope (all located on the Bankside, a region just across the Thames south of the city of London). All these playhouses had to be built outside the jurisdiction of the city of London because many civic officials were hostile to the performance of drama and repeatedly petitioned the royal council to abolish it.

The theaters erected on the Bankside (a region under the authority of the Church of England, whose head was the monarch) shared the neighborhood with houses of prostitution and with the Paris Garden, where the blood sports of bearbaiting and bullbaiting were carried on. There may have been no clear distinction between playhouses and buildings for such sports, for we know that the Hope was used for both plays and baiting and that Philip Henslowe, owner of the Rose and, later, partner in the ownership of the Fortune, was also a partner in a monopoly on baiting. All these forms of entertainment were easily accessible to Londoners by boat across the Thames or over London Bridge.

Evidently Shakespeare's company prospered on the Bankside. They moved there in 1599. Threatened by difficulties in renewing the lease on the land where their first theater (the Theatre) had been built, Shakespeare's company took advantage of the Christmas holiday in 1598 to dismantle the Theatre and transport its timbers across the Thames to the Bankside, where, in 1599, these timbers were used in the building of the Globe. The weather in late December 1598 is recorded as having been especially harsh. It was so cold that the Thames was "nigh [nearly] frozen," and there was heavy snow. Perhaps the weather aided Shakespeare's company in eluding their landlord, the snow hiding their activity and the freezing of the Thames allowing them to slide the timbers across to the Bankside without paying tolls for repeated trips over London Bridge. Attractive as this narrative is, it remains just as likely that the heavy snow hampered transport of the timbers in wagons through the London streets to the river. It also must be remembered that the Thames was, according to report, only "nigh frozen" and therefore as impassable as it ever was. Whatever the precise circumstances of this fascinating event in English theater history, Shakespeare's company was able to begin playing at their new Globe theater on the Bankside in 1599. After the first Globe burned down in 1613 during the staging of Shakespeare's *Henry VIII* (its thatch roof was set alight by cannon fire called for by

A stage play.
From [William Alabaster,] *Roxana tragœdia . . .* (1632).

the performance), Shakespeare's company immediately rebuilt on the same location. The second Globe seems to have been a grander structure than its predecessor. It remained in use until the beginning of the English Civil War in 1642, when Parliament officially closed the theaters. Soon thereafter it was pulled down.

The public theaters of Shakespeare's time were very different buildings from our theaters today. First of all, they were open-air playhouses. As recent excavations of the Rose and the Globe confirm, some were polygonal or roughly circular in shape; the Fortune, however, was square. The most recent estimates of their size put the diameter of these buildings at 72 feet (the Rose) to 100 feet (the Globe), but we know that they held vast audiences of two or three thousand, who must have been squeezed together quite tightly. Some of these spectators paid extra to sit or stand in the two or three levels of roofed galleries that extended, on the upper levels, all the way around the theater and surrounded an open space. In this space were the stage and, perhaps, the tiring house (what we would call dressing rooms), as well as the so-called yard. In the yard stood the spectators who chose to pay less, the ones whom Hamlet contemptuously called "groundlings." For a roof they had only the sky, and so they were exposed to all kinds of weather. They stood on a floor that was sometimes made of mortar and sometimes of ash mixed with the shells of hazelnuts. The latter provided a porous and therefore dry footing for the crowd, and the shells may have been more comfortable to stand on because they were not as hard as mortar. Availability of shells may not have been a problem if hazelnuts were a favorite food for Shakespeare's audiences to munch on as they watched his plays. Archaeologists who are today unearthing the remains of theaters from this period have discovered quantities of these nutshells on theater sites.

Unlike the yard, the stage itself was covered by a roof. Its ceiling, called "the heavens," is thought to have been elaborately painted to depict the sun, moon, stars, and planets. Just how big the stage was remains hard to determine. We have a single sketch of part of the interior of the Swan. A Dutchman named Johannes de Witt visited this theater around 1596 and sent a sketch of it back to his friend, Arend van Buchel. Because van Buchel found de Witt's letter and sketch of interest, he copied both into a book. It is van Buchel's copy, adapted, it seems, to the shape and size of the page in his book, that survives. In this sketch, the stage appears to be a large rectangular platform that thrusts far out into the yard, perhaps even as far as the center of the circle formed by the surrounding galleries. This drawing, combined with the specifications for the size of the stage in the building contract for the Fortune, has led scholars to conjecture that the stage on which Shakespeare's plays were performed must have measured approximately 43 feet in width and 27 feet in depth, a vast acting area. But the digging up of a large part of the Rose by archaeologists has provided evidence of a quite different stage design. The Rose stage was a platform tapered at the corners and much shallower than what seems to be depicted in the van Buchel sketch. Indeed, its measurements seem to be about 37.5 feet across at its widest point and only 15.5 feet deep. Because the surviving indications of stage size and design differ from each other so much, it is possible that the stages in other theaters, like the Theatre, the Curtain, and the Globe (the outdoor playhouses where we know that Shakespeare's plays were performed), were different from those at both the Swan and the Rose.

After about 1608 Shakespeare's plays were staged not only at the Globe but also at an indoor or private playhouse in Blackfriars. This theater had been constructed in 1596 by James Burbage in an upper hall of a former Dominican priory or monastic house. Although Henry VIII had dissolved all English monasteries in the 1530s (shortly after he had founded the Church of England), the area remained under church, rather than hostile civic, control. The hall that Burbage had purchased and renovated was a large one in which Parliament had once met. In the private theater that he constructed, the stage, lit by candles, was built across the narrow end of the hall, with boxes flanking it. The rest of the hall offered seating room only. Because there was no provision for standing room, the largest audience it could hold was less than a thousand, or about a quarter of what the Globe could accommodate. Admission to Blackfriars was correspondingly more expensive. Instead of a penny to stand in the yard at the Globe, it cost a minimum of sixpence to get into Blackfriars. The best seats at the Globe (in the Lords' Room in the gallery above and behind the stage) cost sixpence; but the boxes flanking the stage at Blackfriars were half a crown, or five times sixpence. Some spectators who were particularly interested in displaying themselves paid even more to sit on stools on the Blackfriars stage.

Whether in the outdoor or indoor playhouses, the stages of Shakespeare's time were different from ours. They were not separated from the audience by the dropping of a curtain between acts and scenes. Therefore the playwrights of the time had to find other ways of signaling to the audience that one scene (to be imagined as occurring in one location at a given time) had ended and the next (to be imagined at perhaps a different location at a later time) had begun. The customary way used by Shakespeare and many of his contemporaries was to have everyone onstage exit at the end of one scene and have one or more different characters enter to begin the next. In a few cases, where characters remain onstage from one scene to another, the dialogue or stage action makes the change of location clear, and the characters are generally to be imagined as having moved from one place to another. For example, in *Romeo and Juliet*, Romeo and his friends remain onstage in Act 1 from scene 4 to scene 5, but they are represented as having moved between scenes from the street that leads to Capulet's house into Capulet's house itself. The new location is signaled in part by the appearance onstage of Capulet's servingmen carrying napkins, something they would not take into the streets. Playwrights had to be quite resourceful in the use of hand properties, like the napkin, or in the use of dialogue to specify where the action was taking place in their plays because, in contrast to most of today's theaters, the playhouses of Shakespeare's time did not use movable scenery to dress the stage and make the setting precise. As another consequence of this difference, however, the playwrights of Shakespeare's time did not have to specify exactly where the action of their plays was set when they did not choose to do so, and much of the action of their plays is tied to no specific place.

Usually Shakespeare's stage is referred to as a "bare stage," to distinguish it from the stages of the last two or three centuries with their elaborate sets. But the stage in Shakespeare's time was not completely bare. Philip Henslowe, owner of the Rose, lists in his inventory of stage properties a rock, three tombs, and two mossy banks. Stage directions in plays of the time also call for such things as thrones (or "states"), banquets (presumably tables with plaster replicas of food on them), and beds and tombs to be pushed onto the stage. Thus the stage often held more than the actors.

The actors did not limit their performing to the stage alone. Occasionally they went beneath the stage, as the Ghost appears to do in the first act of *Hamlet*. From there they could emerge onto the stage through a trapdoor. They could retire behind the hangings across the back of the stage (or the front of the tiring house), as, for example, the actor playing Polonius does when he hides behind the arras. Sometimes the hangings could be drawn back during a performance to "discover" one or more actors behind them. When performance required that an actor appear "above," as when Juliet is imagined to stand at the window of her chamber in the famous and misnamed "balcony scene," then the actor probably climbed the stairs to the gallery over the back of the stage and temporarily shared it with some of the spectators. The stage was also provided with ropes and winches so that actors could descend from, and reascend to, the "heavens."

Perhaps the greatest difference between dramatic performances in Shakespeare's time and ours was that in Shakespeare's England the roles of women were played by boys. (Some of these boys grew up to take male roles in their maturity.) There were no women in the acting companies, only in the audience. It had not always been so in the history of the English stage. There are records of women on English stages in the thirteenth and fourteenth centuries, two hundred years before Shakespeare's plays were performed. After the accession of James I in 1603, the queen of England and her ladies took part in entertainments at court called masques, and with the reopening of the theaters in 1660 at the restoration of Charles II, women again took their place on the public stage.

The chief competitors for the companies of adult

actors such as the one to which Shakespeare belonged and for which he wrote were companies of exclusively boy actors. The competition was most intense in the early 1600s. There were then two principal children's companies: the Children of Paul's (the choirboys from St. Paul's Cathedral, whose private playhouse was near the cathedral); and the Children of the Chapel Royal (the choirboys from the monarch's private chapel, who performed at the Blackfriars theater built by Burbage in 1596, which Shakespeare's company had been stopped from using by local residents who objected to crowds). In *Hamlet* Shakespeare writes of "an aerie [nest] of children, little eyases [hawks], that cry out on the top of question and are most tyrannically clapped for 't. These are now the fashion and . . . berattle the common stages [attack the public theaters]." In the long run, the adult actors prevailed. The Children of Paul's dissolved around 1606. By about 1608 the Children of the Chapel Royal had been forced to stop playing at the Blackfriars theater, which was then taken over by the King's Men, Shakespeare's own troupe.

Acting companies and theaters of Shakespeare's time were organized in different ways. For example, Philip Henslowe owned the Rose and leased it to companies of actors, who paid him from their takings. Henslowe would act as manager of these companies, initially paying playwrights for their plays and buying properties, recovering his outlay from the actors. Shakespeare's company, however, managed itself, with the principal actors, Shakespeare among them, having the status of "sharers" and the right to a share in the takings, as well as the responsibility for a part of the expenses. Five of the sharers themselves, Shakespeare among them, owned the Globe. As actor, as sharer in an acting company and in ownership of theaters, and as playwright, Shakespeare was about as involved in the theatrical industry as one could imagine. Although Shakespeare and his fellows prospered, their status under the law was conditional upon the protection of powerful patrons. "Common players"—those who did not have patrons or masters—were classed in the language of the law with "vagabonds and sturdy beggars." So the actors had to secure for themselves the official rank of servants of patrons. Among the patrons under whose protection Shakespeare's company worked were the lord chamberlain and, after the accession of King James in 1603, the king himself.

We are now perhaps on the verge of learning a great deal more about the theaters in which Shakespeare and his contemporaries performed—or at least of opening up new questions about them. Already about 70 percent of the Rose has been excavated, as has about 10 percent of the second Globe, the one built in 1614. It is to be hoped that soon more will be available for study. These are exciting times for students of Shakespeare's stage.

# The Publication of Shakespeare's Plays

Eighteen of Shakespeare's plays found their way into print during the playwright's lifetime, but there is nothing to suggest that he took any interest in their publication. These eighteen appeared separately in editions called quartos. Their pages were not much larger than the one you are now reading, and these little books were sold unbound for a few pence. The earliest of the quartos that still survive were printed in

1594, the year that both *Titus Andronicus* and a version of the play now called *2 King Henry VI* became available. While almost every one of these early quartos displays on its title page the name of the acting company that performed the play, only about half provide the name of the playwright, Shakespeare. The first quarto edition to bear the name Shakespeare on its title page is *Love's Labor's Lost* of 1598. A few of these quartos were popular with the book-buying public of Shakespeare's lifetime; for example, quarto *Richard II* went through five editions between 1597 and 1615. But most of the quartos were far from best-sellers; *Love's Labor's Lost* (1598), for instance, was not reprinted in quarto until 1631. After Shakespeare's death, two more of his plays appeared in quarto format: *Othello* in 1622 and *The Two Noble Kinsmen*, coauthored with John Fletcher, in 1634.

In 1623, seven years after Shakespeare's death, *Mr. William Shakespeares Comedies, Histories, & Tragedies* was published. This printing offered readers in a single book thirty-six of the thirty-eight plays now thought to have been written by Shakespeare, including eighteen that had never been printed before. And it offered them in a style that was then reserved for serious literature and scholarship. The plays were arranged in double columns on pages nearly a foot high. This large page size is called "folio," as opposed to the smaller "quarto," and the 1623 volume is usually called the Shakespeare First Folio. It is reputed to have sold for the lordly price of a pound. (One copy at the Folger Library is marked fifteen shillings—that is, three-quarters of a pound.)

In a preface to the First Folio entitled "To the great Variety of Readers," two of Shakespeare's former fellow actors in the King's Men, John Heminge and Henry Condell, wrote that they themselves had collected their dead companion's plays. They suggested that they had seen his own papers: "we have scarce received from him a blot in his papers." The title page of the Folio declared that the plays within it had been printed "according to the True Original Copies." Comparing the Folio to the quartos, Heminge and Condell disparaged the quartos, advising their readers that "before you were abused with divers stolen and surreptitious copies, maimed, and deformed by the frauds and stealths of injurious impostors." Many Shakespeareans of the eighteenth and nineteenth centuries believed Heminge and Condell and regarded the Folio plays as superior to anything in the quartos.

Once we begin to examine the Folio plays in detail, it becomes less easy to take at face value the word of Heminge and Condell about the superiority of the Folio texts. For example, of the first nine plays in the Folio (one-quarter of the entire collection), four were essentially reprinted from earlier quarto printings that Heminge and Condell had disparaged; and four have now been identified as printed from copies written in the hand of a professional scribe of the 1620s named Ralph Crane; the ninth, *The Comedy of Errors*, was apparently also printed from a manuscript, but one whose origin cannot be readily identified. Evidently then, eight of the first nine plays in the First Folio were not printed, in spite of what the Folio title page announces, "according to the True Original Copies," or Shakespeare's own papers, and the source of the ninth is unknown. Since today's editors have been forced to treat Heminge and Condell's pronouncements with skepticism, they must choose whether to base their own editions upon quartos or the Folio on grounds other than Heminge and Condell's story of where the quarto and Folio versions originated.

Editors have often fashioned their own narratives to

explain what lies behind the quartos and Folio. They have said that Heminge and Condell meant to criticize only a few of the early quartos, the ones that offer much shorter and sometimes quite different, often garbled, versions of plays. Among the examples of these are the 1600 quarto of *Henry V* (the Folio offers a much fuller version) or the 1603 *Hamlet* quarto (in 1604 a different, much longer form of the play got into print as a quarto). Early in this century editors speculated that these questionable texts were produced when someone in the audience took notes from the plays' dialogue during performances and then employed "hack poets" to fill out the notes. The poor results were then sold to a publisher and presented in print as Shakespeare's plays. More recently this story has given way to another in which the shorter versions are said to be re-creations from memory of Shakespeare's plays by actors who wanted to stage them in the provinces but lacked manuscript copies. Most of the quartos offer much better texts than these so-called bad quartos. Indeed, in most of the quartos we find texts that are at least equal to or better than what is printed in the Folio. Many of this century's Shakespeare enthusiasts have persuaded themselves that most of the quartos were set into type directly from Shakespeare's own papers, although there is nothing on which to base this conclusion except the desire for it to be true. Thus speculation continues about how the Shakespeare plays got to be printed. All that we have are the printed texts.

The book collector who was most successful in bringing together copies of the quartos and the First Folio was Henry Clay Folger, founder of the Folger Shakespeare Library in Washington, D.C. While it is estimated that there survive around the world only about 230 copies of the First Folio, Mr. Folger was able to acquire more than seventy-five copies, as well as a large number of fragments, for the library that bears his name. He also amassed a substantial number of quartos. For example, only fourteen copies of the First Quarto of *Love's Labor's Lost* are known to exist, and three are at the Folger Shakespeare Library. As a consequence of Mr. Folger's labors, twentieth-century scholars visiting the Folger Library have been able to learn a great deal about sixteenth- and seventeenth-century printing and, particularly, about the printing of Shakespeare's plays. And Mr. Folger did not stop at the First Folio, but collected many copies of later editions of Shakespeare, beginning with the Second Folio (1632), the Third (1663–64), and the Fourth (1685). Each of these later folios was based on its immediate predecessor and was edited anonymously. The first editor of Shakespeare whose name we know was Nicholas Rowe, whose first edition came out in 1709. Mr. Folger collected this edition and many, many more by Rowe's successors.

# An Introduction to This Text

*Antony and Cleopatra* was first printed in the 1623 collection of Shakespeare's plays now known as the First Folio. The present edition is based directly upon that printing.\* For the convenience of the reader, we have modernized the punctuation and the spelling of the Folio. Sometimes we go so far as to modernize certain old forms of words; for example, usually when

---

\*We have also consulted the computerized text of the First Folio provided by the Text Archive of the Oxford University Computing Centre, to which we are grateful.

*a* means *he,* we change it to *he;* we change *mo* to *more,* and *ye* to *you.* But it is not our practice in editing any of the plays to modernize words that sound distinctly different from modern forms. For example, when the early printed texts read *sith* or *apricocks* or *porpentine,* we have not modernized to *since, apricots, porcupine.* When the forms *an, and,* or *and if* appear instead of the modern form *if,* we have reduced *and* to *an* but have not changed any of these forms to their modern equivalent, *if.* We also modernize and, where necessary, correct passages in foreign languages, unless an error in the early printed text can be reasonably explained as a joke.

Whenever we change the wording of the First Folio or add anything to its stage directions, we mark the change by enclosing it in superior half-brackets ( ⌐ ¬ ). We want our readers to be immediately aware when we have intervened. (Only when we correct an obvious typographical error in the First Folio does the change not get marked.) Whenever we change either the First Folio's wording or its punctuation so that meaning changes, we list the change in the textual notes at the back of the book, even if all we have done is fix an obvious error.

We regularize spellings of a number of the proper names, as is the usual practice in editions of the play. In doing so we have referred to the spelling of names in Shakespeare's principal source for *Antony and Cleopatra,* Thomas North's translation of Plutarch's *Life of Marcus Antonius* (1579), and to usage in classical literature. For example, the Folio sometimes calls *Cleopatra* by the name "Cleopater" but we use the spelling "Cleopatra" throughout the text. The Folio employs the spellings "Ventigius," "Menes," "Camidius," and "Camidias," which we normalize or regularize to "Ventidius," "Menas," and "Canidius."

This edition differs from many earlier ones in its efforts to aid the reader in imagining the play as a performance rather than as a series of actual events. Thus stage directions that we as editors add to the play's text are written, like those printed in the Folio, with reference to the stage. For example, the Folio's stage directions sometimes specify that opposing parties arriving to negotiate their differences should enter by separate stage doors: *"Enter Pompey . . . at one door, with Drum and Trumpet; at another Caesar, Lepidus, Antony. . . ."* (2.6.0 SD). However, when Antony and Caesar enter in 2.2 to discuss Caesar's grievances against Antony, it is clear that they must enter separately, but the Folio does not refer to stage doors. In this case, to aid the reader in imagining the play as a performance, we supplement the Folio's stage directions: *"Enter, ⌈at one door,⌉ Antony and Ventidius"* and *"Enter, ⌈at another door,⌉ Caesar, Maecenas, and Agrippa."* Whenever it is reasonably certain, in our view, that a speech is accompanied by a particular action, we provide a stage direction describing the action, setting the added direction in brackets to signal that it is not found in the Folio. (Occasional exceptions to this rule occur when the action is so obvious that to add a stage direction would insult the reader.) Stage directions for the entrance of a character in mid-scene are, with rare exceptions, placed so that they immediately precede the character's participation in the scene, even though these entrances may appear somewhat earlier in the early printed texts. Whenever we move a stage direction, we record this change in the textual notes. Latin stage directions (e.g., *Exeunt*) are translated into English (e.g., *They exit*).

We expand the often severely abbreviated forms of names used as speech headings in early printed texts into the full names of the characters. We also regularize the speakers' names in speech headings, using only a single designation for each character, even though the early printed texts sometimes use a variety of designations. Variations in the speech headings of the early printed texts are recorded in the textual notes.

In the present edition, as well, we mark with a dash any change of address within a speech, unless a stage direction intervenes. When the *-ed* ending of a word is to be pronounced, we mark it with an accent. Like editors for the past two centuries, we print metrically linked lines in the following way:

CLEOPATRA
  Pray you stand farther from me.
ANTONY                        What's the matter?
                                (1.3.22–23)

However, when there are a number of short verse-lines that can be linked in more than one way, we do not, with rare exceptions, indent any of them.

## The Explanatory Notes

The notes that appear on the pages facing the text are designed to provide readers with the help that they may need to enjoy the play. Whenever the meaning of a word in the text is not readily accessible in a good contemporary dictionary, we offer the meaning in a note. Sometimes we provide a note even when the relevant meaning is to be found in the dictionary but when the word has acquired since Shakespeare's time other potentially confusing meanings. In our notes, we try to offer modern synonyms for Shakespeare's words. We also try to indicate to the reader the connection between the word in the play and the modern synonym. For example, Shakespeare sometimes uses the word *head* to mean *source*, but, for modern readers, there may be no connection evident between these two words. We provide the connection by explaining Shakespeare's usage as follows: "**head:** fountainhead, source." On some occasions, a whole phrase or clause needs explanation. Then we rephrase in our own words the difficult passage, and add at the end synonyms for individual words in the passage. When scholars have been unable to determine the meaning of a word or phrase, we acknowledge the uncertainty.

# ANTONY
### AND
# CLEOPATRA

# Characters in the Play

ANTONY, a triumvir of Rome
CLEOPATRA, Queen of Egypt

OCTAVIUS CAESAR, a triumvir of Rome
OCTAVIA, sister to Caesar, later wife to Antony
LEPIDUS, a triumvir of Rome

ENOBARBUS, also called DOMITIUS
VENTIDIUS
SILIUS
EROS
CANIDIUS
SCARUS                         *accompanying Antony in*
DERCETUS                       *Egypt and elsewhere*
DEMETRIUS
PHILO
A SCHOOLMASTER, Antony's
   AMBASSADOR to Caesar

CHARMIAN
IRAS
ALEXAS                         *serving in Cleopatra's*
MARDIAN, *a Eunuch*            *court*
SELEUCUS, *Cleopatra's treasurer*
DIOMEDES

MAECENAS
AGRIPPA
TAURUS
THIDIAS       *supporting and accompanying Caesar*
DOLLABELLA
GALLUS
PROCULEIUS

3

SEXTUS POMPEIUS, also called POMPEY
MENAS
MENECRATES
VARRIUS

MESSENGERS
SOLDIERS
SENTRIES
GUARDSMEN
A SOOTHSAYER
SERVANTS
A BOY
A CAPTAIN
AN EGYPTIAN
A COUNTRYMAN

*Ladies, Eunuchs, Captains, Officers, Soldiers, Attendants,
Servants (Lamprius, Rannius, Lucillius: mute characters
named in the opening stage direction to 1.2)*

# ANTONY

## AND

# CLEOPATRA

ACT 1

**1.1** Antony refuses to hear the messengers from Rome and declares that nothing matters but his love for Cleopatra.

———————

2. **measure:** limit, bounds

3. **files and musters of the war:** i.e., ranks of troops

4. **plated:** armored; **Mars:** the Roman god of war (See page 46.)

5. **office:** attention; function; service, duty

6. **tawny:** brown-skinned (See longer note, page 277.) **front:** forehead

8. **reneges all temper:** abandons all moderation (perhaps with wordplay on **temper** in its sense of "hardness" in steel)

10. **gypsy's:** Egyptian's (Gypsies were believed, wrongly, to have come originally from Egypt.)

10 SD. **Flourish:** a trumpet fanfare to announce the entrance of royalty

13. **triple pillar of the world:** i.e., triumvir (one of the three allies ruling the Roman Empire) See page 50.

14. **fool:** dupe, plaything

16. **that can be reckoned:** i.e., whose worth can be calculated

17. **bourn:** limit, boundary

# ACT 1

## Scene 1
*Enter Demetrius and Philo.*

PHILO
   Nay, but this dotage of our general's
   O'erflows the measure. Those his goodly eyes,
   That o'er the files and musters of the war
   Have glowed like plated Mars, now bend, now turn
   The office and devotion of their view                                  5
   Upon a tawny front. His captain's heart,
   Which in the scuffles of great fights hath burst
   The buckles on his breast, reneges all temper
   And is become the bellows and the fan
   To cool a gypsy's lust.                                                 10

*Flourish. Enter Antony, Cleopatra, her Ladies, the Train,*
*with Eunuchs fanning her.*

                     Look where they come.
   Take but good note, and you shall see in him
   The triple pillar of the world transformed
   Into a strumpet's fool. Behold and see.

CLEOPATRA
   If it be love indeed, tell me how much.                                15

ANTONY
   There's beggary in the love that can be reckoned.

CLEOPATRA
   I'll set a bourn how far to be beloved.

7

18–19. **new . . . earth:** Compare Revelation 21.1: "And I saw a new heaven and a new earth."

21. **Grates me, the sum:** i.e., this irritates me; therefore briefly summarize your news

22. **them:** i.e., the news (regarded as a plural)

23. **Fulvia:** Antony's wife

24. **scarce-bearded Caesar:** i.e., Octavius Caesar, who has only recently been old enough to grow a beard (a contemptuous reference to the young Octavius, twenty years the junior of Antony, who was then past forty)

26. **Take in:** conquer

27. **we:** i.e., I (the royal "we"); **damn:** condemn

28. **How:** an exclamation

29. **like:** i.e., likely

30. **dismission:** discharge (from service)

32. **process:** summons (ordering a defendant to appear in court)

36. **homager:** tenant or vassal (to a feudal lord)

38. **Tiber:** See map of Rome, page xix.

39. **ranged:** ordered; widely extensive

42–43. **thus . . . do 't:** Many editors follow Alexander Pope, the second editor of Shakespeare, in printing a stage direction for Antony to embrace Cleopatra here, but others doubt that Cleopatra's mood in the scene would allow for an embrace.

ANTONY
  Then must thou needs find out new heaven, new
    earth.

*Enter a Messenger.*

MESSENGER   News, my good lord, from Rome.	20
ANTONY   Grates me, the sum.
CLEOPATRA   Nay, hear them, Antony.
  Fulvia perchance is angry. Or who knows
  If the scarce-bearded Caesar have not sent
  His powerful mandate to you: "Do this, or this;	25
  Take in that kingdom, and enfranchise that.
  Perform 't, or else we damn thee."
ANTONY                                       How, my love?
CLEOPATRA   Perchance? Nay, and most like.
  You must not stay here longer; your dismission	30
  Is come from Caesar. Therefore hear it, Antony.
  Where's Fulvia's process? Caesar's, I would say—
    both?
  Call in the messengers. As I am Egypt's queen,
  Thou blushest, Antony, and that blood of thine	35
  Is Caesar's homager; else so thy cheek pays shame
  When shrill-tongued Fulvia scolds. The messengers!
ANTONY
  Let Rome in Tiber melt and the wide arch
  Of the ranged empire fall. Here is my space.
  Kingdoms are clay. Our dungy earth alike	40
  Feeds beast as man. The nobleness of life
  Is to do thus; when such a mutual pair
  And such a twain can do 't, in which I bind,
  On pain of punishment, the world to weet
  We stand up peerless.	45
CLEOPATRA                   Excellent falsehood!
  Why did he marry Fulvia, and not love her?
  I'll seem the fool I am not. Antony
  Will be himself.

51. **Love:** Venus, the Roman goddess of love; **hours:** with wordplay on the Hours, Venus' handmaids in mythology

52. **confound:** waste, spoil; **conference:** conversation

55. **ambassadors:** i.e., messengers (See line 34.)

65. **with:** i.e., by; **slight:** poorly, contemptuously

67. **property:** distinctive quality

68. **still:** always

69. **full:** very

70. **approves:** i.e., confirms what is said by

72. **Of:** i.e., for; **Rest you happy:** i.e., good-bye

**1.2** Antony learns that Fulvia, his wife, has died. That and other news, especially news of Pompey's threat to Caesar, make him decide to return to Rome.

Mark Antony.
From Jacobus de Strada, *Epitome thesauri antiquitatum . . .* (1557).

ANTONY                But stirred by Cleopatra.                    50
    Now for the love of Love and her soft hours,
    Let's not confound the time with conference harsh.
    There's not a minute of our lives should stretch
    Without some pleasure now. What sport tonight?
CLEOPATRA
    Hear the ambassadors.                                         55
ANTONY                        Fie, wrangling queen,
    Whom everything becomes—to chide, to laugh,
    To weep; ⌜whose⌝ every passion fully strives
    To make itself, in thee, fair and admired!
    No messenger but thine, and all alone              60
    Tonight we'll wander through the streets and note
    The qualities of people. Come, my queen,
    Last night you did desire it. ⌜*To the Messenger.*⌝
        Speak not to us.
                ⌜*Antony and Cleopatra*⌝ *exit with the Train.*
DEMETRIUS
    Is Caesar with Antonius prized so slight?                     65
PHILO
    Sir, sometimes when he is not Antony
    He comes too short of that great property
    Which still should go with Antony.
DEMETRIUS                        I am full sorry
    That he approves the common liar who              70
    Thus speaks of him at Rome; but I will hope
    Of better deeds tomorrow. Rest you happy!
                                        *They exit.*


                    ⌜Scene 2⌝
*Enter Enobarbus, Lamprius, a Soothsayer, Rannius,*
*Lucillius, Charmian, Iras, Mardian the Eunuch, Alexas,*
                ⌜*and Servants.*⌝

CHARMIAN  Lord Alexas, sweet Alexas, most anything
    Alexas, almost most absolute Alexas, where's the

**4–5. charge his horns with garlands:** i.e., wear **garlands** on his **horns** (See page 64.) Horns were imaged as growing from the forehead of a cuckold, i.e., a husband whose wife was unfaithful to him.

**7. Your will:** i.e., what do you wish

**12. banquet:** dessert, including fruit and wine

**18. fairer:** more likely to succeed (The next two lines play on other meanings of **fairer** as "more plump" and as "more beautiful.")

**20. paint:** i.e., use cosmetics

**25. liver:** Regarded as the seat of the passions, the **liver** would be heated by love as well as by drink.

**27. Good now:** an exclamation of encouragement

**28. forenoon:** morning

**29–30. Herod of Jewry:** Herod, king of Judea at the time of the birth of Christ (See longer note, page 277, and illustrations, pages 124 and 198.)

**30. Find me:** i.e., discover by looking at my hand (This example of the "ethical dative" is an abbreviated form of "find to or for me.")

**30–31. to marry me with:** i.e., that I will marry

**31–32. companion . . . mistress:** i.e., become the fellow or equal of Queen Cleopatra

soothsayer that you praised so to th' Queen? O, that
I knew this husband which you say must ⌜charge⌝
his horns with garlands!    5

ALEXAS  Soothsayer!

SOOTHSAYER  Your will?

CHARMIAN
Is this the man?—Is 't you, sir, that know things?

SOOTHSAYER
In nature's infinite book of secrecy
A little I can read.    10

ALEXAS, ⌜*to Charmian*⌝  Show him your hand.

ENOBARBUS, ⌜*to Servants*⌝
Bring in the banquet quickly, wine enough
Cleopatra's health to drink.

CHARMIAN, ⌜*giving her hand to the Soothsayer*⌝  Good sir,
give me good fortune.    15

SOOTHSAYER  I make not, but foresee.

CHARMIAN  Pray then, foresee me one.

SOOTHSAYER
You shall be yet far fairer than you are.

CHARMIAN  He means in flesh.

IRAS  No, you shall paint when you are old.    20

CHARMIAN  Wrinkles forbid!

ALEXAS  Vex not his prescience. Be attentive.

CHARMIAN  Hush.

SOOTHSAYER
You shall be more beloving than beloved.

CHARMIAN  I had rather heat my liver with drinking.    25

ALEXAS  Nay, hear him.

CHARMIAN  Good now, some excellent fortune! Let me
be married to three kings in a forenoon and widow
them all. Let me have a child at fifty to whom Herod
of Jewry may do homage. Find me to marry me    30
with Octavius Caesar, and companion me with my
mistress.

34. **figs:** a cure for the onset of wrinkles, according to the 1582 book *Batman vppon Bartholome,* and associated since classical times with the erotic because of the fruit's resemblance to human genitalia

35. **proved:** experienced

37. **belike:** perhaps

40. **every:** i.e., every one

41. **fertile every wish:** i.e., if every wish were fertile

42. **Out:** an expression of indignant reproach; **forgive . . . witch:** (1) acquit you of any charge of witchcraft, for you are none if this is the best you can do; or (2) forgive you for your honesty because you are a witch

51. **Nilus:** Nile River, whose floods irrigated the crops that fed the population (See picture, page 82.) **presageth:** presages, portends

54–55. **fruitful prognostication:** i.e., a portent of fruitfulness

59. **I have said:** i.e., I have nothing more to say

64. **worser:** i.e., worse, indecent

SOOTHSAYER
  You shall outlive the lady whom you serve.
CHARMIAN   O, excellent! I love long life better than figs.
SOOTHSAYER
  You have seen and proved a fairer former fortune       35
  Than that which is to approach.
CHARMIAN   Then belike my children shall have no
      names. Prithee, how many boys and wenches must
      I have?
SOOTHSAYER
  If every of your wishes had a womb,                    40
  And ⌈fertile⌉ every wish, a million.
CHARMIAN   Out, fool! I forgive thee for a witch.
ALEXAS   You think none but your sheets are privy to
      your wishes.
CHARMIAN, ⌈to Soothsayer⌉  Nay, come. Tell Iras hers.    45
ALEXAS   We'll know all our fortunes.
ENOBARBUS   Mine, and most of our fortunes tonight,
      shall be—drunk to bed.
IRAS, ⌈giving her hand to the Soothsayer⌉  There's a palm
      presages chastity, if nothing else.                50
CHARMIAN   E'en as the o'erflowing Nilus presageth
      famine.
IRAS   Go, you wild bedfellow, you cannot soothsay.
CHARMIAN   Nay, if an oily palm be not a fruitful prog-
      nostication, I cannot scratch mine ear.—Prithee    55
      tell her but a workaday fortune.
SOOTHSAYER   Your fortunes are alike.
IRAS   But how, but how? Give me particulars.
SOOTHSAYER   I have said.
IRAS   Am I not an inch of fortune better than she?      60
CHARMIAN   Well, if you were but an inch of fortune
      better than I, where would you choose it?
IRAS   Not in my husband's nose.
CHARMIAN   Our worser thoughts heavens mend. Alexas—
      come, his fortune, his fortune! O, let him marry a  65

66. **go:** (1) walk; (2) become pregnant (The word **go** was also used in a variety of phrases describing the sexual act.) **Isis:** principal Egyptian goddess, associated, among other things, with the earth, the moon, and fertility (See below.)

69. **fiftyfold:** fifty times over; **hear me:** i.e., hear (See longer note, page 277.)

73. **heartbreaking:** i.e., heartbreak

74. **loose-wived:** married to a wife who is unfaithful

75. **foul:** ugly; **uncuckolded:** i.e., with a wife who is faithful (See note to lines 4–5 above.)

76. **keep decorum:** i.e., act appropriately; **fortune him:** i.e., assign him his fortunes

79–80. **they would . . . do 't:** i.e., they would make me a cuckold even if they had to make themselves whores

83. **my lord:** i.e., Antony

92. **We, us:** i.e., I, me (the royal "we")

The goddess Isis. (1.2.66–71, 3.6.18)
From [Guillaume Rouillé,] . . . *Prima pars promptuarii iconum* . . . (1553).

16

woman that cannot go, sweet Isis, I beseech thee, and
let her die, too, and give him a worse, and let worse
follow worse, till the worst of all follow him laughing
to his grave, fiftyfold a cuckold. Good Isis, hear me
this prayer, though thou deny me a matter of more    70
weight, good Isis, I beseech thee!

IRAS   Amen, dear goddess, hear that prayer of the
people. For, as it is a heartbreaking to see a hand-
some man loose-wived, so it is a deadly sorrow to
behold a foul knave uncuckolded. Therefore, dear    75
Isis, keep decorum and fortune him accordingly.

CHARMIAN   Amen.

ALEXAS   Lo now, if it lay in their hands to make me a
cuckold, they would make themselves whores but
they'd do 't.    80

ENOBARBUS   Hush, here comes Antony.

CHARMIAN   Not he. The Queen.

*Enter Cleopatra.*

CLEOPATRA   ⌜Saw⌝ you my lord?

ENOBARBUS   No, lady.

CLEOPATRA   Was he not here?    85

CHARMIAN   No, madam.

CLEOPATRA
He was disposed to mirth, but on the sudden
A Roman thought hath struck him.—Enobarbus!

ENOBARBUS   Madam?

CLEOPATRA
Seek him and bring him hither.—Where's Alexas?    90

ALEXAS
Here at your service. My lord approaches.

*Enter Antony with a Messenger.*

CLEOPATRA
We will not look upon him. Go with us.
⌜*All but Antony and the Messenger*⌝ *exit.*

93. **came . . . field:** commenced military operations

96. **time's state:** circumstances at that time

97. **jointing their force:** i.e., combining their armies

99. **better issue:** greater success

99–100. **from Italy . . . drave them:** i.e., drove Fulvia and Lucius out of Italy at **the first encounter**

101. **what worst:** i.e., what's the worst of your news

103. **On:** i.e., go on

106. **as:** i.e., as if

107. **Labienus:** See longer note, page 278.

109. **Extended:** seized; **Asia:** i.e., western region of what is now called Asia Minor (**Asia** has three syllables here.) See map, pages xvi–xvii. **Euphrates:** A river in what is now southwestern Asia, **Euphrates** is accented on the first and third syllables.

110–11. **Syria . . . Ionia: Syria** is just east of the Mediterranean; **Ionia** and **Lydia** were in present-day Asia Minor (See map, pages xvi–xvii.)

115. **home:** directly; **mince not:** i.e., do not euphemistically report; **general tongue:** i.e., what the (Roman) people are saying

117. **in Fulvia's phrase:** i.e., using the language Fulvia would use

118. **full license:** i.e., total freedom

119–21. **we bring . . . earing:** This difficult metaphor compares humans as moral beings to an ecosystem. Like soil when it is not swept by **winds**, we produce **weeds.** Being told of our misdeeds is like plowing the weeds under. **quick:** brisk, sharp **ills:** misdeeds **earing:** plowing (Compare this passage to

*(continued)*

MESSENGER
  Fulvia thy wife first came into the field.
ANTONY   Against my brother Lucius?
MESSENGER   Ay.                                                                 95
  But soon that war had end, and the time's state
  Made friends of them, jointing their force 'gainst
    Caesar,
  Whose better issue in the war from Italy
  Upon the first encounter drave them.                                          100
ANTONY   Well, what worst?
MESSENGER
  The nature of bad news infects the teller.
ANTONY
  When it concerns the fool or, coward. On.
  Things that are past are done, with me. 'Tis thus:
  Who tells me true, though in his tale lie death,                              105
  I hear him as he flattered.
MESSENGER                    Labienus—
  This is stiff news—hath with his Parthian force
  Extended Asia: from Euphrates
  His conquering banner shook, from Syria                                       110
  To Lydia and to Ionia,
  Whilst—
ANTONY      "Antony," thou wouldst say?
MESSENGER                              O, my lord!
ANTONY
  Speak to me home; mince not the general tongue.                              115
  Name Cleopatra as she is called in Rome;
  Rail thou in Fulvia's phrase, and taunt my faults
  With such full license as both truth and malice
  Have power to utter. O, then we bring forth weeds
  When our quick winds lie still, and our ills told us                          120
  Is as our earing. Fare thee well awhile.
MESSENGER   At your noble pleasure.   *Messenger exits.*

*Henry VI, Part 3:* "For what doth cherish weeds but gentle air?" and to the proverb: "Weeds come forth on the fattest soil if it is untilled.") See below.

124. **Sicyon:** a town in Greece

126. **stays . . . will:** i.e., is waiting until you want to hear him

130. **What:** i.e., who

135. **Importeth thee:** i.e., it concerns you

136. **Forbear me:** i.e., leave me

138. **contempts:** actions of contemning or despising; **doth:** i.e., do

139. **present:** immediately available

140. **By revolution lowering:** i.e., in due course of time decreasing in desirability (literally, descending as if by the turning of a wheel)

142. **could:** i.e., would now be willing to

144. **ills:** disasters

Earing (plowing) a field. (1.2.121)
From Joseph Blagrave, *The epitomie of the art of husbandry . . .* (1685).

*Enter another Messenger.*

ANTONY
From Sicyon how the news? Speak there.

⌜SECOND⌝ MESSENGER
The man from Sicyon—

⌜ANTONY⌝                    Is there such an one?          125

SECOND MESSENGER
He stays upon your will.

ANTONY                    Let him appear.
                         ⌜*Second Messenger exits.*⌝
These strong Egyptian fetters I must break,
Or lose myself in dotage.

*Enter another Messenger with a letter.*

                         What are you?          130

THIRD MESSENGER
Fulvia thy wife is dead.

ANTONY                    Where died she?

⌜THIRD⌝ MESSENGER    In Sicyon.
Her length of sickness, with what else more serious
Importeth thee to know, this bears.          135
                    ⌜*He hands Antony the letter.*⌝

ANTONY                    Forbear me.
                    ⌜*Third Messenger exits.*⌝
There's a great spirit gone! Thus did I desire it.
What our contempts doth often hurl from us,
We wish it ours again. The present pleasure,
By revolution lowering, does become          140
The opposite of itself. She's good, being gone.
The hand could pluck her back that shoved her on.
I must from this enchanting queen break off.
Ten thousand harms more than the ills I know
My idleness doth hatch.—How now, Enobarbus!          145

*Enter Enobarbus.*

157. **moment:** cause or motive for action

158. **mettle:** vigor, ardor

160. **dying:** with wordplay on **dying** as "experiencing sexual orgasm"

167. **Jove:** i.e., Jupiter, king of the gods in Roman mythology, and god of thunder, lightning, and rain (See page 170.)

168. **Would:** i.e., I wish

171. **withal:** with; **travel:** Travelers were notorious for telling tales of wonders.

179–80. **tailors of the earth:** Like **tailors,** who fashion new replacements **when old robes are worn out** (lines 180–81), the gods create new persons in place of old.

Cleopatra, "Egypt's queen." (1.1.34)
From Jacobus de Strada, *Epitome thesauri antiquitatum . . .* (1557).

22

ENOBARBUS   What's your pleasure, sir?

ANTONY   I must with haste from hence.

ENOBARBUS   Why then we kill all our women. We see
     how mortal an unkindness is to them. If they suffer
     our departure, death's the word.                                    150

ANTONY   I must be gone.

ENOBARBUS   Under a compelling occasion, let women
     die. It were pity to cast them away for nothing,
     though between them and a great cause, they
     should be esteemed nothing. Cleopatra, catching    155
     but the least noise of this, dies instantly. I have seen
     her die twenty times upon far poorer moment. I do
     think there is mettle in death which commits some
     loving act upon her, she hath such a celerity in
     dying.                                                                       160

ANTONY   She is cunning past man's thought.

ENOBARBUS   Alack, sir, no, her passions are made of
     nothing but the finest part of pure love. We cannot
     call her winds and waters sighs and tears; they are
     greater storms and tempests than almanacs can    165
     report. This cannot be cunning in her; if it be, she
     makes a shower of rain as well as Jove.

ANTONY   Would I had never seen her!

ENOBARBUS   O, sir, you had then left unseen a wonder-
     ful piece of work, which not to have been blest    170
     withal would have discredited your travel.

ANTONY   Fulvia is dead.

ENOBARBUS   Sir?

ANTONY   Fulvia is dead.

ENOBARBUS   Fulvia?                                                     175

ANTONY   Dead.

ENOBARBUS   Why, sir, give the gods a thankful sacrifice.
     When it pleaseth their deities to take the wife of a
     man from him, it shows to man the tailors of the

180. **therein:** in this respect

181. **members:** limbs of the body (with wordplay on sexual organs)

183. **cut:** blow (with possible wordplay on "fashion" or "style")

184, 185. **smock, petticoat:** Distinctively feminine garments, they here refer to women themselves: Fulvia and Cleopatra.

185–86. **the tears . . . onion that:** i.e., only feigned **tears**

187. **broachèd:** started (In line 189, the word is repeated with wordplay on its meaning of "pierced.")

191. **abode:** remaining

193. **notice:** i.e., notice of; **break:** make known

194. **expedience:** (1) haste; (2) expedition

196. **with . . . touches:** i.e., together with more pressing concerns

197. **Do:** i.e., does

198. **many our contriving friends:** i.e., many of the people who are making plans on our behalf

199. **at home:** i.e., to come home; **Sextus Pompeius:** i.e., Pompey

200. **given the dare to:** i.e., challenged

200–201. **commands . . . of:** i.e., controls

204. **Pompey the Great:** i.e., the name of Pompey the Great (Cneius Pompeius Magnus [106–48 BCE] was, with Julius Caesar and Crassus, a member of the first triumvirate. After being defeated in civil war, he fled to Egypt, where he was murdered.) See page 96.

206. **blood and life:** courage and spirit

206–7. **stands . . . soldier:** i.e., ranks as the greatest **soldier**

*(continued)*

earth; comforting therein, that when old robes are 180
worn out, there are members to make new. If there
were no more women but Fulvia, then had you
indeed a cut, and the case to be lamented. This grief
is crowned with consolation; your old smock brings
forth a new petticoat, and indeed the tears live in an 185
onion that should water this sorrow.

ANTONY
The business she hath broachèd in the state
Cannot endure my absence.

ENOBARBUS    And the business you have broached here
cannot be without you, especially that of Cleopa- 190
tra's, which wholly depends on your abode.

ANTONY
No more light answers. Let our officers
Have notice what we purpose. I shall break
The cause of our expedience to the Queen
And get her ⌈leave⌉ to part. For not alone        195
The death of Fulvia, with more urgent touches,
Do strongly speak to us, but the letters too
Of many our contriving friends in Rome
Petition us at home. Sextus Pompeius
⌈Hath⌉ given the dare to Caesar and commands        200
The empire of the sea. Our slippery people,
Whose love is never linked to the deserver
Till his deserts are past, begin to throw
Pompey the Great and all his dignities
Upon his son, who—high in name and power,        205
Higher than both in blood and life—stands up
For the main soldier; whose quality, going on,
The sides o' th' world may danger. Much is
    breeding
Which, like the courser's hair, hath yet but life        210
And not a serpent's poison. Say our pleasure,

207–8. **whose quality . . . danger:** i.e., whose nature and condition, if not restrained, may endanger the whole **world** (The world is imaged here, as often in this play, as an architectural construction.)

210–11. **courser's hair . . . poison:** Antony plays on the belief that a horse's **hair** submerged in standing water becomes a living creature, a worm, which he images as capable of later growing to be a poisonous serpent.

**1.3** Cleopatra, after accusing Antony of hypocrisy and betrayal, gives him leave to depart from Egypt.

———————

4. **sad:** serious, grave, sober

6. **sudden:** i.e., suddenly

7. **methinks:** i.e., it seems to me

8. **hold:** adhere to

10. **should I do:** i.e., should I do that

11. **give him way:** i.e., give way to him; **cross:** oppose

13. **I wish, forbear:** i.e., I wish that you would desist

17. **breathing:** utterance

To such whose ⌜place is⌝ under us, ⌜requires⌝
Our quick remove from hence.
ENOBARBUS    I shall do 't.

⌜*They exit.*⌝


⌜Scene 3⌝
*Enter Cleopatra, Charmian, Alexas, and Iras.*

CLEOPATRA
  Where is he?
CHARMIAN        I did not see him since.
CLEOPATRA, ⌜*to Alexas*⌝
  See where he is, who's with him, what he does.
  I did not send you. If you find him sad,
  Say I am dancing; if in mirth, report                          5
  That I am sudden sick. Quick, and return.

⌜*Alexas exits.*⌝

CHARMIAN
  Madam, methinks, if you did love him dearly,
  You do not hold the method to enforce
  The like from him.
CLEOPATRA            What should I do I do not?        10
CHARMIAN
  In each thing give him way; cross him in nothing.
CLEOPATRA
  Thou teachest like a fool: the way to lose him.
CHARMIAN
  Tempt him not so too far. I wish, forbear.
  In time we hate that which we often fear.

*Enter Antony.*

  But here comes Antony.                                          15
CLEOPATRA                    I am sick and sullen.
ANTONY
  I am sorry to give breathing to my purpose—

19–20. **It cannot . . . it:** i.e., my condition cannot last long; my constitution will not be able to hold up under it

25–26. **What, says . . . to come:** See longer note, page 278. **What:** an interjection introducing a question or exclamation

35. **shake the thronèd gods:** See longer note, page 278.

36. **Who:** i.e., you, who; **Riotous madness:** i.e., it was extravagant foolishness on my part

37. **mouth-made:** rather than heartfelt

38. **in swearing:** i.e., as they are being sworn

41. **color . . . going:** i.e., excuse for your unjustifiable departure

42. **sued staying:** pleaded to stay

44. **our:** i.e., my (the royal "we")

45. **our brows' bent:** i.e., the curve of my eyebrows; **none our parts:** i.e., none of my features or qualities was

46. **a race of heaven:** i.e., descended from heaven

CLEOPATRA
  Help me away, dear Charmian! I shall fall.
  It cannot be thus long; the sides of nature
  Will not sustain it.                      20
ANTONY          Now, my dearest queen—
CLEOPATRA
  Pray you stand farther from me.
ANTONY                 What's the matter?
CLEOPATRA
  I know by that same eye there's some good news.
  What, says the married woman you may go?      25
  Would she had never given you leave to come.
  Let her not say 'tis I that keep you here.
  I have no power upon you. Hers you are.
ANTONY
  The gods best know—
CLEOPATRA          O, never was there queen    30
  So mightily betrayed! Yet at the first
  I saw the treasons planted.
ANTONY              Cleopatra—
CLEOPATRA
  Why should I think you can be mine, and true—
  Though you in swearing shake the thronèd gods—  35
  Who have been false to Fulvia? Riotous madness,
  To be entangled with those mouth-made vows
  Which break themselves in swearing!
ANTONY                  Most sweet
  queen—                          40
CLEOPATRA
  Nay, pray you seek no color for your going,
  But bid farewell and go. When you sued staying,
  Then was the time for words. No going then!
  Eternity was in our lips and eyes,
  Bliss in our brows' bent; none our parts so poor    45
  But was a race of heaven. They are so still,

51. **a heart in Egypt:** (1) a person with courage in **Egypt**; (2) courage in Cleopatra, queen of **Egypt**

55. **in use:** in trust

56. **civil swords:** i.e., swords drawn in civil wars

57. **the port of Rome:** Ostia

58. **two domestic powers:** i.e., Pompey's and the triumvirs; or, Octavius Caesar's and Lepidus' (Antony's fellow triumvirs)

59. **Breed scrupulous faction:** i.e., breeds quarrels over trivial things (Literally, a scruple is 1/24 of an ounce.)

61. **Are newly grown to love:** i.e., have recently become popular; **condemned Pompey:** Pompey had been proscribed by the Roman Senate.

64. **Upon . . . state:** i.e., under the current government (of the triumvirs)

65. **purge:** purify or heal itself (See longer note, page 278.)

66. **particular:** i.e., personal (reason for going)

67. **safe:** i.e., make safe

73. **garboils:** confusions, brawls

76–77. **sacred vials . . . water:** i.e., bottles (**vials**) of tears sometimes put by Romans into the urn of a friend

Or thou, the greatest soldier of the world,
Art turned the greatest liar.

ANTONY                            How now, lady?

CLEOPATRA

I would I had thy inches. Thou shouldst know          50
There were a heart in Egypt.

ANTONY                           Hear me, queen:
The strong necessity of time commands
Our services awhile, but my full heart
Remains in use with you. Our Italy                   55
Shines o'er with civil swords; Sextus Pompeius
Makes his approaches to the port of Rome;
Equality of two domestic powers
Breed scrupulous faction; the hated grown to
   strength                                          60
Are newly grown to love; the condemned Pompey,
Rich in his father's honor, creeps apace
Into the hearts of such as have not thrived
Upon the present state, whose numbers threaten;
And quietness, grown sick of rest, would purge       65
By any desperate change. My more particular,
And that which most with you should safe my going,
Is Fulvia's death.

CLEOPATRA

Though age from folly could not give me freedom,
It does from childishness. Can Fulvia die?           70

ANTONY   She's dead, my queen. ⌜*He shows her papers.*⌝
Look here, and at thy sovereign leisure read
The garboils she awaked; at the last, best,
See when and where she died.

CLEOPATRA                      O, most false love!    75
Where be the sacred vials thou shouldst fill
With sorrowful water? Now I see, I see,
In Fulvia's death, how mine received shall be.

ANTONY

Quarrel no more, but be prepared to know

80–81. **are . . . advice:** i.e., I will carry out or not according to your judgment

81–82. **the fire / That . . . slime:** i.e., the sun, which **quickens** (gives life) to **Nilus' slime** (See note to 1.2.51.)

84. **affects:** prefers

85. **lace:** cord that draws closed the bodice of her dress (a famous anachronism in this play, since Roman dress did not have bodices closed with cords)

87. **So:** i.e., (1) since; or (2) in the same (erratic) way

89. **evidence:** witness

94. **Egypt:** i.e., me

97. **heat my blood:** i.e., make me angry

98. **meetly:** suitable (to the role in which Cleopatra has cast him in lines 92–96 above)

100. **target:** shield, buckler (See longer note, page 279.) **mends:** improves

102. **Herculean:** Hercules-like (In Greek mythology, Hercules was a hero of extraordinary strength and courage. See longer note, page 279, and picture, page 194.)

102–3. **does become . . . chafe:** i.e., plays so well the role of an angry man **carriage:** deportment, bearing **chafe:** rage, fury

109. **oblivion:** (1) forgetfulness; (2) state of being forgotten (See longer note, page 279.)

110. **all:** entirely

112. **idleness:** silliness, foolishness (Replying, Cleopatra plays on the word's senses of "inactivity" or "indolence.")

The purposes I bear, which are or cease          80
As you shall give th' advice. By the fire
That quickens Nilus' slime, I go from hence
Thy soldier, servant, making peace or war
As thou affects.
CLEOPATRA          Cut my lace, Charmian, come!          85
But let it be; I am quickly ill and well;
So Antony loves.
ANTONY          My precious queen, forbear,
And give true evidence to his love, which stands
An honorable trial.          90
CLEOPATRA          So Fulvia told me.
I prithee turn aside and weep for her,
Then bid adieu to me, and say the tears
Belong to Egypt. Good now, play one scene
Of excellent dissembling, and let it look          95
Like perfect honor.
ANTONY          You'll heat my blood. No more!
CLEOPATRA
You can do better yet, but this is meetly.
ANTONY
Now by ⌜my⌝ sword—
CLEOPATRA          And target. Still he mends.          100
But this is not the best. Look, prithee, Charmian,
How this Herculean Roman does become
The carriage of his chafe.
ANTONY   I'll leave you, lady.
CLEOPATRA   Courteous lord, one word.          105
Sir, you and I must part, but that's not it;
Sir, you and I have loved, but there's not it;
That you know well. Something it is I would—
O, my oblivion is a very Antony,
And I am all forgotten.          110
ANTONY          But that your Royalty
Holds idleness your subject, I should take you
For idleness itself.

**114–15. labor / To bear:** i.e., work to endure (with wordplay on **labor** as "labor pains" and on **bear** as "give birth to")

**117. my becomings:** i.e., (even) the things that befit or grace me

**118. Eye:** appear

**120–22. Upon . . . feet:** The allusion here is to the Roman custom in which a wreath of laurel crowned a conqueror and flowers or laurel branches were **strewed before** the conqueror's **feet.** (See page 200.)

**1.4** Octavius Caesar condemns Antony's behavior in Egypt, and, in the face of attacks by Pompey, Menas, and Menecrates, he wishes for Antony's return.

———————

**3. competitor:** (1) partner, associate; (2) rival

**6. the queen of Ptolemy:** i.e., Cleopatra, referred to by the name of her former, now-dead husband, **Ptolemy**

**7. hardly gave audience:** i.e., he was harsh in receiving our messengers (Compare 1.1 and 1.2.)

**9. there:** i.e., in this letter

**10. abstract:** epitome

CLEOPATRA       'Tis sweating labor
  To bear such idleness so near the heart      115
  As Cleopatra this. But, sir, forgive me,
  Since my becomings kill me when they do not
  Eye well to you. Your honor calls you hence;
  Therefore be deaf to my unpitied folly,
  And all the gods go with you. Upon your sword   120
  Sit laurel victory, and smooth success
  Be strewed before your feet.
ANTONY           Let us go. Come.
  Our separation so abides and flies
  That thou, residing here, goes yet with me,   125
  And I, hence fleeting, here remain with thee.
  Away!

                        *They exit.*


⌜Scene 4⌝
*Enter Octavius ⌜Caesar,⌝ reading a letter,*
*Lepidus, and their Train.*

CAESAR
  You may see, Lepidus, and henceforth know,
  It is not Caesar's natural vice to hate
  ⌜Our⌝ great competitor. From Alexandria
  This is the news: he fishes, drinks, and wastes
  The lamps of night in revel, is not more manlike   5
  Than Cleopatra, nor the queen of Ptolemy
  More womanly than he; hardly gave audience, or
  ⌜Vouchsafed⌝ to think he had partners. You shall
    find there
  A man who is th' ⌜abstract⌝ of all faults   10
  That all men follow.
LEPIDUS         I must not think there are
  Evils enough to darken all his goodness.

14. **spots of heaven:** i.e., stars

15. **More fiery by:** i.e., that appear more fiery by contrast to

16. **purchased:** acquired

20. **for a mirth:** i.e., in return for pleasure or amusement

21. **keep . . . tippling:** i.e., keep pace, drink for drink

22. **reel:** i.e., stagger drunkenly through; **stand the buffet:** i.e., exchange blows, brawl

23. **smells:** i.e., smell

25. **composure:** temperament, that which constitutes him

28. **foils:** disgraces, stigmas

29. **in his lightness:** i.e., because of his frivolity, thoughtlessness, lewdness

29–32. **If he . . . for 't:** i.e., if he gratified himself in his leisure time, let him suffer for it in a sick body **vacancy:** leisure time, idleness **surfeits:** sicknesses arising from excessive eating and drinking **dryness of his bones:** a symptom associated with old age or with venereal diseases

32–34. **But . . . ours:** i.e., but by wasting time now, he puts all three of us in danger of losing power **confound:** waste **sport:** amusement (but also sexual gratification) **state:** high rank and power (as a triumvir)

34–37. **'tis . . . judgment:** i.e., he should be rebuked as boys are who, knowing better, nonetheless heedlessly pursue pleasure **rate:** berate **to judgment:** i.e., against good judgment

42. **of those:** i.e., by those

*(continued)*

His faults in him seem as the spots of heaven,
More fiery by night's blackness, hereditary          15
Rather than purchased, what he cannot change
Than what he chooses.

CAESAR
You are too indulgent. Let's grant it is not
Amiss to tumble on the bed of Ptolemy,
To give a kingdom for a mirth, to sit          20
And keep the turn of tippling with a slave,
To reel the streets at noon and stand the buffet
With knaves that smells of sweat. Say this becomes
    him—
As his composure must be rare indeed          25
Whom these things cannot blemish—yet must
    Antony
No way excuse his foils when we do bear
So great weight in his lightness. If he filled
His vacancy with his voluptuousness,          30
Full surfeits and the dryness of his bones
Call on him for 't. But to confound such time
That drums him from his sport and speaks as loud
As his own state and ours, 'tis to be chid
As we rate boys who, being mature in knowledge,          35
Pawn their experience to their present pleasure
And so rebel to judgment.

*Enter a Messenger.*

LEPIDUS                    Here's more news.
MESSENGER
Thy biddings have been done, and every hour,
Most noble Caesar, shalt thou have report          40
How 'tis abroad. Pompey is strong at sea,
And it appears he is beloved of those
That only have feared Caesar. To the ports
The discontents repair, and men's reports
Give him much wronged.          45

43. **only have feared Caesar:** i.e., been loyal to Caesar only for fear of him

44. **discontents:** discontented men, malcontents

45. **Give him:** i.e., give him out as, represent him as

47. **from the primal state:** i.e., (1) by all political history since the founding of the first government; or, (2) since the primeval days of human society

48. **That he . . . were:** i.e., that a man is regarded as a desirable leader only until he becomes one

49. **ebbed:** decayed; **ne'er worth love:** i.e., no longer powerful

50. **feared:** held in awe (See longer note, page 280.) **This common body:** i.e., the common people

51. **vagabond:** (1) restless; (2) good-for-nothing; **flag:** rush, reed

52. **lackeying:** i.e., in the service of (A lackey's job was to run errands.)

55. **famous:** notorious

56. **Makes:** i.e., make; **ear:** plough

59. **borders maritime:** i.e., coastal regions

60. **Lack blood:** i.e., are pale (with fear); **flush:** lusty, vigorous

62–63. **strikes more . . . resisted:** i.e., costs you more supporters than you would lose if they fought a war against him on your behalf

66. **Modena:** i.e., Mutina, a city in northern Italy

67. **Hirsius and Pansa:** After the assassination of Julius Caesar, Antony and Octavius Caesar became embattled, and the Senate sent the consuls **Hirsius and Pansa** to drive Antony out of Italy. Although both consuls were killed in their battle, their side was victorious and Antony was driven out and forced to cross the Alps.

*(continued)*

CAESAR                         I should have known no less.
It hath been taught us from the primal state
That he which is was wished until he were,
And the ebbed man, ne'er loved till ne'er worth love,
Comes feared by being lacked. This common body,    50
Like to a vagabond flag upon the stream,
Goes to and back, ⌜lackeying⌝ the varying tide
To rot itself with motion.

        ⌜*Enter a Second Messenger.*⌝

⌜SECOND⌝ MESSENGER  Caesar, I bring thee word
  Menecrates and Menas, famous pirates,       55
Makes the sea serve them, which they ear and
    wound
With keels of every kind. Many hot inroads
They make in Italy—the borders maritime
Lack blood to think on 't—and flush youth revolt.    60
No vessel can peep forth but 'tis as soon
Taken as seen, for Pompey's name strikes more
Than could his war resisted.

CAESAR                 Antony,
Leave thy lascivious ⌜wassails.⌝ When thou once    65
Was beaten from Modena, where thou slew'st
Hirsius and Pansa, consuls, at thy heel
Did famine follow, whom thou fought'st against,
Though daintily brought up, with patience more
Than savages could suffer. Thou didst drink    70
The stale of horses and the gilded puddle
Which beasts would cough at. Thy palate then did
    deign
The roughest berry on the rudest hedge.
Yea, like the stag when snow the pasture sheets,    75
The barks of trees thou browsèd. On the Alps
It is reported thou didst eat strange flesh
Which some did die to look on. And all this—

68. **whom:** i.e., which

69. **daintily:** with every comfort; **patience more:** greater composure

70. **could suffer:** i.e., exhibit in suffering

71. **stale:** urine

73. **deign:** condescend to accept; not disdain

74. **roughest:** harshest-tasting; **rudest:** wildest

81. **lanked not:** did not grow hollow or thin

82. **of:** about

85. **i' th' field:** on the battlefield

90. **what:** i.e., what forces; **can be able:** i.e., am able to muster

91. **front:** oppose

95. **stirs:** insurrections, public disturbances

97. **Doubt:** fear; mistrust (me); **bond:** duty

**1.5** Cleopatra receives a pearl and a message from Antony and resolves to send him a letter each day that he's away.

───────────

3. **Ha, ha:** often interpreted by editors as a yawn of boredom; **mandragora:** i.e., narcotic syrup from the mandrake plant

It wounds thine honor that I speak it now—
Was borne so like a soldier that thy cheek          80
So much as lanked not.

LEPIDUS     'Tis pity of him.

CAESAR     Let his shames quickly
Drive him to Rome. 'Tis time we twain
Did show ourselves i' th' field, and to that end          85
Assemble ⌜we⌝ immediate council. Pompey
Thrives in our idleness.

LEPIDUS                              Tomorrow, Caesar,
I shall be furnished to inform you rightly
Both what by sea and land I can be able          90
To front this present time.

CAESAR                              Till which encounter,
It is my business too. Farewell.

LEPIDUS
Farewell, my lord. What you shall know meantime
Of stirs abroad, I shall beseech you, sir,          95
To let me be partaker.

CAESAR
Doubt not, sir. I knew it for my bond.

                                        *They exit.*


⌜Scene 5⌝
*Enter Cleopatra, Charmian, Iras, and Mardian.*

CLEOPATRA     Charmian!

CHARMIAN     Madam?

CLEOPATRA     Ha, ha! Give me to drink mandragora.

CHARMIAN     Why, madam?

CLEOPATRA
That I might sleep out this great gap of time          5
My Antony is away.

CHARMIAN     You think of him too much.

12. **sing:** Eunuchs, or *castrati*, were employed as singers by the church and by patrons in Shakespeare's time.

13. **aught:** anything

14. **unseminared:** castrated

15. **of:** i.e., from; **affections:** desires

19. **honest:** (1) virtuous, upright; (2) chaste

21. **What . . . Mars:** i.e., of lovemaking (**Venus,** the Roman goddess of love, and **Mars,** the Roman god of war, were famous lovers trapped by Venus' husband in the act of lovemaking. See Ovid's *Metamorphoses* 4.171–89.)

23. **he:** i.e., Antony

26. **Do bravely:** i.e., make a splendid show of yourself; **wot'st:** know

28. **The demi-Atlas . . . earth:** i.e., the one who carries half the weight of the world on his shoulders (In mythology, the god **Atlas** shoulders the whole of this weight. See page 104.) **arm:** support (that which one relies upon for support or assistance) See longer note, page 280.

29. **burgonet:** light steel helmet, expertly designed to protect the neck of its wearer

33. **with Phoebus' . . . black:** i.e., tanned by the sun (Phoebus Apollo is the Roman god of the sun; Africans were then thought by some to have darker skin because of the sun's heat near the Equator.) See longer note to 1.1.6, page 277.

34. **Broad-fronted Caesar:** a reference to the wide forehead of Julius Caesar (See page 72.)

36. **great Pompey:** another of Cleopatra's past lovers (not Pompey the Great, but his son, the elder brother to the Pompey who appears in the play)

*(continued)*

42

CLEOPATRA
  O, 'tis treason!
CHARMIAN         Madam, I trust not so.
CLEOPATRA
  Thou, eunuch Mardian!                             10
MARDIAN             What's your Highness' pleasure?
CLEOPATRA
  Not now to hear thee sing. I take no pleasure
  In aught an eunuch has. 'Tis well for thee
  That, being unseminared, thy freer thoughts
  May not fly forth of Egypt. Hast thou affections?     15
MARDIAN    Yes, gracious madam.
CLEOPATRA    Indeed?
MARDIAN
  Not in deed, madam, for I can do nothing
  But what indeed is honest to be done.
  Yet have I fierce affections, and think                 20
  What Venus did with Mars.
CLEOPATRA                  O, Charmian,
  Where think'st thou he is now? Stands he, or sits he?
  Or does he walk? Or is he on his horse?
  O happy horse, to bear the weight of Antony!       25
  Do bravely, horse, for wot'st thou whom thou
    mov'st?
  The demi-Atlas of this earth, the arm
  And burgonet of men. He's speaking now,
  Or murmuring "Where's my serpent of old Nile?"    30
  For so he calls me. Now I feed myself
  With most delicious poison. Think on me
  That am with Phoebus' amorous pinches black,
  And wrinkled deep in time? Broad-fronted Caesar,
  When thou wast here above the ground, I was      35
  A morsel for a monarch. And great Pompey
  Would stand and make his eyes grow in my brow;
  There would he anchor his aspect, and die
  With looking on his life.

37. **grow:** become ineradicably fixed

38. **aspect:** gaze (accent on second syllable)

42–43. **that great . . . thee:** Cleopatra compares Antony to the philosopher's stone or elixir (**med'cine**) reputed by alchemists to have the power to turn base metals to gold, and suggests that Alexas has been covered in gold (**gilded**) by having been with Antony. **tinct:** (1) tincture, immaterial substance; (2) color

44. **brave:** splendid

51. **firm:** constant, unwavering; **Egypt:** i.e., Cleopatra

53. **piece:** i.e., piece out, extend, enlarge

56. **arm-gaunt:** perhaps, fit and trim from service in battle (This word is not recorded as occurring elsewhere; its meaning is thus uncertain, and it has often been emended by editors.)

58. **dumbed:** i.e., silenced

61. **nor sad:** i.e., neither sad

62. **Note him:** i.e., observe (Alexas' description of) Antony

66. **make . . . by his:** i.e., fashion their expressions according to his

67. **remembrance:** memory

*Enter Alexas from* ⌈*Antony.*⌉

ALEXAS   Sovereign of Egypt, hail!                                    40
CLEOPATRA
  How much unlike art thou Mark Antony!
  Yet coming from him, that great med'cine hath
  With his tinct gilded thee.
  How goes it with my brave Mark Antony?
ALEXAS   Last thing he did, dear queen,                               45
  He kissed—the last of many doubled kisses—
  This orient pearl. His speech sticks in my heart.
CLEOPATRA
  Mine ear must pluck it thence.
ALEXAS                              "Good friend," quoth
    he,                                                              50
  "Say the firm Roman to great Egypt sends
  This treasure of an oyster; at whose foot,
  To mend the petty present, I will piece
  Her opulent throne with kingdoms. All the East,
  Say thou, shall call her mistress." So he nodded     55
  And soberly did mount an arm-gaunt steed,
  Who neighed so high that what I would have spoke
  Was beastly ⌈dumbed⌉ by him.
CLEOPATRA   What, was he sad, or merry?
ALEXAS
  Like to the time o' th' year between th' extremes    60
  Of hot and cold, he was nor sad nor merry.
CLEOPATRA
  O, well-divided disposition!—Note him,
  Note him, good Charmian, 'tis the man! But note
    him:
  He was not sad, for he would shine on those          65
  That make their looks by his; he was not merry,
  Which seemed to tell them his remembrance lay
  In Egypt with his joy; but between both.

69. **mingle:** mixture
71. **posts:** messengers
72. **several:** individual
79. **brave:** See line 44 and note.
80. **emphasis:** emphatic expression
84. **paragon:** compare
87. **after you:** i.e., according to your tune

Mars, the Roman god of war. (1.1.4)
From Vincenzo Cartari, *Le imagini de i dei . . .* (1587).

O, heavenly mingle!—Be'st thou sad or merry,
The violence of either thee becomes,                    70
So does it no man's else.—Met'st thou my posts?

ALEXAS
Ay, madam, twenty several messengers.
Why do you send so thick?

CLEOPATRA                    Who's born that day
When I forget to send to Antony                         75
Shall die a beggar.—Ink and paper, Charmian.—
Welcome, my good Alexas.—Did I, Charmian,
Ever love Caesar so?

CHARMIAN                O, that brave Caesar!

CLEOPATRA
Be choked with such another emphasis!                   80
Say "the brave Antony."

CHARMIAN                The valiant Caesar!

CLEOPATRA
By Isis, I will give thee bloody teeth
If thou with Caesar paragon again
My man of men.                                          85

CHARMIAN        By your most gracious pardon,
I sing but after you.

CLEOPATRA        My salad days,
When I was green in judgment, cold in blood,
To say as I said then. But come, away,                  90
Get me ink and paper.
He shall have every day a several greeting,
Or I'll unpeople Egypt.

                                        *They exit.*

# ANTONY

### AND

# CLEOPATRA

ACT 2

**2.1** Pompey learns that Antony has left Egypt for Rome, and fears that Antony and Caesar will unite against him.

----

5. **suitors:** petitioners
13. **powers:** armed forces; **crescent:** increasing, waxing (like the moon); **auguring:** prophesying
14. **it:** i.e., the crescent new moon (of my **powers**)
16. **without doors:** out of doors, outside (i.e., Antony's only wars will be, in a highly conventional figure of speech from Shakespeare's time, wars of love)
17. **both:** i.e., Antony and Caesar
21. **in the field:** engaged in military operations

The Triumvirate of Octavius Caesar, Antony, and Lepidus. (1.1.13)
From Jacobus de Strada, *Epitome thesauri antiquitatum . . .* (1557).

# ⌜ACT 2⌝

---

## ⌜Scene 1⌝

*Enter Pompey, Menecrates, and Menas,*
*in warlike manner.*

**POMPEY**
 If the great gods be just, they shall assist
 The deeds of justest men.
**MENAS**                         Know, worthy Pompey,
 That what they do delay they not deny.
**POMPEY**
 Whiles we are suitors to their throne, decays          5
 The thing we sue for.
**MENAS**                    We, ignorant of ourselves,
 Beg often our own harms, which the wise powers
 Deny us for our good; so find we profit
 By losing of our prayers.                               10
**POMPEY**                    I shall do well.
 The people love me, and the sea is mine;
 My powers are crescent, and my auguring hope
 Says it will come to th' full. Mark Antony
 In Egypt sits at dinner, and will make                  15
 No wars without doors. Caesar gets money where
 He loses hearts. Lepidus flatters both,
 Of both is flattered; but he neither loves,
 Nor either cares for him.
**MENAS**                    Caesar and Lepidus           20
 Are in the field. A mighty strength they carry.

51

25. **Looking for Antony:** i.e., hoping for Antony's return

26. **Salt:** lecherous; **wanned:** dark (See longer note, page 280.)

29. **brain fuming:** The fumes of wine were then thought to rise from the stomach to the brain.

30. **cloyless sauce:** sauce that does not cloy or satiate

31. **prorogue his honor:** i.e., defer any consideration of his duty

32. **Even . . . dullness:** i.e., until he has sunk into oblivion (The Lethe was a river in the Underworld of classical mythology whose name means "forgetfulness." The dead who drank from it totally forgot the past.)

35. **every:** i.e., each

38. **less matter:** i.e., news of less substance

43. **opinion:** i.e., opinion of ourselves

46. **cannot hope:** do not expect

49. **His brother:** Antony's brother Lucius Antonius, who joined Fulvia in her war against Caesar and Lepidus

**POMPEY**
  Where have you this? 'Tis false.
**MENAS**                                    From Silvius, sir.
**POMPEY**
  He dreams. I know they are in Rome together,
  Looking for Antony. But all the charms of love,          25
  Salt Cleopatra, soften thy wanned lip!
  Let witchcraft join with beauty, lust with both;
  Tie up the libertine in a field of feasts;
  Keep his brain fuming. Epicurean cooks
  Sharpen with cloyless sauce his appetite,          30
  That sleep and feeding may prorogue his honor
  Even till a Lethe'd dullness—

                    *Enter Varrius.*

                              How now, Varrius?
**VARRIUS**
  This is most certain that I shall deliver:
  Mark Antony is every hour in Rome          35
  Expected. Since he went from Egypt 'tis
  A space for farther travel.
**POMPEY**   I could have given less matter
  A better ear.—Menas, I did not think
  This amorous surfeiter would have donned his helm     40
  For such a petty war. His soldiership
  Is twice the other twain. But let us rear
  The higher our opinion, that our stirring
  Can from the lap of Egypt's widow pluck
  The ne'er lust-wearied Antony.          45
**MENAS**                              I cannot hope
  Caesar and Antony shall well greet together.
  His wife that's dead did trespasses to Caesar;
  His brother ⌜warred⌝ upon him, although I think
  Not moved by Antony.          50
**POMPEY**                    I know not, Menas,

54. **pregnant:** clear, obvious; **square:** fall out, quarrel

56. **entertainèd:** received

58. **cement:** accent on first syllable

60–61. **It only . . . hands:** i.e., our very survival depends upon our using the greatest force we can

**2.2** Antony agrees to marry Caesar's sister Octavia as a way of cementing the newly reestablished bond between the men. Enobarbus predicts that Antony will nonetheless return to Cleopatra.

---

5. **like himself:** i.e., in a way that is appropriate to his greatness; **move:** provoke, anger

6. **Let Antony . . . head:** The implication is that Antony is taller and more imposing than Octavius Caesar.

8–9. **Were . . . today:** i.e., I would defy Caesar by remaining unshaven (Editors are divided as to whether Antony is to be seen as thus openly tempting Caesar to pluck his beard and thus begin a fight, or as showing Caesar disrespect by failing to shave.)

10. **stomaching:** cherishing of bitterness

How lesser enmities may give way to greater.
Were 't not that we stand up against them all,
'Twere pregnant they should square between
    themselves,                                                55
For they have entertainèd cause enough
To draw their swords. But how the fear of us
May cement their divisions and bind up
The petty difference, we yet not know.
Be 't as our gods will have 't. It only stands             60
Our lives upon to use our strongest hands.
Come, Menas.

                                                *They exit.*


⌜Scene 2⌝
*Enter Enobarbus and Lepidus.*

LEPIDUS
  Good Enobarbus, 'tis a worthy deed,
  And shall become you well, to entreat your captain
  To soft and gentle speech.
ENOBARBUS                    I shall entreat him
  To answer like himself. If Caesar move him,           5
  Let Antony look over Caesar's head
  And speak as loud as Mars. By Jupiter,
  Were I the wearer of Antonio's beard,
  I would not shave 't today.
LEPIDUS
  'Tis not a time for private stomaching.               10
ENOBARBUS  Every time serves for the matter that is
    then born in 't.
LEPIDUS
  But small to greater matters must give way.
ENOBARBUS  Not if the small come first.
LEPIDUS
  Your speech is passion; but pray you stir             15
  No embers up. Here comes the noble Antony.

18. **compose:** i.e., reach an agreement; **Parthia:** a region east of Syria (See map, page xvii.)

23. **What's:** i.e., whatever is

25. **loud:** i.e., loudly

26. **healing:** i.e., trying to heal

27. **The rather for:** The more so because

29. **Nor . . . matter:** i.e., and do not allow ill temper to enter into the discussion

31. **to fight:** i.e., be about to fight

32. **do thus:** Perhaps Antony here embraces or shakes hands with Octavius Caesar; or perhaps **I should do thus** means simply "I would speak as moderately as you [Lepidus] counsel."

39. **being:** i.e., if they are **ill** (i.e., reprehensible)

41. **or for nothing:** i.e., either for nothing

Octavius Caesar.
From Thomas Treterus, *Romanorum imperatorum effigies . . .* (1590).

*Enter, ⌈at one door,⌉ Antony and Ventidius.*

ENOBARBUS   And yonder Caesar.

*Enter, ⌈at another door,⌉ Caesar,*
*Maecenas, and Agrippa.*

ANTONY, ⌈*to Ventidius*⌉
  If we compose well here, to Parthia.
  Hark, Ventidius.                    ⌈*They talk aside.*⌉
CAESAR, ⌈*to Maecenas*⌉
  I do not know, Maecenas. Ask Agrippa.                    20
LEPIDUS, ⌈*to Caesar and Antony*⌉   Noble friends,
  That which combined us was most great, and let not
  A leaner action rend us. What's amiss,
  May it be gently heard. When we debate
  Our trivial difference loud, we do commit                    25
  Murder in healing wounds. Then, noble partners,
  The rather for I earnestly beseech,
  Touch you the sourest points with sweetest terms,
  Nor curstness grow to th' matter.
ANTONY                    'Tis spoken well.                    30
  Were we before our armies, and to fight,
  I should do thus.                    *Flourish.*
CAESAR   Welcome to Rome.
ANTONY   Thank you.
CAESAR   Sit.                    35
ANTONY   Sit, sir.
CAESAR   Nay, then.                    ⌈*They sit.*⌉
ANTONY
  I learn you take things ill which are not so,
  Or, being, concern you not.
CAESAR                    I must be laughed at                    40
  If or for nothing or a little, I
  Should say myself offended, and with you
  Chiefly i' th' world; more laughed at, that I should

44. **derogately:** derogatorily, disparagingly

50. **practice on my state:** scheme against my power and position

51. **my question:** i.e., a subject of discussion that concerns me

55–56. **their contestation ... war:** i.e., they warred on your behalf and in your name

58. **urge me in:** i.e., present my name in justification of; **inquire:** i.e., inquire into

59. **learning:** information; **true reports:** trustworthy reporters

61. **with:** i.e., along with

62. **stomach:** inclination, desire

63. **Having ... cause:** i.e., I having the same reason to be offended as you

64. **Before ... you:** i.e., have already provided sufficient proof

64–65. **If ... with:** i.e., if it is your wish to quarrel with me over something substantial (See longer note, page 281.) **patch:** put together, make up from scraps (In line 69 the phrase **patched up** carries this same meaning, with the added sense of mending as if with patches.)

71–72. **I know ... thought:** i.e., I know that you must have thought

73. **he:** i.e., Antony's brother

74. **with ... attend:** i.e., look with favor on

Once name you derogately when to sound your
　　name                                            45
It not concerned me.

**ANTONY**
My being in Egypt, Caesar, what was 't to you?

**CAESAR**
No more than my residing here at Rome
Might be to you in Egypt. Yet if you there
Did practice on my state, your being in Egypt         50
Might be my question.

**ANTONY**                         How intend you, practiced?

**CAESAR**
You may be pleased to catch at mine intent
By what did here befall me. Your wife and brother
Made wars upon me, and their contestation             55
Was theme for you; you were the word of war.

**ANTONY**
You do mistake your business. My brother never
Did urge me in his act. I did inquire it,
And have my learning from some true reports
That drew their swords with you. Did he not rather    60
Discredit my authority with yours,
And make the wars alike against my stomach,
Having alike your cause? Of this my letters
Before did satisfy you. If you'll patch a quarrel,
As matter whole you have to make it with,             65
It must not be with this.

**CAESAR**                     You praise yourself
By laying defects of judgment to me; but
You patched up your excuses.

**ANTONY**                         Not so, not so.      70
I know you could not lack—I am certain on 't—
Very necessity of this thought, that I,
Your partner in the cause 'gainst which he fought,
Could not with graceful eyes attend those wars

**77–78. The third . . . wife:** i.e., you can manage a third of the world more easily than **such a wife** (These lines compare both **the third o' th' world** and **such a wife** to horses.) **snaffle:** a simple form of bridle-bit, with less restraining power than one provided with a curb **pace:** train to pace **easy:** easily

**81. So much uncurbable:** i.e., she being so unmanageable; **garboils:** uproars, disturbances

**82. not wanted:** i.e., did not lack

**83. of policy:** i.e., as a scheme (to get me back from Egypt)

**84. Did:** caused; **For:** i.e., as for

**87. rioting:** i.e., you were reveling

**89. missive:** messenger

**92–93. did want . . . was:** i.e., was not the person I was (Feasting involved much drinking of wine.)

**94. told . . . myself:** i.e., offered him an explanation of my earlier state

**96. Be nothing of:** i.e., not be considered in

**97. question:** quarrel

**99. The article of your oath:** i.e., a part of our sworn agreement

**101. Soft:** i.e., wait

**103. talks on:** i.e., talks of

**104. But on:** i.e., but go on

**106. required:** asked for

Which fronted mine own peace. As for my wife,                    75
I would you had her spirit in such another.
The third o' th' world is yours, which with a snaffle
You may pace easy, but not such a wife.
ENOBARBUS   Would we had all such wives, that the men
     might go to wars with the women!                            80
ANTONY
So much uncurbable, her garboils, Caesar,
Made out of her impatience—which not wanted
Shrewdness of policy too—I grieving grant
Did you too much disquiet. For that you must
But say I could not help it.                                     85
CAESAR                       I wrote to you
When rioting in Alexandria; you
Did pocket up my letters, and with taunts
Did gibe my missive out of audience.
ANTONY                                   Sir,                     90
He fell upon me ere admitted, then;
Three kings I had newly feasted, and did want
Of what I was i' th' morning. But next day
I told him of myself, which was as much
As to have asked him pardon. Let this fellow                     95
Be nothing of our strife; if we contend,
Out of our question wipe him.
CAESAR                           You have broken
The article of your oath, which you shall never
Have tongue to charge me with.                                   100
LEPIDUS   Soft, Caesar!
ANTONY   No, Lepidus, let him speak.
The honor is sacred which he talks on now,
Supposing that I lacked it.—But on, Caesar:
The article of my oath?                                          105
CAESAR
To lend me arms and aid when I required them,
The which you both denied.

109–10. **bound . . . knowledge:** i.e., restricted my self-understanding

112. **make poor:** abase; lessen

113. **it:** perhaps, **honesty;** or, perhaps, **greatness**

115. **motive:** mover, moving cause

118. **noble:** i.e., nobly

119. **enforce:** emphasize, urge

120. **griefs:** grievances

122. **atone:** reconcile

131. **presence:** high-ranking company

132. **Go to:** an expression introducing a contemptuous concession; **Your:** i.e., I am your

135. **conditions:** dispositions, natures

ANTONY                         Neglected, rather;
  And then when poisoned hours had bound me up
  From mine own knowledge. As nearly as I may          110
  I'll play the penitent to you. But mine honesty
  Shall not make poor my greatness, nor my power
  Work without it. Truth is that Fulvia,
  To have me out of Egypt, made wars here,
  For which myself, the ignorant motive, do            115
  So far ask pardon as befits mine honor
  To stoop in such a case.
LEPIDUS                      'Tis noble spoken.
MAECENAS
  If it might please you to enforce no further
  The griefs between you, to forget them quite         120
  Were to remember that the present need
  Speaks to atone you.
LEPIDUS               Worthily spoken, Maecenas.
ENOBARBUS   Or, if you borrow one another's love for
    the instant, you may, when you hear no more words  125
    of Pompey, return it again. You shall have time to
    wrangle in when you have nothing else to do.
ANTONY
  Thou art a soldier only. Speak no more.
ENOBARBUS   That truth should be silent I had almost
    forgot.                                            130
ANTONY
  You wrong this presence; therefore speak no more.
ENOBARBUS   Go to, then. Your considerate stone.
CAESAR
  I do not much dislike the matter, but
  The manner of his speech; for 't cannot be
  We shall remain in friendship, our conditions        135
  So diff'ring in their acts. Yet if I knew
  What hoop should hold us staunch, from edge to
    edge
  O' th' world I would pursue it.

142. **sister . . . side:** i.e., half-sister

146–47. **your reproof . . . rashness:** i.e., you would deserve reprimand for your thoughtlessness

157. **jealousies:** suspicions, mistrusts

158. **import:** bring with them

159. **tales:** i.e., common talk

160. **half-tales be truths:** i.e., mere gossip is accepted as true

163. **a studied . . . thought:** i.e., something upon which I have deliberated, not something I just now thought of

166. **touched:** affected

167. **is spoke:** i.e., has been spoken

A bull with horns "charge[d] . . . with garlands." (1.2.5)
From Guillaume Du Choul, *Discours de la religion des anciens Romains . . .* (1556).

AGRIPPA   Give me leave, Caesar.                            140
CAESAR   Speak, Agrippa.
AGRIPPA
  Thou hast a sister by the mother's side,
  Admired Octavia. Great Mark Antony
  Is now a widower.
CAESAR                    Say not ⌜so,⌝ Agrippa.              145
  If Cleopatra heard you, your ⌜reproof⌝
  Were well deserved of rashness.
ANTONY
  I am not married, Caesar. Let me hear
  Agrippa further speak.
AGRIPPA
  To hold you in perpetual amity,                           150
  To make you brothers, and to knit your hearts
  With an unslipping knot, take Antony
  Octavia to his wife, whose beauty claims
  No worse a husband than the best of men;
  Whose virtue and whose general graces speak               155
  That which none else can utter. By this marriage
  All little jealousies, which now seem great,
  And all great fears, which now import their dangers,
  Would then be nothing. Truths would be tales,
  Where now half-tales be truths. Her love to both          160
  Would each to other and all loves to both
  Draw after her. Pardon what I have spoke,
  For 'tis a studied, not a present thought,
  By duty ruminated.
ANTONY                    Will Caesar speak?                 165
CAESAR
  Not till he hears how Antony is touched
  With what is spoke already.
ANTONY   What power is in Agrippa,
  If I would say "Agrippa, be it so,"
  To make this good?                                        170

174. **so fairly shows:** i.e., seems so promising
176. **grace:** goodwill
178. **sway:** rule
180. **bequeath:** deliver to, commend to
183. **Fly . . . loves:** i.e., may our concord desert us
186. **strange:** rare, surprising
187. **thank him only:** i.e., only thank him
188. **remembrance:** i.e., reputation
189. **At heel of:** immediately after
191. **Of:** i.e., by; **presently:** at once
194. **Mount Misena:** a promontory on the western coast of Italy, south of Rome
198. **fame:** common report, rumor

CAESAR                    The power of Caesar, and
His power unto Octavia.

ANTONY                    May I never
To this good purpose, that so fairly shows,
Dream of impediment. Let me have thy hand.                    175
Further this act of grace; and from this hour
The heart of brothers govern in our loves
And sway our great designs.

CAESAR                    There's my hand.
⌐*They clasp hands.*⌐

A sister I bequeath you whom no brother                    180
Did ever love so dearly. Let her live
To join our kingdoms and our hearts; and never
Fly off our loves again.

LEPIDUS                    Happily, amen!

ANTONY
I did not think to draw my sword 'gainst Pompey,                    185
For he hath laid strange courtesies and great
Of late upon me. I must thank him only,
Lest my remembrance suffer ill report;
At heel of that, defy him.

LEPIDUS                    Time calls upon 's.                    190
Of us must Pompey presently be sought,
Or else he seeks out us.

ANTONY   Where lies he?

CAESAR   About the Mount Misena.

ANTONY   What is his strength by land?                    195

CAESAR   Great and increasing;
But by sea he is an absolute master.

ANTONY   So is the fame.
Would we had spoke together. Haste we for it.
Yet, ere we put ourselves in arms, dispatch we                    200
The business we have talked of.

CAESAR                    With most gladness,

203. **do:** i.e., I do

204. **straight:** straightway, immediately

212. **digested:** settled; **stayed well by 't:** perhaps, held up well under all the feasting

213–14. **sleep . . . of countenance:** i.e., disconcerted the daytime by sleeping through it

214. **light:** (1) bright with artificial light; (2) merry; (3) light-headed

217. **by:** in comparison to

220. **triumphant:** notable, noble, splendid

221. **square to:** i.e., accurate in describing

223. **pursed up his heart:** put his heart in her purse; **Cydnus:** a river flowing south through Cilicia into the Mediterranean (See map, page xvii.)

224. **appeared indeed:** perhaps, made a spectacular appearance (Some editors think that a word is missing from the line.)

225. **devised:** invented

228. **poop:** i.e., poop deck

A mermaid. (2.2.245, 247)
From August Casimir Redel, *Apophtegmata symbolica* . . . [n.d.].

And do invite you to my sister's view,
Whither straight I'll lead you.

ANTONY
Let us, Lepidus, not lack your company.                    205

LEPIDUS
Noble Antony, not sickness should detain me.
                *Flourish. All but Enobarbus, Agrippa, and*
                                    *Maecenas exit.*

MAECENAS, ⌈*to Enobarbus*⌉ Welcome from Egypt, sir.

ENOBARBUS Half the heart of Caesar, worthy
    Maecenas!—My honorable friend Agrippa!

AGRIPPA  Good Enobarbus!                                   210

MAECENAS  We have cause to be glad that matters are so
    well digested. You stayed well by 't in Egypt.

ENOBARBUS  Ay, sir, we did sleep day out of counte-
    nance and made the night light with drinking.

MAECENAS  Eight wild boars roasted whole at a break- 215
    fast, and but twelve persons there. Is this true?

ENOBARBUS  This was but as a fly by an eagle. We had
    much more monstrous matter of feast, which wor-
    thily deserved noting.

MAECENAS  She's a most triumphant lady, if report be 220
    square to her.

ENOBARBUS  When she first met Mark Antony, she
    pursed up his heart upon the river of Cydnus.

AGRIPPA  There she appeared indeed, or my reporter
    devised well for her.                                  225

ENOBARBUS  I will tell you.
    The barge she sat in like a burnished throne
    Burned on the water. The poop was beaten gold,
    Purple the sails, and so perfumed that
    The winds were lovesick with them. The oars were  230
        silver,
    Which to the tune of flutes kept stroke, and made
    The water which they beat to follow faster,

234. **As:** i.e., as if; **For:** i.e., as for

236. **cloth-of-gold, of tissue:** i.e., colored silk woven of twisted threads to enrich its texture, and interwoven with threads of gold

237. **O'erpicturing that Venus:** i.e., surpassing any artist's representation of Venus

238. **fancy:** (the artist's) imagination; **side her:** i.e., side of her

239. **like:** in the roles of; **Cupids:** Cupid was the Roman god of love. (See page 98.)

241. **glow:** heat

244. **Nereides:** sea-nymphs, akin to **mermaids** but fully human in shape, daughters of the sea-god Nereus

245. **So many:** i.e., as if they were so many; **tended . . . eyes:** (1) attended to and obeyed her every glance; (2) waited on her beneath her gaze (It is possible that **eyes** here has the nautical meaning of "bow of the ship," not otherwise recorded before the nineteenth century.)

246. **made . . . adornings:** i.e., adorned Cleopatra by bowing to her so gracefully

247. **A seeming mermaid:** i.e., a servant in the guise of a **mermaid** (See page 68.) **tackle:** i.e., such ship's gear as sails, ropes, and cables

249. **yarely:** skillfully; **office:** the functions (of sailors)

254. **but for vacancy:** i.e., if a vacuum were not impossible (Proverbial: Nature abhors a vacuum.)

264. **ordinary:** meal (used sarcastically here, because **ordinary** was a fixed-price meal in an eating house or tavern)

265. **eat:** i.e., ate (pronounced "et")

As amorous of their strokes. For her own person,
It beggared all description: she did lie                    235
In her pavilion—cloth-of-gold, of tissue—
O'erpicturing that Venus where we see
The fancy outwork nature. On each side her
Stood pretty dimpled boys, like smiling Cupids,
With divers-colored fans, whose wind did seem              240
To ⌐glow¬ the delicate cheeks which they did cool,
And what they undid did.

AGRIPPA                    O, rare for Antony!

ENOBARBUS
Her ⌐gentlewomen,¬ like the Nereides,
So many mermaids, tended her i' th' eyes,                  245
And made their bends adornings. At the helm
A seeming mermaid steers. The silken tackle
Swell with the touches of those flower-soft hands
That yarely frame the office. From the barge
A strange invisible perfume hits the sense                250
Of the adjacent wharfs. The city cast
Her people out upon her; and Antony,
Enthroned i' th' market-place, did sit alone,
Whistling to th' air, which but for vacancy
Had gone to gaze on Cleopatra too                         255
And made a gap in nature.

AGRIPPA                          Rare Egyptian!

ENOBARBUS
Upon her landing, Antony sent to her,
Invited her to supper. She replied
It should be better he became her guest,                  260
Which she entreated. Our courteous Antony,
Whom ne'er the word of "No" woman heard speak,
Being barbered ten times o'er, goes to the feast,
And for his ordinary pays his heart
For what his eyes eat only.                                265

AGRIPPA                          Royal wench!

267. **great Caesar:** Julius Caesar (See below.)

268. **cropped:** bore fruit (i.e., had a child)

272. **That:** i.e., in such a way that; **defect:** i.e., her breathlessness

276. **stale:** render stale

280. **Become themselves:** i.e., are attractive; **that:** so that

281. **riggish:** licentious

284. **lottery:** gift of fortune

**2.3** Antony promises Octavia that he will henceforth live according to the rule. A Soothsayer advises Antony to keep his distance from Caesar. Antony admits to himself that he will return to Egypt.

---

Julius Caesar. (1.5.34, 79)
From Thomas Treterus, *Romanorum imperatorum effigies . . .* (1590).

She made great Caesar lay his sword to bed;
He ploughed her, and she cropped.

ENOBARBUS                              I saw her once
Hop forty paces through the public street,                    270
And having lost her breath, she spoke and panted,
That she did make defect perfection,
And breathless pour breath forth.

MAECENAS
Now Antony must leave her utterly.

ENOBARBUS   Never. He will not.                               275
Age cannot wither her, nor custom stale
Her infinite variety. Other women cloy
The appetites they feed, but she makes hungry
Where most she satisfies. For vilest things
Become themselves in her, that the holy priests           280
Bless her when she is riggish.

MAECENAS
If beauty, wisdom, modesty can settle
The heart of Antony, Octavia is
A blessèd lottery to him.

AGRIPPA                          Let us go.                   285
Good Enobarbus, make yourself my guest
Whilst you abide here.

ENOBARBUS                     Humbly, sir, I thank you.
                                              *They exit.*


                          ⌜Scene 3⌝
         *Enter Antony, Caesar; Octavia between them.*

ANTONY
The world and my great office will sometimes
Divide me from your bosom.

OCTAVIA                          All which time
Before the gods my knee shall bow my prayers
To them for you.                                               5

7. **Read:** interpret; **in . . . report:** i.e., according to what everyone says

8. **kept my square:** i.e., lived according to **th' rule** (line 9)

13. **sirrah:** term of address to a servant or social inferior

15. **nor you thither:** (1) perhaps, and I wish you had never come to Egypt; or (2) perhaps, I wish you had never come away from Egypt

17–18. **I see . . . tongue:** i.e., I experience it only as an inward prompting or impulse, which I cannot express

23. **dæmon . . . keeps thee:** attendant spirit or **angel** (line 25) that guards and protects (**keeps**) you

25. **Where Caesar's is not:** i.e., when Caesar's attendant spirit is absent

31. **of that:** i.e., as a result of that

32. **thickens:** becomes obscure, dims

33. **by:** nearby

ANTONY, ⌜*to Caesar*⌝        Goodnight, sir.—My Octavia,
Read not my blemishes in the world's report.
I have not kept my square, but that to come
Shall all be done by th' rule. Good night, dear
    lady.—                                                    10
Good night, sir.
CAESAR   Goodnight.                ⌜*Caesar and Octavia*⌝ *exit.*

                *Enter Soothsayer.*

ANTONY
Now, sirrah, you do wish yourself in Egypt?
SOOTHSAYER   Would I had never come from thence,
    nor you thither.                                          15
ANTONY   If you can, your reason?
SOOTHSAYER   I see it in my motion, have it not in my
    tongue. But yet hie you to Egypt again.
ANTONY
Say to me, whose fortunes shall rise higher,
Caesar's or mine?                                             20
SOOTHSAYER   Caesar's.
Therefore, O Antony, stay not by his side.
Thy dæmon—that thy spirit which keeps thee—is
Noble, courageous, high, unmatchable,
Where Caesar's is not. But near him, thy angel              25
Becomes ⌜afeard,⌝ as being o'erpowered. Therefore
Make space enough between you.
ANTONY                               Speak this no more.
SOOTHSAYER
To none but thee; no more but when to thee.
If thou dost play with him at any game,                      30
Thou art sure to lose; and of that natural luck
He beats thee 'gainst the odds. Thy luster thickens
When he shines by. I say again, thy spirit
Is all afraid to govern thee near him;
But he ⌜away,⌝ 'tis noble.                                   35

38. **He shall:** i.e., **Ventidius** shall; **art:** skill in prophecy; **hap:** luck

39. **He hath:** i.e., the Soothsayer has; **obey him:** i.e., obey Caesar

40. **better cunning:** superior ability

41. **chance:** good fortune; **speeds:** prevails

42. **still:** always; **of mine:** i.e., from mine

43. **When . . . naught:** i.e., when the odds are everything to nothing on my side

44. **inhooped:** i.e., confined for their fight within a small low round enclosure; **at odds:** against the odds


**2.4** Lepidus sets off to do battle with Pompey, urging Maecenas and Agrippa to hasten the departures of Antony and Caesar.

---

1. **Trouble . . . further:** a polite dismissal

8. **the Mount:** i.e., Mount Misena (See note to 2.2.194.)

ANTONY                    Get thee gone.
  Say to Ventidius I would speak with him.
                              ⌜*Soothsayer*⌝ *exits.*
  He shall to Parthia. Be it art or hap,
  He hath spoken true. The very dice obey him,
  And in our sports my better cunning faints          40
  Under his chance. If we draw lots, he speeds;
  His cocks do win the battle still of mine
  When it is all to naught, and his quails ever
  Beat mine, inhooped, at odds. I will to Egypt.
  And though I make this marriage for my peace,          45
  I' th' East my pleasure lies.

                    *Enter Ventidius.*

                    O, come, Ventidius.
  You must to Parthia; your commission's ready.
  Follow me and receive 't.
                                        *They exit.*


                    ⌜Scene 4⌝
          *Enter Lepidus, Maecenas, and Agrippa.*

LEPIDUS
  Trouble yourselves no further. Pray you hasten
  Your generals after.
AGRIPPA                    Sir, Mark Antony
  Will e'en but kiss Octavia, and we'll follow.
LEPIDUS
  Till I shall see you in your soldiers' dress,          5
  Which will become you both, farewell.
MAECENAS                              We shall,
  As I conceive the journey, be at ⌜the⌝ Mount
  Before you, Lepidus.

11. **draw . . . about:** i.e., take me much out of the way

**2.5** Cleopatra learns of Antony's marriage and, in her fury, beats the messenger who brought the news.

---

1. **moody:** gloomy, melancholy
2. **trade in:** occupy ourselves with
11. **I'll none:** i.e., I won't play
12. **angle:** fishing gear

"Let's to billiards." (2.5.4)
From Charles Cotton, *The compleat gamester . . .* (1674).

LEPIDUS                      Your way is shorter;            10
  My purposes do draw me much about.
  You'll win two days upon me.
BOTH                          Sir, good success.
LEPIDUS   Farewell.

                                    *They exit.*


                        ⌜Scene 5⌝
        *Enter Cleopatra, Charmian, Iras, and Alexas.*

CLEOPATRA
  Give me some music—music, moody food
  Of us that trade in love.
ALL                          The music, ho!

                *Enter Mardian the eunuch.*

CLEOPATRA
  Let it alone. Let's to billiards. Come, Charmian.
CHARMIAN
  My arm is sore. Best play with Mardian.            5
CLEOPATRA
  As well a woman with an eunuch played
  As with a woman.—Come, you'll play with me, sir?
MARDIAN   As well as I can, madam.
CLEOPATRA
  And when good will is showed, though 't come too
    short,                                            10
  The actor may plead pardon. I'll none now.
  Give me mine angle; we'll to th' river. There,
  My music playing far off, I will betray
  ⌜Tawny-finned⌝ fishes. My bended hook shall pierce
  Their slimy jaws, and as I draw them up             15
  I'll think them every one an Antony
  And say "Aha! You're caught."

25. **drunk:** i.e., drank

26. **tires:** headdresses; or, perhaps, clothes

27. **sword Philippan:** i.e., the sword used by Antony at the battle of Philippi (42 BCE) (See Shakespeare's *Julius Caesar*, act 5.)

34. **yield:** (1) deliver; (2) report

39. **Bring . . . that:** i.e., if you are using "well" to mean "dead"

43. **go to:** an expression of protest

45. **favor:** (1) look; (2) face

47. **Fury . . . snakes:** one of the Erinyes, mythological beings who punished those who broke natural or moral laws (often pictured with snakes twined in their hair) See below.

48. **formal:** normal

The Erinyes, or Furies. (2.5.47)
From Vincenzo Cartari, *Le vere e noue imagini
de gli dei delli antichi . . .* (1615).

CHARMIAN                              'Twas merry when
  You wagered on your angling; when your diver
  Did hang a salt fish on his hook, which he                     20
  With fervency drew up.
CLEOPATRA                    That time?—O, times!—
  I laughed him out of patience; and that night
  I laughed him into patience; and next morn,
  Ere the ninth hour, I drunk him to his bed,                    25
  Then put my tires and mantles on him, whilst
  I wore his sword Philippan.

                    *Enter a Messenger.*

                              O, from Italy!
  Ram thou thy fruitful tidings in mine ears,
  That long time have been barren.                               30
MESSENGER                              Madam, madam—
CLEOPATRA
  Antonio's dead! If thou say so, villain,
  Thou kill'st thy mistress. But well and free,
  If thou so yield him, there is gold, and here
  My bluest veins to kiss, a hand that kings                     35
  Have lipped and trembled kissing.
MESSENGER
  First, madam, he is well.
CLEOPATRA
  Why, there's more gold. But sirrah, mark, we use
  To say the dead are well. Bring it to that,
  The gold I give thee will I melt and pour                      40
  Down thy ill-uttering throat.
MESSENGER   Good madam, hear me.
CLEOPATRA   Well, go to, I will.
  But there's no goodness in thy face—if Antony
  Be free and healthful, so tart a favor                         45
  To trumpet such good tidings! If not well,
  Thou shouldst come like a Fury crowned with snakes,
  Not like a formal man.

58. **honest:** honorable, worthy

62–63. **allay / The good precedence:** i.e., qualify the good news that preceded it

66. **matter:** subject matter

70. **bound:** i.e., in marriage (In the next line, Cleopatra's question implies that **bound unto Octavia** means "obliged to Octavia" for some favor.)

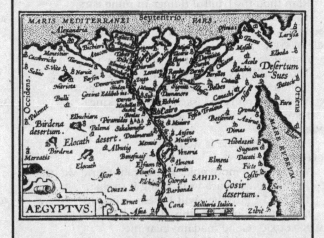

The Nile River.
From Abraham Ortelius, *An epitome of . . . his theatre of the world* [1601?].

MESSENGER                    Will 't please you hear me?

CLEOPATRA

I have a mind to strike thee ere thou speak'st.                    50
Yet if thou say Antony lives, ⌈is⌉ well,
Or friends with Caesar or not captive to him,
I'll set thee in a shower of gold and hail
Rich pearls upon thee.

MESSENGER                    Madam, he's well.                    55

CLEOPATRA                                        Well said.

MESSENGER

And friends with Caesar.

CLEOPATRA                    Th' art an honest man.

MESSENGER

Caesar and he are greater friends than ever.

CLEOPATRA

Make thee a fortune from me.                    60

MESSENGER                              But yet, madam—

CLEOPATRA

I do not like "But yet." It does allay
The good precedence. Fie upon "But yet."
"But yet" is as a jailer to bring forth
Some monstrous malefactor. Prithee, friend,                    65
Pour out the pack of matter to mine ear,
The good and bad together: he's friends with Caesar,
In state of health, thou say'st, and, thou say'st, free.

MESSENGER

Free, madam, no. I made no such report.
He's bound unto Octavia.                    70

CLEOPATRA                    For what good turn?

MESSENGER

For the best turn i' th' bed.

CLEOPATRA                    I am pale, Charmian.

MESSENGER

Madam, he's married to Octavia.

76. **patience:** i.e., remain calm
78. **spurn:** kick
79 SD. **hales:** drags, tugs
82. **pickle:** solution of salt or acid
87. **make thy peace:** reconcile you (to me)
88. **boot thee with:** add, enrich you with; **what:** i.e., whatever
99. **mad:** (1) furious, rabid; (2) insane
100. **afeard:** afraid

Perseus with the head of the Gorgon Medusa. (2.5.144)
From Cesare Ripa, *Noua iconologia . . .* (1618).

CLEOPATRA
  The most infectious pestilence upon thee!          75
                  *Strikes him down.*

MESSENGER   Good madam, patience!

CLEOPATRA   What say you?          *Strikes him.*
  Hence, horrible villain, or I'll spurn thine eyes
  Like balls before me! I'll unhair thy head!
             *She hales him up and down.*
  Thou shalt be whipped with wire and stewed in          80
    brine,
  Smarting in ling'ring pickle.

MESSENGER          Gracious madam,
  I that do bring the news made not the match.

CLEOPATRA
  Say 'tis not so, a province I will give thee          85
  And make thy fortunes proud. The blow thou hadst
  Shall make thy peace for moving me to rage,
  And I will boot thee with what gift beside
  Thy modesty can beg.

MESSENGER          He's married, madam.          90

CLEOPATRA
  Rogue, thou hast lived too long.          *Draw a knife.*

MESSENGER          Nay then, I'll run.
  What mean you, madam? I have made no fault.
                  *He exits.*

CHARMIAN
  Good madam, keep yourself within yourself.
  The man is innocent.          95

CLEOPATRA
  Some innocents 'scape not the thunderbolt.
  Melt Egypt into Nile, and kindly creatures
  Turn all to serpents! Call the slave again.
  Though I am mad, I will not bite him. Call!

CHARMIAN
  He is afeard to come.          100

103. **A meaner:** i.e., someone of lower social rank

107. **gracious:** pleasing, welcome

112. **worser:** i.e., worse

115. **confound:** destroy

118. **So:** i.e., even if

120. **Narcissus:** In mythology, a boy so beautiful that he drowned as he tried to embrace his own reflection in a pool. (See below.)

124. **that:** because

126. **much unequal:** very unfair

127–28. **O . . . sure of:** i.e., it's too bad that Antony's **fault** makes you look like a **knave** when you are not involved in his knavery in marrying Octavia

Narcissus. (2.5.120)
From Geoffrey Whitney, *A choice of emblemes . . .* (1586).

CLEOPATRA                    I will not hurt him.
  These hands do lack nobility that they strike
  A meaner than myself, since I myself
  Have given myself the cause.

*Enter the Messenger again.*

                    Come hither, sir.        105
  Though it be honest, it is never good
  To bring bad news. Give to a gracious message
  An host of tongues, but let ill tidings tell
  Themselves when they be felt.
MESSENGER   I have done my duty.        110
CLEOPATRA   Is he married?
  I cannot hate thee worser than I do
  If thou again say "yes."
MESSENGER                He's married, madam.
CLEOPATRA
  The gods confound thee! Dost thou hold there still?   115
MESSENGER
  Should I lie, madam?
CLEOPATRA          O, I would thou didst,
  So half my Egypt were submerged and made
  A cistern for scaled snakes! Go, get thee hence.
  Hadst thou Narcissus in thy face, to me        120
  Thou wouldst appear most ugly. He is married?
MESSENGER
  I crave your Highness' pardon.
CLEOPATRA                He is married?
MESSENGER
  Take no offense that I would not offend you.
  To punish me for what you make me do        125
  Seems much unequal. He's married to Octavia.
CLEOPATRA
  O, that his fault should make a knave of thee

131. **Are:** i.e., is; **Lie . . . hand:** i.e., I hope you are unable to sell the **merchandise**

132. **undone:** ruined

140. **feature:** physical features (figure and face)

141. **inclination:** nature, natural disposition

143. **him:** i.e., Antony

144–45. **Though . . . Mars:** i.e., although he is painted so that he appears, from one perspective, a **Gorgon** (a mythological figure the sight of whose face brought instant death), from another perspective he is like the god **Mars** (Cleopatra's figure of speech alludes to a particular technique in painting—the double picture—fashionable in Shakespeare's time.) For the **Gorgon**, see page 84; for **Mars**, see page 46.


**2.6** In a prebattle conference, Pompey is offered terms by Caesar, Antony, and Lepidus. After Antony thanks Pompey for his earlier kindness to Antony's mother, Pompey accepts the terms, and feasts are planned. Enobarbus predicts that Antony's marriage will divide rather than unite Caesar and Antony.

———————————

0 SD. **Drum and Trumpet:** i.e., soldiers playing drums and trumpets

That art not what th' art sure of! Get thee hence.
The merchandise which thou hast brought from
   Rome                                                    130
Are all too dear for me. Lie they upon thy hand,
And be undone by 'em!          ⌜*Messenger exits.*⌝
CHARMIAN                    Good your Highness,
   patience.
CLEOPATRA
In praising Antony, I have dispraised Caesar.       135
CHARMIAN   Many times, madam.
CLEOPATRA
I am paid for 't now. Lead me from hence;
I faint. O, Iras, Charmian! 'Tis no matter.—
Go to the fellow, good Alexas. Bid him
Report the feature of Octavia, her years,           140
Her inclination; let him not leave out
The color of her hair. Bring me word quickly.
                              ⌜*Alexas exits.*⌝
Let him forever go—let him not, Charmian.
Though he be painted one way like a Gorgon,
The other way 's a Mars. (⌜*To Mardian.*⌝) Bid you   145
   Alexas
Bring me word how tall she is.—Pity me,
   Charmian,
But do not speak to me. Lead me to my chamber.
                                  *They exit.*


                       ⌜Scene 6⌝
*Flourish. Enter Pompey* ⌜*and*⌝ *Menas at one door,*
*with Drum and Trumpet; at another Caesar, Lepidus,*
*Antony, Enobarbus, Maecenas,* ⌜*and*⌝ *Agrippa,*
*with Soldiers marching.*

POMPEY
Your hostages I have, so have you mine,
And we shall talk before we fight.

3. **Most meet:** i.e., it is most appropriate

5. **written purposes:** proposals or offers in writing

7. **If 'twill:** i.e., if our offer will

8. **much tall:** i.e., many courageous

9. **else:** otherwise

11. **senators alone:** i.e., sole rulers (By calling his opponents "senators," Pompey alludes to the triumvirs' having supplanted the former rulers of the Roman Republic, the Senate.)

12. **factors:** agents

13. **Wherefore:** why; **my father:** Pompey the Great, driven out of Rome by Julius Caesar (See page 96.) **revengers want:** lack avengers (for his assassination)

15–22. **at Philippi . . . man:** The events (and the motivation for them) narrated here are dramatized in Shakespeare's *Julius Caesar.* **ghosted:** haunted **honest:** honorable **courtiers of beauteous freedom:** i.e., those who would serve no other monarch but the ideal of **freedom**

25. **despiteful:** spiteful, cruel

28. **fear:** frighten

30. **o'ercount:** outnumber

32. **Thou . . . house:** Pompey wrests the word **o'ercount** from its meaning in order to suggest that somehow Antony has cheated him of his father's **house** and **land** (line 31). See longer note, page 281.

33. **cuckoo:** a bird that lays its eggs in the nest of another bird (See page 94.)

36. **is from the present:** is irrelevant to the business at hand

CAESAR                                    Most meet
That first we come to words, and therefore have we
Our written purposes before us sent,                      5
Which if thou hast considered, let us know
If 'twill tie up thy discontented sword
And carry back to Sicily much tall youth
That else must perish here.

POMPEY                              To you all three,      10
The senators alone of this great world,
Chief factors for the gods: I do not know
Wherefore my father should revengers want,
Having a son and friends, since Julius Caesar,
Who at Philippi the good Brutus ghosted,                  15
There saw you laboring for him. What was 't
That moved pale Cassius to conspire? And what
Made ⌈the⌉ all-honored, honest, Roman Brutus,
With the armed rest, courtiers of beauteous
    freedom,                                              20
To drench the Capitol, but that they would
Have one man but a man? And that ⌈is⌉ it
Hath made me rig my navy, at whose burden
The angered ocean foams, with which I meant
To scourge th' ingratitude that despiteful Rome          25
Cast on my noble father.

CAESAR                          Take your time.

ANTONY
Thou canst not fear us, Pompey, with thy sails.
We'll speak with thee at sea. At land thou know'st
How much we do o'ercount thee.                           30

POMPEY                            At land indeed
Thou dost o'ercount me of my father's house;
But since the cuckoo builds not for himself,
Remain in 't as thou mayst.

LEPIDUS                        Be pleased to tell us—     35
For this is from the present—how you take
The offers we have sent you.

40. **it is worth embraced:** i.e., our offers would be worth to you if you accepted them

41–42. **And what . . . fortune:** i.e., consider what may happen if you attempt to win **a larger fortune** in battle (Caesar's words can also be read to mean: "consider what **larger fortune** may ensue from our initial offers." It is possible that Caesar is being deliberately ambiguous.)

44. **Sicily, Sardinia:** large islands to the south and to the west of Italy

45. **to send:** i.e., I must send

46. **Measures:** bushels; **'greed:** i.e., agreed

48. **targes:** shields

54. **of it:** i.e., for it (Proverbial: To praise oneself is wrong.) **you must know:** i.e., I would have you know

55. **your brother:** i.e., Antony's **brother** (Lucius)

59. **studied for:** i.e., prepared to offer

63. **thanks to you:** i.e., I thank you

64. **timelier than my purpose:** i.e., earlier than I had intended

69. **counts . . . casts:** i.e., wrinkles or scars are registered (To "cast counts" was to reckon accounts, which were at one time recorded as notches on a stick called a tally.)

CAESAR                              There's the point.
ANTONY
  Which do not be entreated to, but weigh
  What it is worth embraced.                              40
CAESAR                         And what may follow
  To try a larger fortune.
POMPEY                        You have made me offer
  Of Sicily, Sardinia; and I must
  Rid all the sea of pirates; then to send                 45
  Measures of wheat to Rome. This 'greed upon,
  To part with unhacked edges and bear back
  Our targes undinted.
ALL                          That's our offer.
POMPEY                                      Know then        50
  I came before you here a man prepared
  To take this offer. But Mark Antony
  Put me to some impatience.—Though I lose
  The praise of it by telling, you must know
  When Caesar and your brother were at blows,              55
  Your mother came to Sicily and did find
  Her welcome friendly.
ANTONY                       I have heard it, Pompey,
  And am well studied for a liberal thanks,
  Which I do owe you.                                      60
POMPEY                     Let me have your hand.
                   ⌜*They clasp hands.*⌝
  I did not think, sir, to have met you here.
ANTONY
  The beds i' th' East are soft; and thanks to you,
  That called me timelier than my purpose hither,
  For I have gained by 't.                                  65
CAESAR, ⌜*to Pompey*⌝     Since I saw you last,
  There's a change upon you.
POMPEY                         Well, I know not
  What counts harsh Fortune casts upon my face,

74. **composition:** mutual agreement

75. **between:** i.e., among

80. **take the lot:** i.e., draw your **lot; first or last:** i.e., wherever you come in the order

81–82. **shall . . . fame:** i.e., will be the talk of everyone

85. **fair:** unobjectionable

86. **fair:** elegant (Proverbs about **"fair words"** suggest that Antony may be sarcastic here. Of many examples, see, for instance, **"fair words** make me look to my purse" and **"fair words** butter no parsnips.")

88. **Apollodorus:** a friend of Cleopatra's

94. **like:** i.e., likely

95. **toward:** coming, impending

A cuckoo (2.6.33)
From Konrad Gesner, . . . *Historiae animalium* . . . (1585–1604).

But in my bosom shall she never come                    70
To make my heart her vassal.
LEPIDUS                          Well met here.
POMPEY
I hope so, Lepidus. Thus we are agreed.
I crave our composition may be written
And sealed between us.                                   75
CAESAR                    That's the next to do.
POMPEY
We'll feast each other ere we part, and let's
Draw lots who shall begin.
ANTONY                        That will I, Pompey.
POMPEY
No, Antony, take the lot. But, first or last,           80
Your fine Egyptian cookery shall have
The fame. I have heard that Julius Caesar
Grew fat with feasting there.
ANTONY   You have heard much.
POMPEY   I have fair ⌜meanings,⌝ sir.                    85
ANTONY   And fair words to them.
POMPEY   Then so much have I heard.
And I have heard Apollodorus carried—
ENOBARBUS
No more ⌜of⌝ that. He did so.
POMPEY                        What, I pray you?          90
ENOBARBUS
A certain queen to Caesar in a mattress.
POMPEY
I know thee now. How far'st thou, soldier?
ENOBARBUS                                Well,
And well am like to do, for I perceive
Four feasts are toward.                                  95
POMPEY                    Let me shake thy hand.
I never hated thee. I have seen thee fight
When I have envied thy behavior.

103. **Enjoy thy plainness:** take full advantage of speaking frankly

104. **nothing:** not at all

110. **have known:** are acquainted with each other

124. **authority:** i.e., the power to capture criminals; **take:** arrest

124–25. **thieves kissing:** i.e., their clasped hands

126. **true:** honest, trustworthy; **whatsome'er:** whatever (In saying **All men's faces are true,** Menas, perhaps ironically, contradicts proverbial wisdom: "Trust not the face.")

130. **No slander:** i.e., what you say is no slander to women because their beautiful faces **steal hearts**

Pompey the Great. (1.2.204; 2.6.13, 109; 3.7.42)
From [Guillaume Rouillé,] . . . *Prima pars promptuarii iconum* . . . (1553).

ENOBARBUS                 Sir,
  I never loved you much, but I ha' praised you     100
  When you have well deserved ten times as much
  As I have said you did.

POMPEY             Enjoy thy plainness;
  It nothing ill becomes thee.—
  Aboard my galley I invite you all.             105
  Will you lead, lords?

ALL              Show 's the way, sir.

POMPEY                   Come.

*They exit, except for Enobarbus and Menas.*

MENAS, ⌜*aside*⌝ Thy father, Pompey, would ne'er have
  made this treaty.—You and I have known, sir.    110

ENOBARBUS  At sea, I think.

MENAS  We have, sir.

ENOBARBUS  You have done well by water.

MENAS  And you by land.

ENOBARBUS  I will praise any man that will praise me,  115
    though it cannot be denied what I have done by
    land.

MENAS  Nor what I have done by water.

ENOBARBUS  Yes, something you can deny for your own
    safety: you have been a great thief by sea.    120

MENAS  And you by land.

ENOBARBUS  There I deny my land service. But give me
    your hand, Menas. ⌜*They clasp hands.*⌝ If our eyes
    had authority, here they might take two thieves
    kissing.                                125

MENAS  All men's faces are true, whatsome'er their
    hands are.

ENOBARBUS  But there is never a fair woman has a true
    face.

MENAS  No slander. They steal hearts.    130

ENOBARBUS  We came hither to fight with you.

MENAS  For my part, I am sorry it is turned to a

137. **You've said:** i.e., you're right

143. **Pray you:** here, a deferential expression of disbelief

145. **Then is:** i.e., then are

146. **divine of:** conjecture about

148. **policy:** political cunning; contrivance; **made more:** i.e., counted for more

149. **parties:** i.e., Octavia and Antony (or, perhaps, Antony and Octavius Caesar)

152. **is of:** i.e., possesses

153. **still:** quiet; **conversation:** manner

160. **variance:** disagreement, quarrel

160–61. **affection:** lust, passion

161. **but his occasion:** i.e., only for political necessity

163. **health:** toast

164. **take:** i.e., drink; **used:** trained

Cupid. (2.2.239)
From an anonymous engraving tipped into Jacques Callot,
[*La petite passion*, n.d.].

drinking. Pompey doth this day laugh away his
fortune.

ENOBARBUS   If he do, sure he cannot weep 't back      135
again.

MENAS   You've said, sir. We looked not for Mark Antony
here. Pray you, is he married to Cleopatra?

ENOBARBUS   Caesar's sister is called Octavia.

MENAS   True, sir. She was the wife of Caius Marcellus.      140

ENOBARBUS   But she is now the wife of Marcus Antonius.

MENAS   Pray you, sir?

ENOBARBUS   'Tis true.

MENAS   Then is Caesar and he forever knit together.      145

ENOBARBUS   If I were bound to divine of this unity, I
would not prophesy so.

MENAS   I think the policy of that purpose made more in
the marriage than the love of the parties.

ENOBARBUS   I think so, too. But you shall find the band      150
that seems to tie their friendship together will be
the very strangler of their amity. Octavia is of a holy,
cold, and still conversation.

MENAS   Who would not have his wife so?

ENOBARBUS   Not he that himself is not so, which is      155
Mark Antony. He will to his Egyptian dish again.
Then shall the sighs of Octavia blow the fire up in
Caesar, and, as I said before, that which is the
strength of their amity shall prove the immediate
author of their variance. Antony will use his affec-      160
tion where it is. He married but his occasion here.

MENAS   And thus it may be. Come, sir, will you aboard?
I have a health for you.

ENOBARBUS   I shall take it, sir. We have used our throats
in Egypt.      165

MENAS   Come, let's away.

*They exit.*

**2.7**   At the feast on Pompey's galley, Pompey refuses the suggestion that he kill his guests and thus become "lord of all the world." Lepidus is carried off the boat in a drunken stupor.

———————

0 SD. **a banquet:** wine for a carousal

2. **plants:** wordplay on (1) planted trees; (2) soles of feet

4. **high-colored:** red in the face (from drinking)

5. **alms-drink:** a term whose meaning is unclear because no other usage of it is recorded

6. **pinch:** i.e., harass or find fault

11–12. **a name . . . fellowship:** i.e., only the title of "partner" in a company of great men, but no power or influence among them

12. **had as lief:** i.e., would just as soon

13. **partisan:** long-handled bladed weapon

15–16. **are the holes . . . be:** i.e., is like having empty eye sockets

16. **disaster:** i.e., ruin the appearance of (See longer note, page 281.)

16 SD. **sennet:** trumpet signal to announce the arrival of important personages

17. **take:** measure; **flow o' th' Nile:** i.e., the height of the Nile at its annual flood (See page 82.)

18. **certain scales i':** a calibrated line on (Editors have suggested that pyramids are here confused with a pillar used to measure the height of the Nile.)

19. **mean:** middle

20. **foison:** plenty; **Nilus:** the Nile

21. **seedsman:** farmer sowing seed

26. **Your serpent:** i.e., the serpent (An informal use of **your** that Lepidus comically repeats throughout this speech.)

⌜Scene 7⌝
*Music plays. Enter two or three Servants*
*with a banquet.*

FIRST SERVANT  Here they'll be, man. Some o' their
plants are ill-rooted already. The least wind i' th'
world will blow them down.

SECOND SERVANT  Lepidus is high-colored.

FIRST SERVANT  They have made him drink alms-drink.     5

SECOND SERVANT  As they pinch one another by the
disposition, he cries out "No more," reconciles
them to his entreaty and himself to th' drink.

FIRST SERVANT  But it raises the greater war between
him and his discretion.     10

SECOND SERVANT  Why, this it is to have a name in great
men's fellowship. I had as lief have a reed that will
do me no service as a partisan I could not heave.

FIRST SERVANT  To be called into a huge sphere, and not
to be seen to move in 't, are the holes where eyes     15
should be, which pitifully disaster the cheeks.

*A sennet sounded. Enter Caesar, Antony, Pompey,*
*Lepidus, Agrippa, Maecenas, Enobarbus, Menas, with*
*other Captains ⌜and a Boy.⌝*

ANTONY
Thus do they, sir: they take the flow o' th' Nile
By certain scales i' th' Pyramid; they know
By th' height, the lowness, or the mean if dearth
Or foison follow. The higher Nilus swells,     20
The more it promises. As it ebbs, the seedsman
Upon the slime and ooze scatters his grain,
And shortly comes to harvest.

LEPIDUS  You've strange serpents there?

ANTONY  Ay, Lepidus.     25

LEPIDUS  Your serpent of Egypt is bred now of your

32. **out:** i.e., stop

33. **fear me:** i.e., fear

34. **in:** i.e., drunk (a play on words in response to Lepidus' use of **out** in the preceding speech)

35–36. **Ptolemies' pyramises:** pyramids of the Egyptian royal family (**Pyramises** may represent a drunken slurring of "pyramids" or may be an alternative spelling.) See page 106.

42. **Forbear me till anon:** leave me alone for a little while

46. **it own:** i.e., its own

47. **elements:** fire, air, water, earth (the four **elements**, which, compounded within the body, endowed it with life)

47–48. **it transmigrates:** i.e., its soul passes into another body

55. **else:** otherwise

56. **very epicure:** perfect glutton

Crocodile tears. (2.7.44–52)
From Jacob Typot, *Symbola diuina . . .* (1652).

mud by the operation of your sun; so is your
crocodile.

ANTONY  They are so.

POMPEY

Sit, and some wine. A health to Lepidus!  30

LEPIDUS  I am not so well as I should be, but I'll ne'er
out.

ENOBARBUS, ⌈*aside*⌉  Not till you have slept. I fear me
you'll be in till then.

LEPIDUS  Nay, certainly, I have heard the Ptolemies'  35
pyramises are very goodly things. Without contra-
diction I have heard that.

MENAS, ⌈*aside to Pompey*⌉

Pompey, a word.

POMPEY, ⌈*aside to Menas*⌉  Say in mine ear what is 't.

MENAS (*whispers in 's ear*)

Forsake thy seat, I do beseech thee, captain,  40
And hear me speak a word.

POMPEY, ⌈*aside to Menas*⌉

Forbear me till anon.—This wine for Lepidus!

LEPIDUS  What manner o' thing is your crocodile?

ANTONY  It is shaped, sir, like itself, and it is as broad as
it hath breadth. It is just so high as it is, and moves  45
with it own organs. It lives by that which nourisheth
it, and the elements once out of it, it transmigrates.

LEPIDUS  What color is it of?

ANTONY  Of it own color too.  50

LEPIDUS  'Tis a strange serpent.

ANTONY  'Tis so, and the tears of it are wet.

CAESAR, ⌈*aside to Antony*⌉  Will this description satisfy
him?

ANTONY  With the health that Pompey gives him, else he  55
is a very epicure.

57. **Go hang:** a harsh expression of dismissal

63. **held . . . to:** i.e., showed great respect for

64. **faith:** faithfulness, loyalty

67. **quicksands:** Lepidus may stagger or fall at this point. At line 99, Antony gives the order to "bear him ashore."

73. **But entertain it:** i.e., just accept what I have to say

79. **pales:** encompasses; **inclips:** encloses

82. **competitors:** partners (Octavius Caesar, Antony, Lepidus)

83. **cable:** i.e., anchor cable

Atlas carrying the world. (1.5.28)
From Gabriele Simeoni, *Le sententiose imprese . . .* (1560).

POMPEY, ⌜*aside to Menas*⌝
  Go hang, sir, hang! Tell me of that? Away!
  Do as I bid you.—Where's this cup I called for?
MENAS, ⌜*aside to Pompey*⌝
  If for the sake of merit thou wilt hear me,
  Rise from thy stool.                                                    60
POMPEY                    I think th' art mad!
                          ⌜*He rises, and they walk aside.*⌝
                                          The matter?

MENAS
  I have ever held my cap off to thy fortunes.
POMPEY
  Thou hast served me with much faith. What's else
    to say?—                                                             65
  Be jolly, lords.
ANTONY               These quicksands, Lepidus,
  Keep off them, for you sink.
MENAS, ⌜*aside to Pompey*⌝
  Wilt thou be lord of all the world?
POMPEY                                    What sayst thou?    70
MENAS
  Wilt thou be lord of the whole world? That's twice.
POMPEY   How should that be?
MENAS   But entertain it,
  And though thou think me poor, I am the man
  Will give thee all the world.                                          75
POMPEY                    Hast thou drunk well?
MENAS
  No, Pompey, I have kept me from the cup.
  Thou art, if thou dar'st be, the earthly Jove.
  Whate'er the ocean pales or sky inclips
  Is thine, if thou wilt ha 't.                                          80
POMPEY                    Show me which way.
MENAS
  These three world-sharers, these competitors,
  Are in thy vessel. Let me cut the cable,

84. **are put off:** have left the shore

87. **on 't:** i.e., of it

88. **Thou must know:** i.e., I would have you know

95. **palled:** weakened, impaired

99. **him:** i.e., Lepidus; **pledge:** i.e., drink

107–8. **Would . . . wheels:** Proverbial: The world goes **on wheels.** (The proverb may mean "All goes easily.")

109. **reels:** whirling movements

111. **Alexandrian:** i.e., Egyptian

112. **Strike the vessels:** apparently, a call for more drink (perhaps, a call to clink cups or to open more casks of wine)

Pyramids. (2.7.18; 5.2.71)
From Sebastian Münster, *Cosmographiae uniuersalis . . .* (1554).

And when we are put off, fall to their throats.
All there is thine.                                                       85
POMPEY                    Ah, this thou shouldst have done
And not have spoke on 't! In me 'tis villainy;
In thee 't had been good service. Thou must know
'Tis not my profit that does lead mine honor;
Mine honor, it. Repent that e'er thy tongue                  90
Hath so betrayed thine act. Being done unknown,
I should have found it afterwards well done,
But must condemn it now. Desist and drink.
MENAS, ⌜*aside*⌝
For this
I'll never follow thy palled fortunes more.                  95
Who seeks and will not take when once 'tis offered
Shall never find it more.
POMPEY                    This health to Lepidus!
ANTONY, ⌜*to Servant*⌝
Bear him ashore.—I'll pledge it for him, Pompey.
ENOBARBUS
Here's to thee, Menas.                                          100
MENAS                    Enobarbus, welcome.
POMPEY   Fill till the cup be hid.
ENOBARBUS, ⌜*pointing to the Servant carrying Lepidus*⌝
There's a strong fellow, Menas.
MENAS                    Why?
ENOBARBUS                    He bears                           105
The third part of the world, man. Seest not?
MENAS
The third part, then, is drunk. Would it were all,
That it might go on wheels.
ENOBARBUS   Drink thou. Increase the reels.
MENAS   Come.                                                    110
POMPEY
This is not yet an Alexandrian feast.
ANTONY
It ripens towards it. Strike the vessels, ho!
Here's to Caesar.

**114. I could well forbear 't:** i.e., I would gladly refrain from drinking this toast

**118. Possess it, I'll make answer:** i.e., my **answer** is that one should **possess** the **time**, not **be a child o' th' time**

**122. bacchanals:** dances in honor of Bacchus, the Roman god of wine

**126. Till that:** i.e., until

**128. Lethe:** i.e., forgetfulness (See note to 2.1.32.)

**132. holding:** burden, refrain; **beat:** i.e., beat out the rhythm of

**135. pink eyne:** half-shut eyes

**138. Cup us:** supply us with cups

**141. brother:** i.e., brother-in-law, Antony

**142. off:** i.e., to leave (with me)

**144. burnt:** i.e., reddened with drink

CAESAR                I could well forbear 't.
  It's monstrous labor when I wash my brain          115
  And it ⌜grows⌝ fouler.
ANTONY                Be a child o' th' time.
CAESAR   Possess it, I'll make answer.
  But I had rather fast from all, four days,
  Than drink so much in one.                         120
ENOBARBUS, ⌜to Antony⌝        Ha, my brave emperor,
  Shall we dance now the Egyptian bacchanals
  And celebrate our drink?
POMPEY   Let's ha't, good soldier.
ANTONY   Come, let's all take hands                  125
  Till that the conquering wine hath steeped our
    sense
  In soft and delicate Lethe.
ENOBARBUS                All take hands.
  Make battery to our ears with the loud music,      130
  The while I'll place you; then the boy shall sing.
  The holding every man shall beat as loud
  As his strong sides can volley.

  *Music plays. Enobarbus places them hand in hand.*

                *The Song.*
⌜BOY⌝   *Come, thou monarch of the vine,*
        *Plumpy Bacchus, with pink eyne.*           135
        *In thy vats our cares be drowned.*
        *With thy grapes our hairs be crowned.*
⌜ALL⌝   *Cup us till the world go round,*
        *Cup us till the world go round.*
CAESAR
  What would you more?—Pompey, goodnight.—           140
    Good brother,
  Let me request you off. Our graver business
  Frowns at this levity.—Gentle lords, let's part.
  You see we have burnt our cheeks. Strong Enobarb
  Is weaker than the wine, and mine own tongue        145

146. **wild disguise:** (1) disorderly drinking; (2) the **Egyptian bacchanals** (line 122) in which they have taken part

147. **Anticked:** transformed into antics (grotesque performers)

150. **try you:** i.e., further test your capacity for drink

151. **shall:** i.e., you shall; **Give 's:** i.e., give me (literally, give us)

153. **boat:** i.e., ship's rowboat

155. **I'll not:** i.e., I'll not go

158. **Neptune:** Roman god of the sea (See below.)

161. **'a:** i.e., he (Enobarbus may be referring to himself as **'a.**)

Neptune. (2.7.158)
From Johann Basilius Herold, *Heydenweldt* . . . [1554].

Splits what it speaks. The wild disguise hath almost
Anticked us all. What needs more words?
    Goodnight.
Good Antony, your hand.
POMPEY    I'll try you on the shore.                          150
ANTONY    And shall, sir. Give 's your hand.
POMPEY
    O, Antony, you have my ⌜father's⌝ house.
    But what? We are friends! Come down into the boat.
ENOBARBUS
    Take heed you fall not.
                    ⌜*All but Menas and Enobarbus exit.*⌝
                        Menas, I'll not on shore.         155
⌜MENAS⌝
    No, to my cabin. These drums, these trumpets,
        flutes! What!
    Let Neptune hear we bid a loud farewell
    To these great fellows. Sound and be hanged. Sound
        out!                *Sound a flourish, with drums.* 160
ENOBARBUS    Hoo, says 'a! There's my cap!
                    ⌜*He throws his cap in the air.*⌝
MENAS    Hoo! Noble captain, come.
                            *They exit.*

# ANTONY

### AND

# CLEOPATRA

---

## ACT 3

**3.1** Having won a victory for Antony, Ventidius explains why it would be politically unwise to achieve further success. We learn that Antony is on his way to Athens.

---

0 SD. **in triumph:** in a formal procession honoring him and his army for their victory; **Pacorus:** son of Orodes, king of Parthia

1. **darting Parthia: Parthia** is called **darting** because its soldiers used light javelins and arrows (darts) as weapons.

2. **Marcus Crassus' death:** Marcus Crassus, one of the members of the first Roman triumvirate (with Julius Caesar and Pompey the Great), was killed by Orodes after having been defeated in battle by the Parthians.

3. **revenger:** i.e., avenger

8. **The fugitive Parthians follow:** i.e., follow the fleeing Parthians

8–9. **Media, / Mesopotamia:** regions bordering Parthia on the north (**Media**) and the south (**Mesopotamia**) See map, page xvii.

14. **A lower place:** i.e., someone in a lower place, a subordinate

19. **officer:** i.e., officers; **person:** i.e., in person (when they were personally leading troops into battle)

20. **place:** rank; **his:** i.e., Antony's

22. **by th' minute:** i.e., very fast

⌜Scene 1⌝

*Enter Ventidius as it were in triumph, the dead body of
Pacorus borne before him; ⌜with Silius and Soldiers.⌝*

VENTIDIUS
  Now, darting Parthia, art thou struck, and now
  Pleased Fortune does of Marcus Crassus' death
  Make me revenger. Bear the King's son's body
  Before our army. Thy Pacorus, Orodes,
  Pays this for Marcus Crassus.                    5
⌜SILIUS⌝                  Noble Ventidius,
  Whilst yet with Parthian blood thy sword is warm,
  The fugitive Parthians follow. Spur through Media,
  Mesopotamia, and the shelters whither
  The routed fly. So thy grand captain, Antony,      10
  Shall set thee on triumphant chariots and
  Put garlands on thy head.
VENTIDIUS            O, Silius, Silius,
  I have done enough. A lower place, note well,
  May make too great an act. For learn this, Silius:    15
  Better to leave undone than by our deed
  Acquire too high a fame when him we serve 's away.
  Caesar and Antony have ever won
  More in their officer than person. Sossius,
  One of my place in Syria, his lieutenant,      20
  For quick accumulation of renown,
  Which he achieved by th' minute, lost his favor.

115

23. **Who:** i.e., whoever

24–26. **ambition . . . darkens him:** (1) The ambitious subordinate chooses to prefer a military loss to a victory that is so great as to attract his (envious) commander's displeasure; or (2) the ambitious commander prefers his subordinate to suffer a loss rather than achieve so great a victory that it obscures the commander's glory.

28. **offense:** i.e., being offended

30–32. **that / Without . . . distinction:** i.e., wisdom, prudence, shrewdness (without which a soldier can hardly be distinguished from the sword he uses)

37. **horse:** cavalry

38. **jaded . . . field:** driven from the battlefield as if they were jades (broken-down horses)

40. **purposeth to:** i.e., intends to go to

41. **with 's:** i.e., with us

42. **On:** i.e., go on

**3.2** Caesar and Octavia take a tearful farewell of each other, and Antony and Octavia depart for Athens.

———————

1. **are the brothers parted:** i.e., have the brothers-in-law, Antony and Octavius Caesar, departed

2. **dispatched:** finished their business

3. **sealing:** formally affixing their official seals to agreements among them

4. **sad:** grave, serious

6. **greensickness:** a form of anemia usually associated with young unmarried women (here perhaps referring to the pallor of Lepidus' skin caused by the aftereffects of his drunkenness)

Who does i' th' wars more than his captain can
Becomes his captain's captain; and ambition,
The soldier's virtue, rather makes choice of loss          25
Than gain which darkens him.
I could do more to do Antonius good,
But 'twould offend him. And in his offense
Should my performance perish.
⌈SILIUS⌉          Thou hast, Ventidius, that          30
    Without the which a soldier and his sword
    Grants scarce distinction. Thou wilt write to
        Antony?
VENTIDIUS
    I'll humbly signify what in his name,
    That magical word of war, we have effected;          35
    How, with his banners and his well-paid ranks,
    The ne'er-yet-beaten horse of Parthia
    We have jaded out o' th' field.
⌈SILIUS⌉                                    Where is he now?
VENTIDIUS
    He purposeth to Athens, whither, with what haste          40
    The weight we must convey with 's will permit,
    We shall appear before him.—On there, pass along!
                                    *They exit.*


⌈Scene 2⌉
*Enter Agrippa at one door, Enobarbus at another.*

AGRIPPA     What, are the brothers parted?
ENOBARBUS
    They have dispatched with Pompey; he is gone.
    The other three are sealing. Octavia weeps
    To part from Rome. Caesar is sad, and Lepidus,
    Since Pompey's feast, as Menas says, is troubled          5
    With the greensickness.

8. **very fine one:** a pun on the Latin meaning of *lepidus*, which is "elegant"

13. **Arabian bird:** phoenix, a mythical bird, only one of which was alive at any given time (It reproduced itself by reincarnation after burning itself to ashes.) See page 126.

14. **Would you:** i.e., if you would

18–20. **hearts . . . number:** i.e., **hearts** cannot **think, tongues** cannot **speak, figures** cannot **cast** (i.e., numbers cannot sum up, or figures of speech cannot devise), **scribes** cannot **write, bards** cannot **sing, poets** cannot **number** (i.e., count; write in metrical verse)

24. **shards:** patches of dung on which a shard-beetle feeds (Because Shakespeare uses the phrase "shard-borne beetle" in *Macbeth*, some editors have argued that **shards** means the wings of the **beetle**.)

26. **to horse:** i.e., the trumpet signal to mount their horses

28. **No further:** perhaps, (1) there is no need to speak further, or (2) no need to accompany us any further

AGRIPPA                                    'Tis a noble Lepidus.

ENOBARBUS
A very fine one. O, how he loves Caesar!

AGRIPPA
Nay, but how dearly he adores Mark Antony!

ENOBARBUS
Caesar? Why, he's the Jupiter of men.                    10

⌜AGRIPPA⌝
What's Antony? The god of Jupiter.

ENOBARBUS
Spake you of Caesar? How, the nonpareil!

AGRIPPA
O Antony, O thou Arabian bird! — *phoenix*

ENOBARBUS
Would you praise Caesar, say "Caesar." Go no
further.                                                  15

AGRIPPA
Indeed, he plied them both with excellent praises.

ENOBARBUS
But he loves Caesar best, yet he loves Antony.
Hoo, hearts, tongues, ⌜figures,⌝ scribes, bards, poets,
cannot
Think, speak, cast, write, sing, number—hoo!—          20
His love to Antony. But as for Caesar,
Kneel down, kneel down, and wonder.

AGRIPPA                                    Both he loves.

ENOBARBUS
They are his shards and he their beetle.
                        ⌜*Trumpet within.*⌝
                        So,                              25
This is to horse. Adieu, noble Agrippa.

AGRIPPA
Good fortune, worthy soldier, and farewell.

    *Enter Caesar, Antony, Lepidus, and Octavia.*

ANTONY   No further, sir.

**31–32. as my farthest ... approof:** i.e., as I will pledge any amount of money on your proving to be

**33. piece:** example (i.e., model)

**34. cement:** accent on first syllable

**35. ram:** battering ram (See below.)

**37. mean:** (1) means; (2) intermediary agent (i.e., Octavia)

**40. In:** i.e., by

**43. curious:** (1) anxious; (2) minute in inquiry; (3) prying

**44. keep:** protect

**49. all:** completely, entirely

**51–52. The April's ... bring it on:** Proverbial: April showers bring May flowers.

**53. my husband's house:** Since Octavia is a widow, she could here be referring to the **house** of Antony or of her first husband, Caius Marcellus.

A battering ram. (3.2.35)

From Guillaume Du Choul, *Los discursos de la religion . . .* (1579).

CAESAR   *Octavia's brother*
  You take from me a great part of myself.
  Use me well in 't.—Sister, prove such a wife                    30
  As my thoughts make thee, and as my farthest bond
  Shall pass on thy approof.—Most noble Antony,
  Let not the piece of virtue which is set   *vagina*
  Betwixt us, as the cement of our love
  To keep it builded, be the ram to batter                    35
  The fortress of it. For better might we
  Have loved without this mean, if on both parts
  This be not cherished.
ANTONY                    Make me not offended
  In your distrust.                    40
CAESAR          I have said.
ANTONY                    You shall not find,
  Though you be therein curious, the least cause
  For what you seem to fear. So the gods keep you,
  And make the hearts of Romans serve your ends.                    45
  We will here part.
CAESAR
  Farewell, my dearest sister, fare thee well.
  The elements be kind to thee and make
  Thy spirits all of comfort. Fare thee well.
OCTAVIA   My noble brother.                    ⌜*She weeps.*⌝   50
ANTONY
  The April's in her eyes. It is love's spring,
  And these the showers to bring it on.—Be cheerful.
OCTAVIA, ⌜*to Caesar*⌝
  Sir, look well to my husband's house, and—
CAESAR
  What, Octavia?
OCTAVIA          I'll tell you in your ear.                    55
        ⌜*Caesar and Octavia walk aside.*⌝
ANTONY
  Her tongue will not obey her heart, nor can

59. **at the full of tide:** i.e., when the tide is at the height of its flow, just before its ebb (Octavia's speechlessness is like the apparent motionlessness of the sea at this moment; or, perhaps, the conflict in her emotions is like the delicate balance of the tide at the moment between flow and ebb.)

62. **He has . . . face:** i.e., he looks as if he may weep (Enobarbus' reply uses **cloud** in the sense of a dark spot on a horse's face, which lowers a horse's value.)

66–68. **When Antony . . . slain:** See Shakespeare's *Julius Caesar* 3.1 and 5.5.

69. **rheum:** cold

70. **confound:** destroy

73. **still:** continually

74. **Outgo:** go faster than; **on:** i.e., of

77. **here I have you:** Perhaps Antony now embraces Caesar.

Her heart inform her tongue—the swan's-down
    feather
That stands upon the swell at the full of tide
And neither way inclines.                                60
ENOBARBUS, ⌈*aside to Agrippa*⌉ Will Caesar weep?
AGRIPPA    He has a cloud in 's face.
ENOBARBUS
    He were the worse for that were he a horse;
    So is he being a man.
AGRIPPA                    Why, Enobarbus,                65
    When Antony found Julius Caesar dead,
    He cried almost to roaring. And he wept
    When at Philippi he found Brutus slain.
ENOBARBUS
    That year indeed he was troubled with a rheum.
    What willingly he did confound he wailed,        70
    Believe 't, till I ⌈wept⌉ too.
CAESAR, ⌈*coming forward with Octavia*⌉
                        No, sweet Octavia,
    You shall hear from me still. The time shall not
    Outgo my thinking on you.
ANTONY                    Come, sir, come,            75
    I'll wrestle with you in my strength of love.
    Look, here I have you, thus I let you go,
    And give you to the gods.
CAESAR                    Adieu, be happy.
LEPIDUS, ⌈*to Antony*⌉
    Let all the number of the stars give light        80
    To thy fair way.
CAESAR          Farewell, farewell.    *Kisses Octavia.*
ANTONY                        Farewell.
                    *Trumpets sound. They exit.*

**3.3** Cleopatra is reassured by further description of Octavia.

_____

3. **Go to:** an expression of derisive incredulity

3 SD. **Messenger as before:** i.e., the messenger who before brought news of Antony's marriage

5. **Herod of Jewry:** See note to 1.2.29–30, and below.

20. **low:** hushed

"Herod of Jewry." (1.2.29–30, 3.3.5)
From [Guillaume Rouillé,] . . . *Prima pars promptuarii iconum* . . . (1553).

⌜Scene 3⌝

*Enter Cleopatra, Charmian, Iras, and Alexas.*

CLEOPATRA
Where is the fellow?
ALEXAS                    Half afeard to come.
CLEOPATRA
Go to, go to.—Come hither, sir.

*Enter the Messenger as before.*

ALEXAS                              Good Majesty,
Herod of Jewry dare not look upon you                        5
But when you are well pleased.
CLEOPATRA                         That Herod's head
I'll have! But how, when Antony is gone,
Through whom I might command it?—Come thou
     near.                                                    10
MESSENGER
Most gracious Majesty!
CLEOPATRA                    Did'st thou behold Octavia?
MESSENGER
Ay, dread queen.
CLEOPATRA          Where?
MESSENGER                     Madam, in Rome.                 15
I looked her in the face and saw her led
Between her brother and Mark Antony.
CLEOPATRA
Is she as tall as me?
MESSENGER               She is not, madam.
CLEOPATRA
Didst hear her speak? Is she shrill-tongued or low?          20
MESSENGER
Madam, I heard her speak. She is low-voiced.
CLEOPATRA
That's not so good. He cannot like her long.
CHARMIAN
Like her? O Isis, 'tis impossible!

29. **station:** standing still
30. **shows:** seems to be
31. **than a breather:** i.e., rather than a living being
33. **observance:** powers of observation
34–35. **Three . . . note:** i.e., there are not **three** other people **in Egypt** who can observe as well as he

The "Arabian bird," or phoenix. (3.2.13)
From Conrad Lycosthenes, *Prodigiorum . . .* [1557].

CLEOPATRA
　I think so, Charmian: dull of tongue, and
　　dwarfish!—                                              25
　What majesty is in her gait? Remember,
　If e'er thou ⌈looked'st⌉ on majesty.
MESSENGER                                    She creeps.
　Her motion and her station are as one.
　She shows a body rather than a life,                     30
　A statue than a breather.
CLEOPATRA                      Is this certain?
MESSENGER
　Or I have no observance.
CHARMIAN                        Three in Egypt
　Cannot make better note.                                 35
CLEOPATRA                        He's very knowing.
　I do perceive 't. There's nothing in her yet.
　The fellow has good judgment.
CHARMIAN                                  Excellent.
CLEOPATRA, ⌈*to Messenger*⌉  Guess at her years, I         40
　　prithee.
MESSENGER  Madam, she was a widow.
CLEOPATRA  Widow? Charmian, hark.
MESSENGER  And I do think she's thirty.
CLEOPATRA
　Bear'st thou her face in mind? Is 't long or round?      45
MESSENGER  Round even to faultiness.
CLEOPATRA
　For the most part, too, they are foolish that are so.
　Her hair what color?
MESSENGER  Brown, madam, and her forehead
　As low as she would wish it.                             50
CLEOPATRA, ⌈*giving money*⌉     There's gold for thee.
　Thou must not take my former sharpness ill.
　I will employ thee back again. I find thee
　Most fit for business. Go, make thee ready.
　Our letters are prepared.            ⌈*Messenger exits.*⌉  55

56. **proper:** fine, admirable
58. **harried:** mistreated; **by him:** according to him
59. **no such thing:** i.e., nothing to be concerned about
62. **else defend:** forbid otherwise
68. **warrant:** assure

**3.4** At the news of Caesar's hostile actions, Antony begins to prepare for war, but gives Octavia permission to go to Rome to try to heal the new division between Caesar and him.

———

3. **semblable import:** i.e., comparable significance
4–5. **read . . . ear:** presumably to win popularity by proclaiming the benefits the Roman people can expect (Compare Antony's public reading of the dead Julius Caesar's will in Shakespeare's *Julius Caesar* 3.2.)
6. **scantly:** grudgingly
9. **hint:** occasion (to praise)
10. **from his teeth:** formally or feignedly (not from his heart)

CHARMIAN                        A proper man.
CLEOPATRA
  Indeed he is so. I repent me much
  That so I harried him. Why, methinks, by him,
  This creature's no such thing.
CHARMIAN                        Nothing, madam.          60
CLEOPATRA
  The man hath seen some majesty, and should know.
CHARMIAN
  Hath he seen majesty? Isis else defend,
  And serving you so long!
CLEOPATRA
  I have one thing more to ask him yet, good
    Charmian,                                             65
  But 'tis no matter. Thou shalt bring him to me
  Where I will write. All may be well enough.
CHARMIAN   I warrant you, madam.

                                *They exit.*


⌜Scene 4⌝
*Enter Antony and Octavia.*

ANTONY
  Nay, nay, Octavia, not only that—
  That were excusable, that and thousands more
  Of semblable import—but he hath waged
  New wars 'gainst Pompey; made his will and read it
  To public ear;                                          5
  Spoke scantly of me; when perforce he could not
  But pay me terms of honor, cold and sickly
  He vented ⌜them,⌝ most narrow measure lent me;
  When the best hint was given him, he not ⌜took 't,⌝
  Or did it from his teeth.                                10
OCTAVIA                        O, my good lord,

13. **Stomach:** resent
14. **chance:** happen, occur
18. **Undo:** i.e., and then cancel
20. **Prays . . . prayer:** The subject of both **prays** and **destroys the prayer** is **Husband win, win brother.**
23. **draw to:** resort to, join the party of; **that point which:** i.e., the man who (literally, the **point** on a compass)
27. **between 's:** i.e., between us
29. **Shall stain:** i.e., that will eclipse
33. **twain:** two
34. **that:** i.e., as if
36. **When . . . begins:** i.e., when you determine who began this conflict
39. **Provide your going:** make preparation for your departure

Believe not all, or if you must believe,
Stomach not all. A more unhappy lady,
If this division chance, ne'er stood between,
Praying for both parts.                                    15
The good gods will mock me presently
When I shall pray "O, bless my lord and husband!"
Undo that prayer by crying out as loud
"O, bless my brother!" Husband win, win brother
Prays and destroys the prayer; no midway          20
'Twixt these extremes at all.

ANTONY                              Gentle Octavia,
Let your best love draw to that point which seeks
Best to preserve it. If I lose mine honor,
I lose myself; better I were not yours               25
Than ⌜yours⌝ so branchless. But, as you requested,
Yourself shall go between 's. The meantime, lady,
I'll raise the preparation of a war
Shall stain your brother. Make your soonest haste,
So your desires are yours.                                30

OCTAVIA                          Thanks to my lord.
The Jove of power make me, most weak, most weak,
⌜Your⌝ reconciler. Wars 'twixt you twain would be
As if the world should cleave, and that slain men
Should solder up the rift.                                35

ANTONY
When it appears to you where this begins,
Turn your displeasure that way, for our faults
Can never be so equal that your love
Can equally move with them. Provide your going;
Choose your own company, and command what cost   40
Your heart ⌜has⌝ mind to.

                                         *They exit.*

**3.5**   With Caesar having imprisoned Lepidus, Caesar and Antony now divide the rulership of their world. Antony's navy is prepared to sail for Italy.

---

6. **success:** outcome
7. **him:** i.e., Lepidus
8. **presently:** i.e., just as soon as the wars were over (literally, "immediately"); **rivality:** status as a partner
11. **wrote:** i.e., written; **upon . . . appeal:** on the basis of his accusation alone
12. **up:** confined (in prison)
12–13. **enlarge his confine:** set him at liberty
14. **chaps:** jaws
17. **thus:** an invitation to the actor playing Eros to represent Antony's manner of **walking**
19. **threats:** i.e., threatens; **that his officer:** i.e., that officer of his (Titius, who, according to some accounts but not others, was acting on Antony's orders)
22. **Domitius:** i.e., Enobarbus, called by his first name
25. **'Twill be naught:** (1) Antony wants me for nothing important; or, (2) the outcome of all this will be hurtful or evil

⌜Scene 5⌝ *alexandria*

*Enter Enobarbus and Eros.*

ENOBARBUS   How now, friend Eros?

EROS   There's strange news come, sir.

ENOBARBUS   What, man?

EROS   Caesar and Lepidus have made wars upon
    Pompey.                                                                           5

ENOBARBUS   This is old. What is the success?

EROS   Caesar, having made use of him in the wars
    'gainst Pompey, presently denied him rivality,
    would not let him partake in the glory of the action;
    and, not resting here, accuses him of letters he had   10
    formerly wrote to Pompey; upon his own appeal
    seizes him. So the poor third is up, till death enlarge
    his confine.   *Lepidus - alone*

ENOBARBUS
    Then, ⌜world,⌝ thou ⌜hast⌝ a pair of chaps, no more,
    And throw between them all the food thou hast,   15
    They'll grind ⌜the one⌝ the other. Where's Antony?

EROS
    He's walking in the garden, thus, and spurns
    The rush that lies before him; cries "Fool Lepidus!"
    And threats the throat of that his officer
    That murdered Pompey.                                                    20

ENOBARBUS                        Our great navy's rigged.

EROS
    For Italy and Caesar. More, Domitius:
    My lord desires you presently. My news
    I might have told hereafter.

ENOBARBUS                                    'Twill be naught,   25
    But let it be. Bring me to Antony.

EROS   Come, sir.

*They exit.*

**3.6** Octavia arrives in Rome, to be told that Antony has left Athens for Egypt.

-----------

3. **tribunal:** platform

6. **my father's son:** i.e., Julius Caesar's son by Cleopatra (Julius Caesar, in his will, became the adoptive father of Octavius Caesar.)

9. **stablishment:** confirmed possession

10, **lower . . . Lydia: Syria,** a region just east of the Mediterranean; **Cyprus,** an island in the eastern Mediterranean; **Lydia,** a region just east of Ionia in present-day Asia Minor. See map, page xvii.

13. **showplace:** place for public shows or spectacles; **they exercise:** i.e., the people take part in games, shows, etc.

24. **knows:** i.e., know

26. **Who:** i.e., whom

28. **Sextus Pompeius spoiled:** despoiled or seized the land that had been Pompey's; **we:** i.e., I (the royal "we"); **rated him:** assigned to him (as his share)

⌜Scene 6⌝
*Enter Agrippa, Maecenas, and Caesar.*

CAESAR
  Contemning Rome, he has done all this and more
  In Alexandria. Here's the manner of 't:
  I' th' marketplace, on a tribunal silvered,
  Cleopatra and himself in chairs of gold
  Were publicly enthroned. At the feet sat            5
  Caesarion, whom they call my father's son,
  And all the unlawful issue that their lust
  Since then hath made between them. Unto her
  He gave the stablishment of Egypt, made her
  Of lower Syria, Cyprus, Lydia,                      10
  Absolute queen.
MAECENAS               This in the public eye?
CAESAR
  I' th' common showplace where they exercise.
  His sons ⌜he there⌝ proclaimed the ⌜kings⌝ of kings.
  Great Media, Parthia, and Armenia                   15
  He gave to Alexander; to Ptolemy he assigned
  Syria, Cilicia, and Phoenicia. She
  In th' habiliments of the goddess Isis
  That day appeared, and oft before gave audience,
  As 'tis reported, so.                               20
MAECENAS   Let Rome be thus informed.
AGRIPPA
  Who, queasy with his insolence already,
  Will their good thoughts call from him.
CAESAR
  The people knows it and have now received
  His accusations.                                    25
AGRIPPA               Who does he accuse?
CAESAR
  Caesar, and that, having in Sicily
  Sextus Pompeius spoiled, we had not rated him
  His part o' th' isle. Then does he say he lent me

30. **shipping:** ships
31. **of:** i.e., from
32. **being:** i.e., having been deposed; **detain:** retain
33. **revenue:** accent on second syllable
38. **For:** i.e., as for
49. **Like:** in a manner appropriate to
51. **horse:** i.e., horses
57. **prevented:** forestalled

A "triumphant chariot" and "garlands." (3.1.11–12)
From Onofrio Panvinio, . . . *De lvdis circensibvs, libri II.*
*De trivmphis liber vnvs . . .* (1642).

Some shipping, unrestored. Lastly, he frets          30
That Lepidus of the triumvirate
Should be deposed and, being, that we detain
All his revenue.

AGRIPPA                    Sir, this should be answered.

CAESAR
'Tis done already, and the messenger gone.           35
I have told him Lepidus was grown too cruel,
That he his high authority abused
And did deserve his change. For what I have
    conquered,
I grant him part; but then in his Armenia            40
And other of his conquered kingdoms I
Demand the like.

MAECENAS                   He'll never yield to that.

CAESAR
Nor must not then be yielded to in this.

*Enter Octavia with her Train.*

OCTAVIA
Hail, Caesar, and my lord! Hail, most dear Caesar.   45

CAESAR
That ever I should call thee castaway!

OCTAVIA
You have not called me so, nor have you cause.

CAESAR
Why have you stol'n upon us thus? You come not
Like Caesar's sister. The wife of Antony
Should have an army for an usher and               50
The neighs of horse to tell of her approach
Long ere she did appear. The trees by th' way
Should have borne men, and expectation fainted,
Longing for what it had not. Nay, the dust
Should have ascended to the roof of heaven,         55
Raised by your populous troops. But you are come
A market-maid to Rome, and have prevented

58. **ostentation:** spectacular display

59. **should:** i.e., would

60. **stage:** i.e., stage of your journey

66. **withal:** i.e., with the news; **whereon:** i.e., and consequently

67. **pardon:** permission

69. **Being . . . him:** If this line refers to Antony's granting Octavia permission to leave, the word **abstract** might suggest a shortening of the distance between Antony and Cleopatra, the object of his **lust.** If the line instead refers to Octavia herself, the word **abstract** is probably an error for some other word that means "an obstruction." Editors who accept the second option emend the word to "obstruct," which is not recorded as appearing as a noun elsewhere in English.

77. **who:** i.e., and they, Cleopatra and Antony

79. **Libya:** a region in North Africa, just west of Egypt (See map, page xvi.)

80. **Cappadocia:** Like **Paphlagonia** (line 81), **Pont** (i.e., Pontus, line 82), **Comagen** (line 84), and **Lycaonia** (line 85), **Cappadocia** was a region in what is now called Asia Minor, south of the Black Sea.

82. **Arabia:** a region just east of Egypt (See map, page xvii.)

83. **Jewry:** i.e., Judea, a region on the east coast of the Mediterranean (See maps, pages xvii and 198.)

85. **Mede:** i.e., Media, a region in what is now southwestern Asia

86. **more larger:** i.e., larger; **scepters:** i.e., kings

89. **does:** i.e., do

The ostentation of our love, which, left unshown,
Is often left unloved. We should have met you
By sea and land, supplying every stage                    60
With an augmented greeting.
OCTAVIA                          Good my lord,
To come thus was I not constrained, but did it
On my free will. My lord, Mark Antony,
Hearing that you prepared for war, acquainted            65
My grievèd ear withal, whereon I begged
His pardon for return.
CAESAR                      Which soon he granted,
Being an abstract 'tween his lust and him.
OCTAVIA
Do not say so, my lord.                                   70
CAESAR                    I have eyes upon him,
And his affairs come to me on the wind.
Where is he now?
OCTAVIA   My lord, in Athens.
CAESAR
No, my most wrongèd sister. Cleopatra                    75
Hath nodded him to her. He hath given his empire
Up to a whore, who now are levying
The kings o' th' earth for war. He hath assembled
Bocchus, the King of Libya; Archelaus
Of Cappadocia; Philadelphos, King                         80
Of Paphlagonia; the Thracian king, Adallas;
King Manchus of Arabia; King of Pont;
Herod of Jewry; Mithridates, King
Of Comagen; Polemon and Amyntas,
The Kings of Mede and Lycaonia,                           85
With a more larger list of scepters.
OCTAVIA   Ay me, most wretched,
That have my heart parted betwixt two friends
That does afflict each other!
CAESAR                          Welcome hither.           90
Your letters did withhold our breaking forth

92. **wrong led:** i.e., misled (by Antony)

93. **negligent danger:** i.e., **danger** through negligence

96–97. **let determined . . . way:** i.e., allow what is destined to happen to continue unlamented on its way

99. **the mark of thought:** i.e., what can be thought (literally, the limit **of thought**); **high gods:** presented here as a single, unified force

106. **large:** gross, improper, unrestrained

107. **turns you off:** dismisses you

108. **potent regiment:** powerful rule or authority; **trull:** harlot

109. **noises it:** clamors, cries out

112. **Be ever known to patience:** i.e., continue to endure your suffering with composure

**3.7** Over the pleading of his soldiers and officers and encouraged by Cleopatra, Antony decides to fight Caesar by sea.

———————

3. **forspoke:** spoken against

Till we perceived both how you were wrong led
And we in negligent danger. Cheer your heart.
Be you not troubled with the time, which drives
O'er your content these strong necessities,                    95
But let determined things to destiny
Hold unbewailed their way. Welcome to Rome,
Nothing more dear to me. You are abused
Beyond the mark of thought, and the high gods,
To do you justice, makes his ministers                         100
Of us and those that love you. Best of comfort,
And ever welcome to us.
AGRIPPA                              Welcome, lady.
MAECENAS   Welcome, dear madam.
Each heart in Rome does love and pity you;                     105
Only th' adulterous Antony, most large
In his abominations, turns you off
And gives his potent regiment to a trull
That noises it against us.
OCTAVIA, ⌜*to Caesar*⌝          Is it so, sir?                 110
CAESAR
Most certain. Sister, welcome. Pray you
Be ever known to patience. My dear'st sister!
                                        *They exit.*


⌜Scene 7⌝
*Enter Cleopatra and Enobarbus.*

CLEOPATRA
I will be even with thee, doubt it not.
ENOBARBUS   But why, why, why?
CLEOPATRA
Thou hast forspoke my being in these wars
And say'st it ⌜is⌝ not fit.
ENOBARBUS                    Well, is it, is it?              5

6. **denounced:** proclaimed; **us:** i.e., me (the royal "we")

8–11. **Well . . . horse:** These lines are frequently marked by editors as an "aside"—that is, addressed to the audience rather than to Cleopatra.   **serve:** i.e., go to war   **horse:** (male) horses   **merely:** utterly

13. **puzzle:** perplex, bewilder

20. **charge:** (1) responsibility; (2) expense (Historically, Cleopatra paid a large share of the war's cost.)

21. **president:** chief ruler; guardian; presiding deity (in her public role as Isis)

22. **Appear . . . man:** i.e., occupy the position of **a man** in this war

27. **Tarentum, Brundusium:** cities on the heel of the boot of Italy

28. **Ionian Sea:** the southern part of what is now called the Adriatic Sea between the boot of Italy and Greece

29. **take in:** take, capture; **Toryne:** a city on the western coast of Greece; **on 't:** i.e., about it

30. **admired:** wondered at

33. **becomed:** become, been appropriate to

34. **slackness:** slowness, tardiness

CLEOPATRA
⌐Is 't⌐ not denounced against us? Why should not we
Be there in person?

ENOBARBUS                    Well, I could reply:
If we should serve with horse and mares together,
The horse were merely lost. The mares would bear      10
A soldier and his horse.

CLEOPATRA                    What is 't you say?

ENOBARBUS
Your presence needs must puzzle Antony,
Take from his heart, take from his brain, from 's time
What should not then be spared. He is already      15
Traduced for levity, and 'tis said in Rome
That Photinus, an eunuch, and your maids
Manage this war.

CLEOPATRA          Sink Rome, and their tongues rot
That speak against us! A charge we bear i' th' war,      20
And as the president of my kingdom will
Appear there for a man. Speak not against it.
I will not stay behind.

*Enter Antony and Canidius.*

ENOBARBUS                    Nay, I have done.
Here comes the Emperor.      25

ANTONY                    Is it not strange, Canidius,
That from Tarentum and Brundusium
He could so quickly cut the Ionian Sea
And take in Toryne?—You have heard on 't, sweet?

CLEOPATRA
Celerity is never more admired      30
Than by the negligent.

ANTONY                    A good rebuke,
Which might have well becomed the best of men,
To taunt at slackness.—Canidius, we will fight
With him by sea.      35

36. **what else:** certainly

39. **For that:** because

41. **Pharsalia:** a city in Thessaly (a region in central Greece) For Thessaly, see map, page xvi.

42. **Caesar:** i.e., Julius Caesar; **Pompey:** i.e., Pompey the Great

43. **for his vantage:** i.e., to his advantage

47. **Engrossed:** gathered up, collected; **impress:** conscription

49. **yare:** maneuverable

50. **fall:** befall, happen to

54. **absolute . . . land:** "great skill and experience of battles by land" (North's Plutarch, *Life of Marcus Antonius* [1579])

55. **Distract:** divide; **most:** i.e., mostly

56. **footmen:** foot soldiers, infantry; **leave unexecuted:** i.e., be unable to put into practice

58. **assurance:** security

59. **merely:** utterly

64. **full-manned:** i.e., fully manned; **head:** headland, promontory, cape

65. **Actium:** a city on the western coast of Greece, just south of Toryne (See map, page xvi.)

CLEOPATRA            By sea, what else?
CANIDIUS                         Why will
  My lord do so?
ANTONY            For that he dares us to 't.
ENOBARBUS
  So hath my lord dared him to single fight.                    40
CANIDIUS
  Ay, and to wage this battle at Pharsalia,
  Where Caesar fought with Pompey. But these offers,
  Which serve not for his vantage, he shakes off,
  And so should you.
ENOBARBUS            Your ships are not well manned,   45
  Your mariners are muleteers, reapers, people
  Engrossed by swift impress. In Caesar's fleet
  Are those that often have 'gainst Pompey fought.
  Their ships are yare, yours heavy. No disgrace
  Shall fall you for refusing him at sea,                        50
  Being prepared for land.
ANTONY                     By sea, by sea.
ENOBARBUS
  Most worthy sir, you therein throw away
  The absolute soldiership you have by land,
  Distract your army, which doth most consist               55
  Of war-marked footmen, leave unexecuted
  Your own renownèd knowledge, quite forgo
  The way which promises assurance, and
  Give up yourself merely to chance and hazard
  From firm security.                                          60
ANTONY              I'll fight at sea.
CLEOPATRA
  I have sixty sails, Caesar none better.
ANTONY
  Our overplus of shipping will we burn,
  And with the rest full-manned, from th' head of
    Actium                                                    65

72. **power:** armed forces

73. **hold by:** i.e., keep out of the action, remaining in battle formation on

74. **horse:** cavalry

75. **Thetis:** a Nereid or sea-nymph, mother of the Greek warrior Achilles

75 SD. **Soldier:** See longer note, page 282.

78. **misdoubt:** i.e., lack confidence in

80. **Phoenicians:** either inhabitants of what is now the coast of Syria, where the famous cities of Tyre and Sidon were located, or the inhabitants of one of the many Phoenician colonies that dotted the Mediterranean coastline (The **Phoenicians** were famous sailors.) **a-ducking:** diving

85–86. **his whole . . . on 't:** i.e., his entire course of action is cut off from his greatest strength

87. **men:** servingmen

89. **whole:** intact, together as a unit (and therefore uncommitted to battle)

Beat th' approaching Caesar. But if we fail,
We then can do 't at land.

*Enter a Messenger.*

                              Thy business?
MESSENGER
   The news is true, my lord; he is descried.
   Caesar has taken Toryne.              ⌜*He exits.*⌝   70
ANTONY
   Can he be there in person? 'Tis impossible;
   Strange that his power should be. Canidius,
   Our nineteen legions thou shalt hold by land,
   And our twelve thousand horse. We'll to our ship.—
   Away, my Thetis. *Cleo*                                75

*Enter a Soldier.*

                 How now, worthy soldier?
SOLDIER
   O noble emperor, do not fight by sea!
   Trust not to rotten planks. Do you misdoubt
   This sword and these my wounds? Let th' Egyptians
   And the Phoenicians go a-ducking. We               80
   Have used to conquer standing on the earth
   And fighting foot to foot.
ANTONY                        Well, well, away.
              *Antony, Cleopatra, and Enobarbus exit.*
SOLDIER
   By Hercules, I think I am i' th' right.
CANIDIUS
   Soldier, thou art, but his whole action grows       85
   Not in the power on 't. So our leader's led,
   And we are women's men.
SOLDIER                        You keep by land
   The legions and the horse whole, do you not?
⌜CANIDIUS⌝
   Marcus Octavius, Marcus Justeius,                   90

93. **Carries:** i.e., reaches
95. **power:** forces; **distractions:** divided forms

**3.8** Caesar orders his army to provoke no battle by land.

---

7. **jump:** venture, hazard, risk

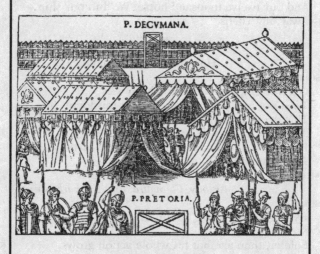

A Roman camp.
From Guillaume Du Choul, *Discours de la religion des anciens Romains* . . . (1556).

Publicola, and Caelius are for sea,
But we keep whole by land. This speed of Caesar's
Carries beyond belief.

SOLDIER                While he was yet in Rome,
His power went out in such distractions as            95
Beguiled all spies.

CANIDIUS                Who's his lieutenant, hear you?

SOLDIER
They say one Taurus.

CANIDIUS                Well I know the man.

*Enter a Messenger.*

MESSENGER   The Emperor calls Canidius.            100

CANIDIUS
With news the time's ⌜in⌝ labor, and throws forth
Each minute some.

                                        *They exit.*


⌜Scene 8⌝
*Enter Caesar with his army, ⌜and Taurus,⌝ marching.*

CAESAR   Taurus!

TAURUS   My lord?

CAESAR
Strike not by land, keep whole. Provoke not battle
Till we have done at sea. Do not exceed
The prescript of this scroll.     ⌜*Hands him a scroll.*⌝   5
                          Our fortune lies
Upon this jump.

                                ⌜*They*⌝ *exit.*

**3.9** Antony sets his squadrons.

_____

1. **squadrons:** bodies of troops drawn up in square formations
2. **In eye:** in sight; **battle:** main (naval) force


**3.10** Antony turns his ship in mid-battle to follow Cleopatra's flight. His officers begin to desert.

_____

0 SD. **going in:** i.e., leaving the stage
1. **Naught:** lost, ruined .
2. **admiral:** flagship (called **Th' Antoniad**)
3. **their sixty:** i.e., sixty Egyptian ships
4. **blasted:** stricken
7. **What's thy passion:** i.e., what's the matter with you (literally, what's your affliction)
8. **cantle:** portion
9. **With very:** through sheer; **kissed away:** lost (by kissing)
12. **tokened pestilence:** i.e., the plague in its advanced stages when spots (called "God's tokens") appeared on the skin
13. **ribaudred:** an apparent error that has never been emended to editors' satisfaction (See longer note, page 282.) **nag:** a term of abuse
14. **o'ertake:** seize
15–16. **vantage . . . elder:** i.e., neither Antony nor Octavius Caesar enjoyed superiority in the battle—or Antony had a slight edge **vantage:** superiority in a contest

⌜Scene 9⌝
*Enter Antony and Enobarbus.*

ANTONY
　Set we our squadrons on yond side o' th' hill
　In eye of Caesar's battle, from which place
　We may the number of the ships behold
　And so proceed accordingly.

⌜*They*⌝ *exit.*

⌜Scene 10⌝
*Canidius marcheth with his land army one way
over the stage, and Taurus the lieutenant of Caesar
the other way. After their going in is heard the
noise of a sea fight.*

*Alarum. Enter Enobarbus.*

ENOBARBUS
　Naught, naught, all naught! I can behold no longer.
　Th' Antoniad, the Egyptian admiral,
　With all their sixty, fly and turn the rudder.
　To see 't mine eyes are blasted.

*Enter Scarus.*

SCARUS　　　　　　　　　　　　Gods and goddesses,　　5
　All the whole synod of them!
ENOBARBUS　　　　　　　　　What's thy passion?
SCARUS
　The greater cantle of the world is lost
　With very ignorance. We have kissed away
　Kingdoms and provinces.　　　　　　　　　　10
ENOBARBUS　　　　　　　How appears the fight?
SCARUS
　On our side, like the tokened pestilence,
　Where death is sure. Yon ribaudred nag of Egypt,
　Whom leprosy o'ertake, i' th' midst o' th' fight,
　When vantage like a pair of twins appeared　　15

17. **breeze:** gadfly (with wordplay, perhaps, on the sense of wind, which fills the sails of Cleopatra's fleeing ships) The image is of a horse (**nag,** line 13) running off after being stung by a fly of the kind that afflict cattle in June.

22. **She . . . loofed:** i.e., as soon as the head of her ship was brought nearer the wind (so as to sail away)

24. **sea-wing:** means of flight by sea

25. **in height:** i.e., when it was most intense

29. **Alack:** an expression of sorrow, regret or alarm

31. **lamentably:** accent on first syllable

32. **himself:** i.e., himself to be

35. **thereabouts:** about that; near to that action (i.e., deserting Antony); **goodnight:** an expression of loss (i.e., the loss of Antony's fortunes)

37. **Peloponnesus:** southern region of Greece

38. **to 't:** i.e., to journey to it; **attend:** wait for

44–45. **my reason . . . me:** i.e., **reason** indicates that I should take the opposite course  **Sits in the wind:** can be perceived to be

Both as the same—or, rather, ours the elder—
The breeze upon her like a cow in ⌜June,⌝
Hoists sails and flies.

ENOBARBUS   That I beheld.
Mine eyes did sicken at the sight and could not          20
Endure a further view.

SCARUS                    She once being loofed,
The noble ruin of her magic, Antony,
Claps on his sea-wing and, like a doting mallard,
Leaving the fight in height, flies after her.          25
I never saw an action of such shame.
Experience, manhood, honor ne'er before
Did violate so itself.

ENOBARBUS             Alack, alack.

*Enter Canidius.*

CANIDIUS
Our fortune on the sea is out of breath          30
And sinks most lamentably. Had our general
Been what he knew himself, it had gone well.
O, ⌜he⌝ has given example for our flight
Most grossly by his own.

ENOBARBUS
Ay, are you thereabouts? Why then goodnight          35
  indeed.

CANIDIUS   Toward Peloponnesus are they fled.

SCARUS
'Tis easy to 't, and there I will attend
What further comes.                    ⌜*He exits.*⌝

CANIDIUS               To Caesar will I render          40
My legions and my horse. Six kings already
Show me the way of yielding.          ⌜*He exits.*⌝

ENOBARBUS                    I'll yet follow
The wounded chance of Antony, though my reason
Sits in the wind against me.          45
                    ⌜*He exits.*⌝

**3.11** Antony, in despair over his action, accuses Cleopatra but then forgives her.

---

3. **I am so lated:** I am so belated (literally, I travel so late at night)

9. **shoulders:** i.e., the backs of their shoulders (as they flee)

13. **that:** i.e., that which

14. **mutiny:** quarrel, contend with each other

15. **rashness:** inconsiderate haste in acting; **they them:** i.e., the brown reprove the white

18. **Sweep your way:** i.e., win you access (to Caesar)

19. **loathness:** reluctance; **hint:** opportunity

22. **possess you:** put you in possession

24. **command:** the authority to give orders (and **command** over himself)

⌜Scene 11⌝
*Enter Antony with Attendants.*

ANTONY
  Hark, the land bids me tread no more upon 't.
  It is ashamed to bear me. Friends, come hither.
  I am so lated in the world that I
  Have lost my way forever. I have a ship
  Laden with gold. Take that, divide it. Fly,          5
  And make your peace with Caesar.
ALL                                    Fly? Not we!
ANTONY
  I have fled myself and have instructed cowards
  To run and show their shoulders. Friends, begone.
  I have myself resolved upon a course                 10
  Which has no need of you. Begone.
  My treasure's in the harbor; take it. O,
  I followed that I blush to look upon!
  My very hairs do mutiny, for the white
  Reprove the brown for rashness, and they them        15
  For fear and doting. Friends, begone. You shall
  Have letters from me to some friends that will
  Sweep your way for you. Pray you look not sad,
  Nor make replies of loathness. Take the hint
  Which my despair proclaims. Let ⌜that⌝ be left       20
  Which leaves itself. To the seaside straightway!
  I will possess you of that ship and treasure.
  Leave me, I pray, a little—pray you, now,
  Nay, do so—for indeed I have lost command.
  Therefore I pray you—I'll see you by and by.        25
        ⌜*Attendants move aside. Antony*⌝ *sits down.*

  *Enter Cleopatra led by Charmian,* ⌜*Iras,*⌝ *and Eros.*

EROS
  Nay, gentle madam, to him, comfort him.

29. **Juno:** in Roman mythology, queen of the gods (See page 166.)

36. **Yes, my lord, yes:** While editors do not agree precisely about these words, there is general agreement that Antony remains lost in his inner dialogue and is not addressing anyone onstage.

37. **like a dancer:** i.e., only for show (Light, sheathed rapiers were part of men's formal wear for dances in Shakespeare's time.)

39. **ended:** killed (More precisely, Antony defeated Brutus in battle and thereby forced him to commit suicide. See Shakespeare's *Julius Caesar,* act 5.)

39–40. **alone . . . lieutenantry:** i.e., merely delegated the fighting to his lieutenants

41. **brave squares:** splendid squadrons

45. **unqualitied:** i.e., not himself (Meanings of "quality" included a person's nature, skills, and accomplishments, all of which Antony is said to be stripped of through his shame.) **with:** by; **very:** absolute, sheer

48. **but:** unless

49. **Your comfort:** (1) your offering her comfort; (2) your finding comfort for yourself

53–56. **See . . . dishonor:** i.e., see how I keep my **shame** from your sight by my brooding on what is destroyed **looking back:** looking back at **'Stroyed:** destroyed

IRAS  Do, most dear queen.

CHARMIAN  Do! Why, what else?

CLEOPATRA  Let me sit down. O Juno! ⌜*She sits down.*⌝

ANTONY  No, no, no, no, no.                                    30

EROS  See you here, sir?

ANTONY  Oh fie, fie, fie!

CHARMIAN  Madam.

IRAS  Madam, O good empress!

EROS  Sir, sir—                                                35

ANTONY
  Yes, my lord, yes. He at Philippi kept
  His sword e'en like a dancer, while I struck
  The lean and wrinkled Cassius, and 'twas I
  That the mad Brutus ended. He alone
  Dealt on lieutenantry, and no practice had          40
  In the brave squares of war, yet now—no matter.

CLEOPATRA
  Ah, stand by.

EROS                    The Queen, my lord, the Queen.

IRAS
  Go to him, madam; speak to him.
  He's unqualitied with very shame.                    45

CLEOPATRA, ⌜*rising*⌝  Well, then, sustain me. O!

EROS
  Most noble sir, arise. The Queen approaches.
  Her head's declined, and death will seize her but
  Your comfort makes the rescue.

ANTONY  I have offended reputation,                          50
  A most unnoble swerving.

EROS                        Sir, the Queen.

ANTONY, ⌜*rising*⌝
  O, whither hast thou led me, Egypt? See
  How I convey my shame out of thine eyes,
  By looking back what I have left behind              55
  'Stroyed in dishonor.

**61. strings:** i.e., heartstrings (in older anatomy, the tendons or nerves thought to brace or sustain the heart)

**68. the young man:** i.e., Octavius Caesar; **treaties:** i.e., offers to negotiate peace

**69. shifts of lowness:** i.e., stratagems used by lowly, powerless people

**73. affection:** passion

**74. on all cause:** i.e., no matter what **cause** I was pursuing

**76. Fall:** let fall; **rates:** has the value of

**3.12** Caesar refuses to grant Antony's petition for clemency, but he agrees to hear Cleopatra's suit if she will banish or kill Antony. Caesar sends Thidias to win Cleopatra from Antony.

A myrtle tree. (3.12.11)
From John Gerard, *The herball . . .* (1597).

CLEOPATRA                    O, my lord, my lord,
  Forgive my fearful sails! I little thought
  You would have followed.

ANTONY                         Egypt, thou knew'st too well     60
  My heart was to thy rudder tied by th' strings,
  And thou shouldst ⌜tow⌝ me after. O'er my spirit
  ⌜Thy⌝ full supremacy thou knew'st, and that
  Thy beck might from the bidding of the gods
  Command me.                                                    65

CLEOPATRA       O, my pardon!

ANTONY                    Now I must
  To the young man send humble treaties, dodge
  And palter in the shifts of lowness, who
  With half the bulk o' th' world played as I pleased,          70
  Making and marring fortunes. You did know
  How much you were my conqueror, and that
  My sword, made weak by my affection, would
  Obey it on all cause.

CLEOPATRA            Pardon, pardon!                            75

ANTONY
  Fall not a tear, I say; one of them rates
  All that is won and lost. Give me a kiss.   ⌜*They kiss.*⌝
  Even this repays me.—
  We sent our schoolmaster. Is he come back?—
  Love, I am full of lead.—Some wine                           80
  Within there, and our viands! Fortune knows
  We scorn her most when most she offers blows.
                                               *They exit.*

⌜Scene 12⌝
*Enter Caesar, Agrippa, ⌜Thidias,⌝ and
Dolabella, with others.*

CAESAR
  Let him appear that's come from Antony.
  Know you him?

4. **An argument:** evidence.

6. **Which:** i.e., who

12. **his grand sea:** i.e., its great sea (the sea from which the dew originally came); or, perhaps, from Antony's **grand sea,** in comparison to which the ambassador-schoolmaster was lately no more than a dewdrop

13. **Declare thine office:** state the business you have been assigned

14. **Lord:** i.e., as lord

15. **Requires:** requests

16. **sues:** petitions

20. **her:** i.e., herself

21. **circle of the Ptolemies:** i.e., crown of Egypt

22. **hazarded . . . grace:** at your mercy

23. **For:** i.e., as for

25. **Of audience . . . fail:** i.e., shall be granted a hearing and her desires; **so:** i.e., provided that

30. **Bring . . . bands:** i.e., safeguard him through the army's camp

31. **try:** test

DOLABELLA          Caesar, 'tis his schoolmaster—
An argument that he is plucked, when hither
He sends so poor a pinion of his wing,                    5
Which had superfluous kings for messengers
Not many moons gone by.

*Enter Ambassador from Antony.*

CAESAR                          Approach, and speak.
AMBASSADOR
  Such as I am, I come from Antony.
  I was of late as petty to his ends                      10
  As is the morn-dew on the myrtle leaf
  To his grand sea.
CAESAR                Be 't so. Declare thine office.
AMBASSADOR
  Lord of his fortunes he salutes thee, and
  Requires to live in Egypt, which not granted,           15
  He ⌈lessens⌉ his requests, and to thee sues
  To let him breathe between the heavens and earth,
  A private man in Athens. This for him.
  Next, Cleopatra does confess thy greatness,
  Submits her to thy might, and of thee craves            20
  The circle of the Ptolemies for her heirs,
  Now hazarded to thy grace.
CAESAR                          For Antony,
  I have no ears to his request. The Queen
  Of audience nor desire shall fail, so she               25
  From Egypt drive her all-disgracèd friend,      A.
  Or take his life there. This if she perform,
  She shall not sue unheard. So to them both.
AMBASSADOR
  Fortune pursue thee!
CAESAR                    Bring him through the bands.     30
              ⌈*Ambassador exits, with Attendants.*⌉
  ⌈*To Thidias.*⌉ To try thy eloquence now 'tis time.
    Dispatch.

36. **want:** destitution

36–37. **perjure . . . vestal:** i.e., force the vestal virgin to break her vow of chastity (A **vestal** virgin was one of six virgin priestesses who tended the sacred fire in Rome's temple of Vesta, goddess of the hearth. See page 186.)

37. **cunning:** skill, expertness, cleverness

38. **Make . . . pains:** i.e., ask whatever you wish as reward for your efforts (**pains**) and your request will have the force in law of an emperor's proclamation

39. **answer as a law:** discharge as if required to do so by law

41. **how Antony . . . flaw:** i.e., how Antony acts in his disaster (literally, a **flaw** is a crack, breach, fissure, rent, rift)

42. **speaks:** indicates

43. **In every . . . moves:** i.e., in every move that he makes

**3.13** Antony has Thidias whipped for kissing Cleopatra's hand, then makes plans to renew his battle with Caesar. Enobarbus decides to find a way to leave Antony.

---

2. **Think:** i.e., take thought, grieve

3. **we:** I (the royal "we"); **in fault:** i.e., at fault

4. **will:** desire

6. **ranges:** rows (of ships in battle formation)

8. **affection:** passion

9. **point:** crisis

*(continued)*

From Antony win Cleopatra. Promise,
And in our name, what she requires; add more,
From thine invention, offers. Women are not                    35
In their best fortunes strong, but want will perjure
The ne'er-touched vestal. Try thy cunning, Thidias.
Make thine own edict for thy pains, which we
Will answer as a law.

THIDIAS                    Caesar, I go.                       40

CAESAR
Observe how Antony becomes his flaw,
And what thou think'st his very action speaks
In every power that moves.

THIDIAS                    Caesar, I shall.
                                        *They exit.*


⌜Scene 13⌝
*Enter Cleopatra, Enobarbus, Charmian, and Iras.*

CLEOPATRA
What shall we do, Enobarbus?

ENOBARBUS                    Think, and die.

CLEOPATRA
Is Antony or we in fault for this?

ENOBARBUS
Antony only, that would make his will
Lord of his reason. What though you fled                       5
From that great face of war, whose several ranges
Frighted each other? Why should he follow?
The itch of his affection should not then
Have nicked his captainship, at such a point,
When half to half the world opposed, he being                  10
The merèd question. 'Twas a shame no less
Than was his loss, to course your flying flags
And leave his navy gazing.

CLEOPATRA                    Prithee, peace.

10–11. **he being / The merèd question:** i.e., his destiny alone being the subject in question (Enobarbus seems to return to his debate with Cleopatra in 3.7 about whether she had a legitimate part to play in the battle of Actium.) **merèd:** sole, entire

14. **peace:** silence

17. **so she:** i.e., so long as she

18. **us:** me (the royal "we")

30. **Under:** i.e., in

32. **caparisons:** trappings, defensive armor (of a horse)

33. **me declined:** i.e., me in my diminished (or aged) condition

35. **like:** i.e., likely; **high-battled Caesar:** i.e., Caesar with his many battalions

36. **Unstate his happiness:** i.e., deprive himself of all the advantages fortune has given him **happiness:** good fortune, success, prosperity; **be staged to th' show:** i.e., be exhibited as if on a stage for a public show

37. **sworder:** gladiator

38. **A parcel of:** i.e., of a piece with

39. **quality:** nature

40. **To suffer all alike:** i.e., so that all—one's **fortunes** and one's **inward** nature—are injured to the same extent

41. **Knowing all measures:** i.e., having experienced all degrees, both prosperity and adversity

42. **Answer:** meet in a fight

*Enter the Ambassador with Antony.*

ANTONY   Is that his answer?                                    15
AMBASSADOR   Ay, my lord.
ANTONY
  The Queen shall then have courtesy, so she
  Will yield us up?
AMBASSADOR         He says so.
ANTONY                 Let her know 't.—         20
  To the boy Caesar send this grizzled head,
  And he will fill thy wishes to the brim
  With principalities.
CLEOPATRA        That head, my lord?
ANTONY, ⌈*to Ambassador*⌉
  To him again. Tell him he wears the rose            25
  Of youth upon him, from which the world should
    note
  Something particular: his coin, ships, legions
  May be a coward's, whose ministers would prevail
  Under the service of a child as soon                 30
  As i' th' command of Caesar. I dare him therefore
  To lay his gay ⌈caparisons⌉ apart
  And answer me declined, sword against sword,
  Ourselves alone. I'll write it. Follow me.
             ⌈*Antony and Ambassador exit.*⌉
ENOBARBUS, ⌈*aside*⌉
  Yes, like enough, high-battled Caesar will          35
  Unstate his happiness and be staged to th' show
  Against a sworder! I see men's judgments are
  A parcel of their fortunes, and things outward
  Do draw the inward quality after them
  To suffer all alike. That he should dream,          40
  Knowing all measures, the full Caesar will
  Answer his emptiness! Caesar, thou hast subdued
  His judgment too.

46. **blown rose:** rose once in bloom
48. **honesty:** honor; **square:** quarrel
50. **faith:** faithfulness; **mere:** utter
55. **apart:** i.e., in private
60. **For us:** i.e., as for us
63. **entreats:** i.e., entreats you

The goddess Juno. (3.11.29)
From Johann Theodor de Bry, *Proscenium
vitae humanae . . .* (1627).

*Enter a Servant.*

SERVANT                    A messenger from Caesar.
CLEOPATRA
What, no more ceremony? See, my women,                    45
Against the blown rose may they stop their nose
That kneeled unto the buds.—Admit him, sir.
                                        ⌜*Servant exits.*⌝

ENOBARBUS, ⌜*aside*⌝
Mine honesty and I begin to square.
The loyalty well held to fools does make
Our faith mere folly. Yet he that can endure                    50
To follow with allegiance a fall'n lord
Does conquer him that did his master conquer,
And earns a place i' th' story.

*Enter Thidias.*

CLEOPATRA                                   Caesar's will?
THIDIAS
Hear it apart.                                                      55
CLEOPATRA          None but friends. Say boldly.
THIDIAS
So haply are they friends to Antony.
ENOBARBUS
He needs as many, sir, as Caesar has,
Or needs not us. If Caesar please, our master
Will leap to be his friend. For us, you know                    60
Whose he is we are, and that is Caesar's.
THIDIAS   So.—
Thus then, thou most renowned: Caesar entreats
Not to consider in what case thou stand'st
Further than he is ⌜Caesar.⌝                                      65
CLEOPATRA                         Go on; right royal.
THIDIAS
He knows that you embrace not Antony
As you did love, but as you feared him.

75. **merely:** only

77. **Sir:** i.e., Antony

81. **require:** request

86. **shroud:** shadow (i.e., protection, although the word usually refers to a corpse's winding-sheet)

87. **landlord:** owner of land (but the word also meant "innkeeper")

91. **in deputation:** as my deputy

94. **all-obeying breath:** i.e., his words, which all must obey

95. **The doom of Egypt:** i.e., his judgment of me (**Doom** does not here necessarily mean condemnation.)

100. **duty:** homage, reverence, respect

A kite (3.13.111)
From Konrad Gesner, . . . *Historiae animalium* . . . (1585–1604).

CLEOPATRA                                          O!

THIDIAS
The scars upon your honor therefore he                    70
Does pity as constrainèd blemishes,
Not as deserved.

CLEOPATRA    ·          He is a god and knows
What is most right. Mine honor was not yielded,
But conquered merely.                                     75

ENOBARBUS, ⌜*aside*⌝          To be sure of that,
I will ask Antony. Sir, sir, thou art so leaky
That we must leave thee to thy sinking, for
Thy dearest quit thee. *Cleo*          *Enobarbus exits.*

THIDIAS                    Shall I say to Caesar         80
What you require of him? For he partly begs
To be desired to give. It much would please him
That of his fortunes you should make a staff
To lean upon. But it would warm his spirits
To hear from me you had left Antony                       85
And put yourself under his shroud,
The universal landlord.

CLEOPATRA                    What's your name?

THIDIAS
My name is Thidias.

CLEOPATRA                    Most kind messenger,         90
Say to great Caesar this in ⌜deputation:⌝
I kiss his conqu'ring hand. Tell him I am prompt
To lay my crown at 's feet, and there to kneel.
Tell him, from his all-obeying breath I hear
The doom of Egypt.                                        95

THIDIAS                    'Tis your noblest course.
Wisdom and fortune combating together,
If that the former dare but what it can,
No chance may shake it. Give me grace to lay
My duty on your hand.                                     100
                    ⌜*She gives him her hand to kiss.*⌝

101. **father:** i.e., Julius Caesar (See note to 3.6.6.)
102. **taking kingdoms in:** conquering **kingdoms**
104. **As:** i.e., as if
106. **What:** i.e., who; **fellow:** a term of contempt
111. **kite:** a term of detestation (literally, a hawk) See page 168.
114. **muss:** a game in which small objects are thrown down to be scrambled for
117. **jack:** fellow; knave
123. **saucy:** presumptuous; wanton
126. **cringe:** contort, wrinkle up

Jove throwing a thunderbolt. (1.2.167, 3.13.105)
From Vincenzo Cartari, *Le vere e noue imagini . . .* (1615).

CLEOPATRA     Your Caesar's father oft,
When he hath mused of taking kingdoms in,
Bestowed his lips on that unworthy place
As it rained kisses.

*Enter Antony and Enobarbus.*

ANTONY               Favors? By Jove that thunders!     105
What art thou, fellow?
THIDIAS             One that but performs
The bidding of the fullest man and worthiest
To have command obeyed.
ENOBARBUS          You will be whipped.     110
ANTONY, ⌜*calling for Servants*⌝
Approach there!—Ah, you kite!—Now, gods and
    devils,
Authority melts from me. Of late when I cried "Ho!"
Like boys unto a muss kings would start forth
And cry "Your will?" Have you no ears? I am     115
Antony yet.

*Enter ⌜Servants.⌝*

       Take hence this jack and whip him.
ENOBARBUS, ⌜*aside*⌝
'Tis better playing with a lion's whelp
Than with an old one dying.
ANTONY             Moon and stars!     120
Whip him! Were 't twenty of the greatest tributaries
That do acknowledge Caesar, should I find them
So saucy with the hand of she here—what's her
    name
Since she was Cleopatra? Whip him, fellows,     125
Till like a boy you see him cringe his face
And whine aloud for mercy. Take him hence.
THIDIAS
Mark Antony—

132. **blasted:** withered

136. **abused:** deceived

137. **feeders:** servants (who eat at their masters' expense)

139. **boggler:** equivocator

141. **seel:** sew shut (as was done to falcons' eyes when the birds were being trained)

144. **confusion:** destruction

149. **vulgar fame:** common report or gossip

150. **Luxuriously:** lasciviously

151. **temperance:** chastity

155. **quit:** repay (**God quit you** was said by servants when given gratuities.)

157. **high:** noble

158. **Basan:** Compare Psalm 22.12–13: "Many young bulls have compassed me: mighty bulls of Bashan have closed me about. They gape upon me with their mouths, as a ramping and roaring lion."

159. **hornèd herd:** i.e., the bulls on the hills of **Basan** (Antony puts himself among them as a horned cuckold. See note to 1.2.4–5.) **savage cause:** i.e., reason to grow **savage**

ANTONY                    Tug him away. Being whipped,
   Bring him again. ⌜This⌝ jack of Caesar's shall          130
   Bear us an errand to him.
                              ⌜*Servants*⌝ *exit with Thidias.*
   ⌜*To Cleopatra.*⌝ You were half blasted ere I knew you.
      Ha!
   Have I my pillow left unpressed in Rome,
   Forborne the getting of a lawful race,                 135
   And by a gem of women, to be abused
   By one that looks on feeders?
CLEOPATRA                    Good my lord—
ANTONY   You have been a boggler ever.
   But when we in our viciousness grow hard—              140
   O, misery on 't!—the wise gods seel our eyes,
   In our own filth drop our clear judgments, make us
   Adore our errors, laugh at 's while we strut
   To our confusion.
CLEOPATRA             O, is 't come to this?               145
ANTONY
   I found you as a morsel cold upon
   Dead Caesar's trencher; nay, you were a fragment
   Of Gneius Pompey's, besides what hotter hours,
   Unregistered in vulgar fame, you have
   Luxuriously picked out. For I am sure,                  150
   Though you can guess what temperance should be,
   You know not what it is.
CLEOPATRA                   Wherefore is this?
ANTONY
   To let a fellow that will take rewards
   And say "God quit you!" be familiar with               155
   My playfellow, your hand, this kingly seal
   And plighter of high hearts! O, that I were
   Upon the hill of Basan, to outroar
   The hornèd herd! For I have savage cause,
   And to proclaim it civilly were like                   160

162. **yare:** brisk, active

167. **repent:** regret

169. **follow . . . triumph:** join Octavius Caesar's train in his triumphal procession through Rome

170. **following him:** being his servant

172. **fever thee:** throw you into a **fever**

174. **entertainment:** treatment; **Look:** i.e., make sure that

179. **stars:** including the planets, the sun, and the moon

180. **orbs:** spheres (See longer note to 2.7.16, pages 281–82.)

181. **mislike:** dislike

183. **enfranchèd:** enfranchised, freed; **bondman:** bondsman, slave (In Plutarch, **Hipparchus,** a dearly loved servant of Antony's, was among the first to desert to Caesar.)

185. **quit:** repay

189. **it:** i.e., the eclipse of the **terrene moon**

A haltered neck which does the hangman thank
For being yare about him.

*Enter a Servant with Thidias.*

                              Is he whipped?
SERVANT   Soundly, my lord.
ANTONY   Cried he? And begged he pardon?                    165
SERVANT   He did ask favor.
ANTONY, ⌜*to Thidias*⌝
   If that thy father live, let him repent
   Thou wast not made his daughter; and be thou sorry
   To follow Caesar in his triumph, since
   Thou hast been whipped for following him.               170
      Henceforth
   The white hand of a lady fever thee;
   Shake thou to look on 't. Get thee back to Caesar.
   Tell him thy entertainment. Look thou say
   He makes me angry with him; for he seems                175
   Proud and disdainful, harping on what I am,
   Not what he knew I was. He makes me angry,
   And at this time most easy 'tis to do 't,
   When my good stars that were my former guides
   Have empty left their orbs and shot their fires         180
   Into th' abysm of hell. If he mislike
   My speech and what is done, tell him he has
   Hipparchus, my enfranchèd bondman, whom
   He may at pleasure whip, or hang, or torture,
   As he shall like to quit me. Urge it thou.              185
   Hence with thy stripes, begone!     *Thidias exits.*
CLEOPATRA                          Have you done yet?
ANTONY
   Alack, our terrene moon is now eclipsed,
   And it portends alone the fall of Antony.
CLEOPATRA   I must stay his time.                          190

**191–92. mingle eyes / With:** exchange glances with, look into the eyes of

**192. his points:** the tagged laces that secure Octavius Caesar's clothes (**Points** tied the hose to the doublet—i.e., the breeches to the jacket—in the male fashion of Shakespeare's day, not in ancient Rome.)

**198. determines:** meets its end (i.e., by dissolving)

**199. The next Caesarion smite:** i.e., may the **next stone** of poisoned **hail** destroy **Caesarion,** my oldest son

**200. memory:** memorials (i.e., children)

**201. brave:** splendid

**202. discandying:** melting

**204. buried them:** (1) consumed them; (2) completely covered their corpses

**206. sits down:** makes his camp; **Alexandria:** See map, pages xx–xxi.

**207. fate:** destiny (to rule the world)

**208. held:** remained united

**209. fleet:** sail; **threat'ning most sealike:** i.e., in a manner as threatening as is the sea itself

**212. field:** battlefield

**214. earn our chronicle:** win our place in history as it is chronicled

**217. be treble-sinewed, -hearted, -breathed:** i.e., have three times my strength, courage, and stamina

**218. maliciously:** fiercely

**219. nice:** perhaps, wanton

**220. Of me for:** i.e., from me in return for

**222. gaudy:** brilliantly fine

ANTONY
  To flatter Caesar, would you mingle eyes
  With one that ties his points?
CLEOPATRA                              Not know me yet?
ANTONY
  Coldhearted toward me?
CLEOPATRA                    Ah, dear, if I be so,                195
  From my cold heart let heaven engender hail
  And poison it in the source, and the first stone
  Drop in my neck; as it determines, so
  Dissolve my life! The next Caesarion ⌈smite,⌉
  Till by degrees the memory of my womb,                     200
  Together with my brave Egyptians all,
  By the discandying of this pelleted storm
  Lie graveless till the flies and gnats of Nile
  Have buried them for prey!
ANTONY                         I am satisfied.                205
  Caesar ⌈sits⌉ down in Alexandria, where
  I will oppose his fate. Our force by land
  Hath nobly held; our severed navy too
  Have knit again, and fleet, threat'ning most sealike.
  Where hast thou been, my heart? Dost thou hear,           210
    lady?
  If from the field I shall return once more
  To kiss these lips, I will appear in blood.
  I and my sword will earn our chronicle.
  There's hope in 't yet.                                    215
CLEOPATRA   That's my brave lord!
ANTONY
  I will be treble-sinewed, -hearted, -breathed,
  And fight maliciously; for when mine hours
  Were nice and lucky, men did ransom lives
  Of me for jests. But now I'll set my teeth                220
  And send to darkness all that stop me. Come,
  Let's have one other gaudy night. Call to me

**226. held it poor:** i.e., done little to celebrate it

**234–35. contend . . . scythe:** i.e., compete with Death in killing people

**236. furious:** raging, frantic

**238. estridge:** perhaps the goshawk, or perhaps the ostrich; **still:** always

An ostrich. (3.13.238)
From Konrad Gesner, . . . *Historiae animalium* . . . (1585–1604).

All my sad captains. Fill our bowls once more.
Let's mock the midnight bell.

CLEOPATRA                              It is my birthday.          225
I had thought t' have held it poor. But since my lord
Is Antony again, I will be Cleopatra.

ANTONY   We will yet do well.

CLEOPATRA
Call all his noble captains to my lord.

ANTONY
Do so; we'll speak to them, and tonight I'll force          230
The wine peep through their scars.—Come on, my
     queen,
There's sap in 't yet. The next time I do fight
I'll make Death love me, for I will contend
Even with his pestilent scythe.                                    235
                              ⌜*All but Enobarbus*⌝ *exit.*

ENOBARBUS
Now he'll outstare the lightning. To be furious
Is to be frighted out of fear, and in that mood
The dove will peck the estridge; and I see still
A diminution in our captain's brain
Restores his heart. When valor preys ⌜on⌝ reason,          240
It eats the sword it fights with. I will seek
Some way to leave him.
                              ⌜*He*⌝ *exits.*

# ANTONY

### AND

# CLEOPATRA

ACT 4

**4.1** Caesar mocks Antony's challenge to single combat and prepares for battle.

---

  1. **as:** i.e., as if
  5. **to:** i.e., against
  9. **rage:** rave in fury
  11. **Make boot:** take advantage; **distraction:** violent disturbance of mind and feelings
  13. **heads:** commanders
  15. **files:** ranks
  16. **but late:** only recently
  17. **fetch him in:** close in on him and take him in
  18. **store:** an abundance of supplies

A Roman foot soldier. (4.10.5)
From Cesare Vecellio, *Degli habiti antichi et moderni . . .* (1590).

# ⌈ACT 4⌝

---

⌈Scene 1⌝

*Enter Caesar, Agrippa, and Maecenas, with his army,*
*Caesar reading a letter.*

**CAESAR**
He calls me "boy," and chides as he had power
To beat me out of Egypt. My messenger
He hath whipped with rods, dares me to personal
  combat,
Caesar to Antony. Let the old ruffian know          5
I have many other ways to die; meantime
Laugh at his challenge.

**MAECENAS**   Caesar must think,
When one so great begins to rage, he's hunted
Even to falling. Give him no breath, but now          10
Make boot of his distraction. Never anger
Made good guard for itself.

**CAESAR**              Let our best heads
Know that tomorrow the last of many battles
We mean to fight. Within our files there are,          15
Of those that served Mark Antony but late,
Enough to fetch him in. See it done,
And feast the army; we have store to do 't,
And they have earned the waste. Poor Antony.

*They exit.*

**4.2** Antony asks his servants to tend him for a few more hours.

---

0 SD. **others:** See longer note, page 282.

7–8. **Or . . . Or:** i.e., either . . . or

8–9. **bathe . . . again:** i.e., bring my **honor** back to life through the **blood** I shed at my death (perhaps an allusion to the belief that bathing in blood was medicinal)

9. **Woo't thou:** i.e., would you (literally, wilt thou)

10. **Take all:** the cry of the desperate gambler betting the last of his money

12 SD. **Servitors:** male domestic servants

15. **honest:** honorable

18. **fellows:** equals

23. **made so many men:** i.e., transformed into as **many men** as you are

⌐Scene 2⌐

*Enter Antony, Cleopatra, Enobarbus, Charmian, Iras,*
*with others.*

ANTONY
  He will not fight with me, Domitius?
ENOBARBUS                  No.
ANTONY   Why should he not?
ENOBARBUS
  He thinks, being twenty times of better fortune,
  He is twenty men to one.                        5
ANTONY                    Tomorrow, soldier,
  By sea and land I'll fight. Or I will live
  Or bathe my dying honor in the blood
  Shall make it live again. Woo't thou fight well?
ENOBARBUS
  I'll strike and cry "Take all."                  10
ANTONY                 Well said. Come on.
  Call forth my household servants.

*Enter three or four Servitors.*

                         Let's tonight
  Be bounteous at our meal.—Give me thy hand;
  Thou hast been rightly honest.—So hast thou,—     15
  Thou,—and thou,—and thou. You have served me
    well,
  And kings have been your fellows.
CLEOPATRA, ⌐*aside to Enobarbus*⌐     What means this?
ENOBARBUS, ⌐*aside to Cleopatra*⌐
  'Tis one of those odd tricks which sorrow shoots     20
  Out of the mind.
ANTONY, ⌐*to another Servitor*⌐
                And thou art honest too.
  I wish I could be made so many men,
  And all of you clapped up together in
  An Antony, that I might do you service     25
  So good as you have done.

30. **fellow:** i.e., fellow servant
31. **suffered:** submitted to
35. **period:** end
36. **if:** i.e., if you do
37. **shadow:** ghost
43. **yield:** reward
45. **discomfort:** discouragement, grief
46. **am onion-eyed:** have eyes full of tears
50. **Grace:** virtue; **hearty:** kind-hearted
53. **comfort:** strengthening, encouragement
54. **hearts:** men of spirit and courage
58. **drown:** i.e., **drown** with wine

A vestal virgin. (3.12.37)
From Johann Basilius Herold, *Heydenweldt* . . . [1554].

ALL ⌜THE SERVITORS⌝          The gods forbid!
ANTONY
  Well, my good fellows, wait on me tonight.
  Scant not my cups, and make as much of me
  As when mine empire was your fellow too          30
  And suffered my command.
CLEOPATRA, ⌜*aside to Enobarbus*⌝ What does he mean?
ENOBARBUS, ⌜*aside to Cleopatra*⌝
  To make his followers weep.
ANTONY, ⌜*to the Servitors*⌝          Tend me tonight;
  May be it is the period of your duty.          35
  Haply you shall not see me more, or if,
  A mangled shadow. Perchance tomorrow
  You'll serve another master. I look on you
  As one that takes his leave. Mine honest friends,
  I turn you not away, but, like a master          40
  Married to your good service, stay till death.
  Tend me tonight two hours—I ask no more—
  And the gods yield you for 't!
ENOBARBUS                    What mean you, sir,
  To give them this discomfort? Look, they weep,          45
  And I, an ass, am onion-eyed. For shame,
  Transform us not to women.
ANTONY                    Ho, ho, ho!
  Now the witch take me if I meant it thus!
  Grace grow where those drops fall! My hearty          50
    friends,
  You take me in too dolorous a sense,
  For I spake to you for your comfort, did desire you
  To burn this night with torches. Know, my hearts,
  I hope well of tomorrow, and will lead you          55
  Where rather I'll expect victorious life
  Than death and honor. Let's to supper, come,
  And drown consideration.
                              *They exit.*

**4.3** Antony's soldiers standing guard hear music indicating that the god Hercules is leaving Antony.

---

2. **determine one way:** i.e., settle the issue one way or the other

5. **Belike:** perhaps, probably

11. **landmen:** infantry

12. **brave:** splendid

12 SD. **hautboys:** powerful double-reed wood-wind instruments, designed for outdoor ceremonials (See below.)

14. **List:** listen

18. **signs:** bodes

21. **Hercules:** See longer note to 1.3.102, page 279, and picture, page 190.

An hautboy. (4.3.12 SD)
From Balthasar Küchler, *Repraesentatio der fürstlichen Auffzug . . .* [1611].

⌜Scene 3⌝
*Enter a company of Soldiers.*

FIRST SOLDIER
  Brother, goodnight. Tomorrow is the day.
SECOND SOLDIER
  It will determine one way. Fare you well.
  Heard you of nothing strange about the streets?
FIRST SOLDIER  Nothing. What news?
SECOND SOLDIER
  Belike 'tis but a rumor. Goodnight to you.                    5
FIRST SOLDIER  Well, sir, goodnight.

  *They meet other Soldiers ⌜who are entering.⌝*

SECOND SOLDIER  Soldiers, have careful watch.
⌜THIRD⌝ SOLDIER  And you. Goodnight, goodnight.

  *They place themselves in every corner of the stage.*

SECOND SOLDIER  Here we; and if tomorrow
  Our navy thrive, I have an absolute hope                      10
  Our landmen will stand up.
FIRST SOLDIER  'Tis a brave army, and full of purpose.

  *Music of the hautboys is under the stage.*

SECOND SOLDIER  Peace. What noise?
FIRST SOLDIER  List, list!
SECOND SOLDIER  Hark!                                           15
FIRST SOLDIER  Music i' th' air.
THIRD SOLDIER  Under the earth.
FOURTH SOLDIER  It signs well, does it not?
THIRD SOLDIER  No.
FIRST SOLDIER  Peace, I say. What should this mean?             20
SECOND SOLDIER
  'Tis the god Hercules, whom Antony loved,
  Now leaves him.

29. **we have quarter:** i.e., our sentry post extends
30. **give off:** cease

**4.4** Cleopatra and Eros arm Antony for battle.

---

3. **chuck:** a term of endearment
4. **thine iron:** i.e., the armor you have brought for me
10. **False:** wrong (referring to a mistake Cleopatra has made in arming him)
11. **Sooth:** an interjection meaning "truly" or "in truth"

Hercules. (3.7.84, 4.3.21)
From Vincenzo Cartari, *Le vere e noue imagini . . .* (1615).

FIRST SOLDIER        Walk. Let's see if other watchmen
 Do hear what we do.

SECOND SOLDIER   How now, masters?   *Speak together.*     25

ALL   How now? How now? Do you hear this?

FIRST SOLDIER   Ay. Is 't not strange?

THIRD SOLDIER   Do you hear, masters? Do you hear?

FIRST SOLDIER
 Follow the noise so far as we have quarter.
 Let's see how it will give off.                                            30

ALL                                          Content. 'Tis strange.
              *They exit.*


⌜Scene 4⌝
*Enter Antony and Cleopatra, with*
⌜*Charmian, and*⌝ *others.*

ANTONY, ⌜*calling*⌝
 Eros! Mine armor, Eros!

CLEOPATRA                          Sleep a little.

ANTONY
 No, my chuck.—Eros, come, mine armor, Eros!

*Enter Eros,* ⌜*carrying armor.*⌝

 Come, good fellow, put thine iron on.
 If fortune be not ours today, it is                                      5
 Because we brave her. Come.

CLEOPATRA                          Nay, I'll help too.
 What's this for?

⌜ANTONY⌝          Ah, let be, let be! Thou art
 The armorer of my heart. False, false. This, this!     10

⌜CLEOPATRA⌝
 Sooth, la, I'll help. Thus it must be.

ANTONY                                      Well, well,
 We shall thrive now.—Seest thou, my good fellow?
 Go, put on thy defenses.

15. **Briefly:** shortly, soon

19. **daff:** doff, throw off

20. **squire:** personal attendant; armor-bearer

21. **tight:** skillful

22. **knew'st:** were conversant with or versed in

23. **The royal occupation:** i.e., warfare

24. **workman:** expert craftsman

26. **him:** i.e., one

27. **betime:** betimes, early

30. **riveted trim:** i.e., armor (One's **trim** is, literally, one's outfit.)

31. **port:** gate

32. **morrow:** morning

34. **'Tis well blown:** i.e., the morning is well in bloom; or, perhaps, the **Trumpets** (line 31 SD) have been **well blown**

37. **Well said:** i.e., well done

40–42. **Rebukable . . . compliment:** i.e., it would be worthy of rebuke and reproof if I engaged in more vulgar ceremonies of leave-taking   **check:** reproof **stand / On:** practice, engage in   **mechanic:** vulgar, low, base

EROS                              Briefly, sir.                    15
CLEOPATRA
  Is not this buckled well?
ANTONY                    Rarely, rarely.
  He that unbuckles this, till we do please
  To daff 't for our repose, shall hear a storm.—
  Thou fumblest, Eros, and my queen's a squire     20
  More tight at this than thou. Dispatch.—O love,
  That thou couldst see my wars today, and knew'st
  The royal occupation, thou shouldst see
  A workman in 't.

            *Enter an armed Soldier.*

                Good morrow to thee. Welcome.    25
  Thou look'st like him that knows a warlike charge.
  To business that we love we rise betime
  And go to 't with delight.
SOLDIER                    A thousand, sir,
  Early though 't be, have on their riveted trim    30
  And at the port expect you. *Shout. Trumpets flourish.*

            *Enter Captains and Soldiers.*

⌐CAPTAIN⌐
  The morn is fair. Good morrow, general.
ALL
  Good morrow, general.
ANTONY                    'Tis well blown, lads.
  This morning, like the spirit of a youth         35
  That means to be of note, begins betimes.
  So, so.—Come, give me that. This way.—Well said.—
  Fare thee well, dame.            ⌐*He kisses her.*⌐
                Whate'er becomes of me,
  This is a soldier's kiss. Rebukable            40
  And worthy shameful check it were to stand
  On more mechanic compliment. I'll leave thee

**4.5** Antony learns that Enobarbus has left, and sends Enobarbus' chest and treasure to him in Caesar's camp.

———————

1. **happy day to:** i.e., fortunate day for

Hercules slaying the Hydra. (1.3.102)
From Guillaume de La Perrière, *Le théâtre des bons engins . . .* [1539].

Now like a man of steel.— You that will fight,
Follow me close. I'll bring you to 't.—Adieu.
⌜*Antony, Eros, Captains, and Soldiers*⌝ *exit.*

CHARMIAN
Please you retire to your chamber?                              45

CLEOPATRA                                    Lead me.
He goes forth gallantly. That he and Caesar might
Determine this great war in single fight,
Then Antony—but now—. Well, on.

                                                    *They exit.*


⌜Scene 5⌝

*Trumpets sound. Enter Antony and Eros,* ⌜*and a Soldier*
*who meets them.*⌝

⌜SOLDIER⌝
The gods make this a happy day to Antony.

ANTONY
Would thou and those thy scars had once prevailed
To make me fight at land.

⌜SOLDIER⌝                          Had'st thou done so,
The kings that have revolted and the soldier             5
That has this morning left thee would have still
Followed thy heels.

ANTONY                    Who's gone this morning?

⌜SOLDIER⌝                                        Who?
One ever near thee. Call for Enobarbus,                   10
He shall not hear thee, or from Caesar's camp
Say "I am none of thine."

ANTONY                    What sayest thou?

SOLDIER                                        Sir,
He is with Caesar.                                        15

EROS                    Sir, his chests and treasure
He has not with him.

21. **Detain no jot:** withhold not the least bit of it
22. **subscribe:** sign (what you write)
25. **honest:** honorable

**4.6**   Enobarbus, faced with Caesar's callousness and Antony's generosity, realizes the magnitude of his fault in deserting Antony.

---

2. **took:** i.e., taken
5. **The time . . . near:** Caesar here prophesies his own future. The *Pax Romana* brought **universal peace** through the consolidation of world power in the hands of this one man, Octavius (soon to be Augustus) Caesar.
6. **three-nooked world:** i.e., Africa, Asia, and Europe (A *nook* is one of the "corners" of the earth.)
7. **olive:** i.e., olive branch, a symbol of peace
11. **vant:** van, vanguard
12. **fury:** wild anger, frenzied rage
14. **revolt:** fall away (from Antony); **Jewry:** Judea
14–15. **on / Affairs of Antony:** i.e., ostensibly on Antony's business

ANTONY                    Is he gone?
SOLDIER                              Most certain.
ANTONY
  Go, Eros, send his treasure after. Do it.                    20
  Detain no jot, I charge thee. Write to him—
  I will subscribe—gentle adieus and greetings.
  Say that I wish he never find more cause
  To change a master. O, my fortunes have
  Corrupted honest men. Dispatch.—Enobarbus!           25
                                      ⌜*They*⌝ *exit.*


                        ⌜Scene 6⌝
              *Flourish. Enter Agrippa, Caesar, with*
                   *Enobarbus and Dolabella.*

CAESAR
  Go forth, Agrippa, and begin the fight.
  Our will is Antony be took alive;
  Make it so known.
AGRIPPA    Caesar, I shall.                    ⌜*He exits.*⌝
CAESAR
  The time of universal peace is near.                    5
  Prove this a prosp'rous day, the three-nooked world
  Shall bear the olive freely.

                   *Enter a Messenger.*

MESSENGER                    Antony
  Is come into the field.
CAESAR                    Go charge Agrippa          10
  Plant those that have revolted in the vant
  That Antony may seem to spend his fury
  Upon himself.                    ⌜*All but Enobarbus*⌝ *exit.*
ENOBARBUS
  Alexas did revolt and went to Jewry on

**15–17. dissuade . . . Antony:** i.e., persuade Herod the Great away from his allegiance to Antony and toward following Caesar

**17. this:** i.e., these

**19. entertainment:** employment

**20. ill:** evil, wrong

**25. His bounty overplus:** his gift in addition

**26. on my guard:** i.e., while I was on guard

**29. Mock:** jest

**30. safed:** conducted safely

**31. host:** army; **mine office:** i.e., to my duty

**38. blows:** swells

**40. thought:** grief (as also in line 41); **mean:** means

**41. outstrike:** deal swifter or heavier blows than

A map of the Holy Land. (1.2.30)
From the Geneva Bible (1562).

Affairs of Antony, there did dissuade                    15
Great Herod to incline himself to Caesar
And leave his master Antony. For this pains,
Caesar hath hanged him. Canidius and the rest
That fell away have entertainment but
No honorable trust. I have done ill,                     20
Of which I do accuse myself so sorely
That I will joy no ⌜more.⌝

                *Enter a Soldier of Caesar's.*

SOLDIER                         Enobarbus, Antony
Hath after thee sent all thy treasure, with
His bounty overplus. The messenger                       25
Came on my guard, and at thy tent is now
Unloading of his mules.
ENOBARBUS   I give it you.
SOLDIER   Mock not, Enobarbus.
I tell you true. Best you safed the bringer              30
Out of the host. I must attend mine office
Or would have done 't myself. Your emperor
Continues still a Jove.                    *He exits.*
ENOBARBUS
I am alone the villain of the earth,
And feel I am so most. O Antony,                         35
Thou mine of bounty, how wouldst thou have paid
My better service, when my turpitude
Thou dost so crown with gold! This blows my
    heart.
If swift thought break it not, a swifter mean            40
Shall outstrike thought, but thought will do 't, I feel.
I fight against thee? No. I will go seek
Some ditch wherein to die; the foul'st best fits
My latter part of life.
                                        *He exits.*

**4.7** Antony and his soldiers rejoice in a victory.

---

0 SD. **Alarum:** a call to arms

2. **work:** trouble; **our oppression:** i.e., the force that crushes us

5. **droven:** i.e., driven

6. **clouts:** rags, i.e., bandages (The word could also mean "blows" or "cuffs.")

9. **H:** the sound of the name of this letter made a pun on *ache* (in early modern pronunciation)

11. **bench-holes:** privies

14. **fair:** (1) clear; (2) promising

17. **runner:** one who runs away

19. **comfort:** encouragement

21. **halt:** limp

"Upon your sword / Sit laurel victory." (1.3.120–21)
From Jacobus a Bruck, *Emblemata moralia & bellica . . .* (1615).

⌜Scene 7⌝
*Alarum, Drums and Trumpets. Enter Agrippa,*
⌜*with other of Caesar's soldiers.*⌝

AGRIPPA
Retire! We have engaged ourselves too far.
Caesar himself has work, and our oppression
Exceeds what we expected.           ⌜*They*⌝ *exit.*

*Alarums. Enter Antony, and Scarus wounded.*

SCARUS
O my brave emperor, this is fought indeed!
Had we done so at first, we had droven them home     5
With clouts about their heads.
ANTONY                              Thou bleed'st apace.
SCARUS
I had a wound here that was like a T,
But now 'tis made an H.     ⌜*Sound of retreat*⌝ *far off.*
ANTONY                    They do retire.     10
SCARUS
We'll beat 'em into bench-holes. I have yet
Room for six scotches more.

*Enter Eros.*

EROS
They are beaten, sir, and our advantage serves
For a fair victory.
SCARUS                    Let us score their backs     15
And snatch 'em up as we take hares, behind.
'Tis sport to maul a runner.
ANTONY                    I will reward thee
Once for thy sprightly comfort and tenfold
For thy good valor. Come thee on.     20
SCARUS                              I'll halt after.
                                        *They exit.*

**4.8** Antony orders a march through Alexandria to celebrate their victory.

---

2. **gests:** notable deeds
4. **see 's:** i.e., see us
6. **doughty-handed: Doughty** means courageous, formidable.
7–8. **as 't . . . mine:** i.e., as if it had been **each man's** personal interest, as it is **mine**
8. **shown:** i.e., shown yourselves to be; **Hectors:** Hector was a prince of Troy and the greatest of its warriors in the Trojan War. (See below.)
9. **Clip:** embrace
14. **fairy:** enchantress
15. **day:** light
18. **proof of harness:** impenetrable armor
21. **virtue:** courage
26. **something:** somewhat
27. **ha' we:** i.e., have I

Hector. (4.8.8)
From [Guillaume Rouillé,] . . . *Prima pars promptuarii iconum* . . . (1553).

⌜Scene 8⌝

*Alarum. Enter Antony again in a march;*
*Scarus, with others.*

ANTONY

We have beat him to his camp. Run one before
And let the Queen know of our ⌜gests.⌝

⌜*A Soldier exits.*⌝

Tomorrow

Before the sun shall see 's, we'll spill the blood
That has today escaped. I thank you all,                    5
For doughty-handed are you, and have fought
Not as you served the cause, but as 't had been
Each man's like mine. You have shown all Hectors.
Enter the city. Clip your wives, your friends.
Tell them your feats, whilst they with joyful tears         10
Wash the congealment from your wounds and kiss
The honored gashes whole.

*Enter Cleopatra.*

⌜*To Scarus.*⌝                    Give me thy hand.
To this great fairy I'll commend thy acts,
Make her thanks bless thee.—O, thou day o' th'           15
    world,
Chain mine armed neck. Leap thou, attire and all,
Through proof of harness to my heart, and there
Ride on the pants triumphing.

CLEOPATRA                    Lord of lords!                 20
O infinite virtue, com'st thou smiling from
The world's great snare uncaught?

ANTONY                    Mine nightingale,
We have beat them to their beds. What, girl, though
    gray                                                    25
Do something mingle with our younger brown, yet
    ha' we

28. **nerves:** sinews

29. **Get . . . youth:** i.e., match younger men's output in a contest

36. **An armor . . . gold:** i.e., **armor** made entirely of **gold**

37. **carbuncled:** adorned with red gems

38. **holy Phoebus' car:** the chariot of the Roman god of the sun

40–41. **Bear . . . them:** (1) carry our shields that are as hacked as the men who own them; or, (2) carry our hacked shields in the spirited fashion appropriate to the men who own them

43. **camp this host:** accommodate or harbor this army

44. **carouses:** toasts

45. **royal peril:** danger on a grand scale

46. **brazen:** (1) brass; (2) shameless

47. **Make mingle with:** i.e., mix in; **taborins:** drums

**4.9** Enobarbus dies expressing his remorse for turning his back on Antony.

————————

2. **court of guard:** place where the guard musters

3. **embattle:** arm; or, perhaps, take to the battlefield

A brain that nourishes our nerves and can
Get goal for goal of youth. Behold this man.
Commend unto his lips thy favoring hand.—          30
Kiss it, my warrior.          ⌜*Scarus kisses her hand.*⌝
                    He hath fought today
As if a god in hate of mankind had
Destroyed in such a shape.
CLEOPATRA, ⌜*to Scarus*⌝          I'll give thee, friend,          35
An armor all of gold. It was a king's.

ANTONY
He has deserved it, were it carbuncled
Like holy Phoebus' car. Give me thy hand.
Through Alexandria make a jolly march.
Bear our hacked targets like the men that owe          40
    them.
Had our great palace the capacity
To camp this host, we all would sup together
And drink carouses to the next day's fate,
Which promises royal peril.—Trumpeters,          45
With brazen din blast you the city's ear.
Make mingle with our rattling taborins,
That heaven and earth may strike their sounds
    together,
Applauding our approach.          50
                              *They exit.*


                    ⌜Scene 9⌝
*Enter a Sentry and his company. Enobarbus follows.*

SENTRY
If we be not relieved within this hour,
We must return to th' court of guard. The night
Is shiny, and they say we shall embattle
By th' second hour i' th' morn.

5. **shrewd:** hard, harmful, dangerous

8. **Stand close:** i.e., remain concealed; **list:** i.e., listen to

10. **revolted:** i.e., who have fallen away from their allegiance; **record:** accent on the second syllable

16. **dispunge:** discharge

20. **Which:** i.e., **my heart** (line 18)

23. **in thine own particular:** i.e., in your own case

36. **raught:** reached, seized

FIRST WATCH   This last day was a shrewd one to 's.                5
ENOBARBUS   O, bear me witness, night—
SECOND WATCH   What man is this?
FIRST WATCH   Stand close, and list him.
ENOBARBUS
  Be witness to me, O thou blessèd moon,
  When men revolted shall upon record                           10
  Bear hateful memory, poor Enobarbus did
  Before thy face repent.
SENTRY   Enobarbus?
SECOND WATCH   Peace! Hark further.
ENOBARBUS
  O sovereign mistress of true melancholy,                     15
  The poisonous damp of night dispunge upon me,
  That life, a very rebel to my will,
  May hang no longer on me. Throw my heart
  Against the flint and hardness of my fault,
  Which, being dried with grief, will break to powder        20
  And finish all foul thoughts. O Antony,
  Nobler than my revolt is infamous,
  Forgive me in thine own particular,
  But let the world rank me in register
  A master-leaver and a fugitive.                               25
  O Antony! O Antony!                        ⌜*He dies.*⌝
FIRST WATCH   Let's speak to him.
SENTRY   Let's hear him, for the things he speaks may
    concern Caesar.
SECOND WATCH   Let's do so. But he sleeps.                          30
SENTRY
  Swoons rather, for so bad a prayer as his
  Was never yet for sleep.
FIRST WATCH                    Go we to him.
SECOND WATCH   Awake, sir, awake! Speak to us.
FIRST WATCH   Hear you, sir?                                       35
SENTRY
  The hand of death hath raught him.   *Drums afar off.*

38. **Demurely:** in a subdued manner

**4.10** Antony places himself so that he can watch his galleys doing battle at sea.

_____

4. **fire, air:** The enemy being prepared on the **sea** (line 1) and on **land** (line 2), Antony imagines carrying the battle to the elements of **fire** and **air,** which along with water and earth were thought to compose the world.

5. **foot:** foot soldiers, infantry (See page 182.)

7. **for . . . given:** i.e., **for** the **sea** battle has already been **given**

9. **appointment:** purpose

**4.11** Caesar orders his land forces to remain quiet unless attacked.

_____

1. **But being charged:** i.e., unless we are attacked; **still:** quiet

2. **shall:** i.e., shall be quiet

4. **hold . . . advantage:** i.e., take up and maintain positions that are most advantageous

                             Hark, the drums
Demurely wake the sleepers. Let us bear him
To th' court of guard; he is of note. Our hour
Is fully out.                                        40
SECOND WATCH   Come on then. He may recover yet.
               *They exit, ⌜carrying Enobarbus' body.⌝*


⌜Scene 10⌝
*Enter Antony and Scarus, with their army.*

ANTONY
  Their preparation is today by sea;
  We please them not by land.
SCARUS                 For both, my lord.
ANTONY
  I would they'd fight i' th' fire or i' th' air;
  We'd fight there too. But this it is: our foot         5
  Upon the hills adjoining to the city
  Shall stay with us—order for sea is given;
  They have put forth the haven—
  Where their appointment we may best discover
  And look on their endeavor.                   10
                                  *They exit.*


⌜Scene 11⌝
*Enter Caesar and his army.*

CAESAR
  But being charged, we will be still by land—
  Which, as I take 't, we shall, for his best force
  Is forth to man his galleys. To the vales,
  And hold our best advantage.
                                  *They exit.*

**4.12** Antony watches as his ships desert him and join Caesar's. He vows to kill Cleopatra, on whom he blames this treachery.

---

3. **Straight:** straightaway, immediately
6. **grimly:** grim
9. **fretted:** (1) vexed; (2) worn
15. **Triple-turned:** Having **turned** from Julius Caesar to Gneius Pompey and then to Antony, Cleopatra, says Antony, has turned a third time, this time to Octavius Caesar.
18. **revenged:** avenged; **charm:** enchantment (Cleopatra)
23. **spanieled me:** i.e., followed me like spaniels
24. **discandy:** melt

Augurs. (4.12.5)
From Guillaume Du Choul, *Discours de la religion des anciens Romains . . .* (1556).

⌜Scene 12⌝
*Enter Antony and Scarus.*

ANTONY
Yet they are not joined. Where yond pine does stand,
I shall discover all. I'll bring thee word
Straight how 'tis like to go.               *He exits.*
               *Alarum afar off, as at a sea fight.*
SCARUS                    Swallows have built
In Cleopatra's sails their nests. The ⌜augurs⌝          5
Say they know not, they cannot tell, look grimly
And dare not speak their knowledge. Antony
Is valiant and dejected, and by starts
His fretted fortunes give him hope and fear
Of what he has and has not.               10

*Enter Antony.*

ANTONY                    All is lost!
This foul Egyptian hath betrayèd me.
My fleet hath yielded to the foe, and yonder
They cast their caps up and carouse together
Like friends long lost. Triple-turned whore! 'Tis thou     15
Hast sold me to this novice, and my heart
Makes only wars on thee. Bid them all fly—
For when I am revenged upon my charm,
I have done all. Bid them all fly. Begone!
               ⌜*Scarus exits.*⌝

O sun, thy uprise shall I see no more.          20
Fortune and Antony part here; even here
Do we shake hands. All come to this? The hearts
That ⌜spanieled⌝ me at heels, to whom I gave
Their wishes, do discandy, melt their sweets
On blossoming Caesar, and this pine is barked     25
That overtopped them all. Betrayed I am.
O, this false soul of Egypt! This grave charm,

28. **becked:** beckoned

30. **crownet:** coronet

31. **right:** true; **gypsy:** See note to 1.1.10. **fast and loose:** a cheating game involving apparently tight (i.e., **fast**) knots that are actually **loose** (sometimes called "gypsies' knots")

32. **loss:** destruction, ruin

34. **Avaunt:** begone

37. **blemish Caesar's triumph:** i.e., keep Caesar from displaying you as a captive in his triumphal procession (by killing you)

38. **plebeians:** accent on first syllable

39–40. **spot / Of:** i.e., blot on

41. **poor'st diminutives:** most insignificant commoners

45–47. **better 'twere . . . many:** i.e., it would have been better if I had killed you in my wild anger, for your death might have saved others from death (See longer note, page 283.)

48–53. **The shirt . . . self:** Antony here alludes to the mythological narrative of Hercules' (or **Alcides'**) torment at the hands of **Nessus.** (See longer note, page 283, and also the longer note to 1.3.102, page 279.) **club:** Hercules' usual weapon (See page 190.)

53. **witch:** i.e., Cleopatra

Whose eye becked forth my wars and called them
    home,
Whose bosom was my crownet, my chief end,        30
Like a right gypsy hath at fast and loose
Beguiled me to the very heart of loss.—
What Eros, Eros!

*Enter Cleopatra.*

          Ah, thou spell! Avaunt!

CLEOPATRA
Why is my lord enraged against his love?        35

ANTONY
Vanish, or I shall give thee thy deserving
And blemish Caesar's triumph. Let him take thee
And hoist thee up to the shouting plebeians!
Follow his chariot, like the greatest spot
Of all thy sex; most monster-like be shown        40
For poor'st diminutives, for dolts, and let
Patient Octavia plow thy visage up
With her preparèd nails.          *Cleopatra exits.*
               'Tis well th' art gone,
If it be well to live. But better 'twere        45
Thou fell'st into my fury, for one death
Might have prevented many.—Eros, ho!—
The shirt of Nessus is upon me. Teach me,
Alcides, thou mine ancestor, thy rage.
Let me lodge Lichas on the horns o' th' moon,        50
And with those hands that grasped the heaviest
    club
Subdue my worthiest self. The witch shall die.
To the young Roman boy she hath sold me, and I
    fall        55
Under this plot. She dies for 't.—Eros, ho!
                    *He exits.*

**4.13** Cleopatra, in terror, flees to her monument and sends Antony word that she is dead.

———————

2. **Telamon:** i.e., the Greek warrior Telamonian Ajax, who became so enraged that he killed himself when he was not awarded the **shield** that had belonged to Achilles (See Ovid's *Metamorphoses*, book 13.) **boar of Thessaly:** the fierce **boar** sent by Diana to ravage Calydon (See *Metamorphoses*, book 8.)

3. **embossed:** a hunting term describing an animal driven to extremity or foaming at the mouth with exhaustion

4. **th' monument:** i.e., the tomb that Cleopatra had already had built for herself

8. **going off:** suddenly departing


**4.14** Antony, receiving the news that Cleopatra has taken her own life, orders Eros to kill him. Eros instead kills himself. Antony then stabs himself but does not die. When a new message comes that Cleopatra is alive, he asks to be taken to her.

———————

1. **thou . . . me:** i.e., am I still visible to you
3. **dragonish:** shaped like a dragon
4. **vapor:** mist
8. **mock:** delude, deceive
10. **vesper's:** evening's

⌈Scene 13⌉

*Enter Cleopatra, Charmian, Iras, ⌈and⌉ Mardian.*

CLEOPATRA
  Help me, my women! O, he's more mad
  Than Telamon for his shield; the boar of Thessaly
  Was never so embossed.

CHARMIAN             To th' monument!
  There lock yourself and send him word you are    5
    dead.
  The soul and body rive not more in parting
  Than greatness going off.

CLEOPATRA           To th' monument!—
  Mardian, go tell him I have slain myself.    10
  Say that the last I spoke was "Antony,"
  And word it, prithee, piteously. Hence, Mardian,
  And bring me how he takes my death.—To th'
    monument!

                             *They exit.*


⌈Scene 14⌉

*Enter Antony and Eros.*

ANTONY
  Eros, thou yet behold'st me?

EROS                Ay, noble lord.

ANTONY
  Sometime we see a cloud that's dragonish,
  A vapor sometime like a bear or lion,
  A ⌈towered⌉ citadel, a pendent rock,    5
  A forkèd mountain, or blue promontory
  With trees upon 't that nod unto the world
  And mock our eyes with air. Thou hast seen these
    signs.
  They are black vesper's pageants.    10

EROS                   Ay, my lord.

13. **rack:** wisp of cloud; **dislimns:** effaces, blots out

16. **knave:** boy (usually, as here, referring to a boy servant)

19. **Egypt:** i.e., Cleopatra

23. **Packed cards:** i.e., conspired (literally, made a cheating arrangement); **false-played:** treacherously dealt away

24. **triumph:** with wordplay on the **triumph** (or "trump") card

30. **her fortunes mingled:** i.e., she joined **her fortunes**

32. **saucy:** insolent

33. **die the death:** a biblical phrase meaning "be put to death"

34. **Death . . . once:** Proverbial: "A man can die but once."

35. **discharged:** paid

36. **done unto thy hand:** without any exertion on your part; **spake:** spoke

38–41. **a tearing groan . . . in her:** i.e., in the middle of uttering your name, she groaned and died, with the result that your name was **divided / Between her heart,** where as your lover she kept your name, **and lips,** which were uttering your name; thus as she died she gave up to the living world your name, which had been **buried in her**

ANTONY
  That which is now a horse, even with a thought
  The rack dislimns and makes it indistinct
  As water is in water.

EROS                       It does, my lord.           15

ANTONY
  My good knave Eros, now thy captain is
  Even such a body. Here I am Antony,
  Yet cannot hold this visible shape, my knave.
  I made these wars for Egypt, and the Queen,
  Whose heart I thought I had, for she had mine—   20
  Which whilst it was mine had annexed unto 't
  A million more, now lost—she, Eros, has
  Packed cards with ⌈Caesar⌉ and false-played my glory
  Unto an enemy's triumph.
  Nay, weep not, gentle Eros. There is left us   25
  Ourselves to end ourselves.

*Enter Mardian.*

                        O, thy vile lady!
  She has robbed me of my sword.

MARDIAN                    No, Antony,
  My mistress loved thee and her fortunes mingled   30
  With thine entirely.

ANTONY                Hence, saucy eunuch! Peace!
  She hath betrayed me and shall die the death.

MARDIAN
  Death of one person can be paid but once,
  And that she has discharged. What thou wouldst do   35
  Is done unto thy hand. The last she spake
  Was "Antony, most noble Antony."
  Then in the midst a tearing groan did break
  The name of Antony; it was divided
  Between her heart and lips. She rendered life   40
  Thy name so buried in her.

48. **sevenfold . . . Ajax:** According to Homer in *The Iliad*, book 7, the **shield** of the Greek warrior **Ajax** was composed of seven overlaid bulls' hides, the outermost covered with a layer of bronze.

50. **once:** i.e., for once; **continent:** container

52. **pieces:** i.e., **pieces** of armor

56. **length:** i.e., **length** of life

58–59. **very . . . strength:** i.e., intense effort impedes itself with the **strength** exerted

59. **Seal:** i.e., affix the seal (the last act in finalizing an official document)

61. **Where . . . flowers:** i.e., in the Elysian Fields, where, in classical mythology, heroes enjoy an afterlife

62. **port:** bearing

63. **Dido and her Aeneas:** See page 224 and longer note to 1.3.25–26, page 278. **troops:** i.e., of spectators, admirers

69. **green Neptune's:** i.e., the ocean's (Neptune was the Roman god of the sea.)

70. **With ships made cities:** i.e., assembled what appeared to be entire **cities** composed of **ships**

ANTONY                    Dead, then?
MARDIAN                                   Dead.
ANTONY
    Unarm, Eros. The long day's task is done,
    And we must sleep.—That thou depart'st hence safe     45
    Does pay thy labor richly. Go.          *Mardian exits.*
                        Off, pluck off!
            ⌈*Eros begins to remove Antony's armor.*⌉
    The sevenfold shield of Ajax cannot keep
    The battery from my heart. O, cleave, my sides!
    Heart, once be stronger than thy continent;     50
    Crack thy frail case. Apace, Eros, apace!
    No more a soldier. Bruisèd pieces, go.
    You have been nobly borne.—From me awhile.
                                    *Eros exits.*
    I will o'ertake thee, Cleopatra, and
    Weep for my pardon. So it must be, for now     55
    All length is torture. Since the torch is out,
    Lie down and stray no farther. Now all labor
    Mars what it does; yea, very force entangles
    Itself with strength. Seal, then, and all is done.—
    Eros!—I come, my queen.—Eros!—Stay for me.     60
    Where souls do couch on flowers, we'll hand in hand,
    And with our sprightly port make the ghosts gaze.
    Dido and her Aeneas shall want troops,
    And all the haunt be ours.—Come, Eros, Eros!

                    *Enter Eros.*

EROS
    What would my lord?     65
ANTONY                    Since Cleopatra died
    I have lived in such dishonor that the gods
    Detest my baseness. I, that with my sword
    Quartered the world and o'er green Neptune's back
    With ships made cities, condemn myself to lack     70

71. **less noble mind:** i.e., **condemn myself** to have a **less noble mind**

72. **which:** i.e., who

74. **exigent:** exigency, time of extreme necessity

76. **inevitable prosecution:** inescapable pursuit

81. **withhold:** prevent

82. **Parthian darts:** See note to 3.1.1.

83. **enemy:** i.e., **enemy darts**

85. **windowed:** placed in a window

86. **pleached:** folded

86–87. **bending . . . neck:** i.e., **his neck** bowed in submission **corrigible:** submissive to correction

88. **wheeled seat:** i.e., chariot (in the triumphal procession) See page 136.

89–90. **branded . . . ensued:** i.e., marked the debased state of him who followed

93. **honest:** honorable

98. **precedent:** previous, former (accent on second syllable)

99. **But accidents unpurposed:** i.e., to no purpose

101. **Wherein . . . lies:** i.e., in which is to be found what **the whole world** honors

The courage of a woman—less noble mind
Than she which, by her death, our Caesar tells
"I am conqueror of myself." Thou art sworn, Eros,
That when the exigent should come, which now
Is come indeed, when I should see behind me          75
Th' inevitable prosecution of
Disgrace and horror, that on my command
Thou then wouldst kill me. Do 't. The time is come.
Thou strik'st not me; 'tis Caesar thou defeat'st.
Put color in thy cheek.          80

EROS                         The gods withhold me!
Shall I do that which all the Parthian darts,
Though enemy, lost aim and could not?

ANTONY                                    Eros,
Wouldst thou be windowed in great Rome and see          85
Thy master thus with pleached arms, bending down
His corrigible neck, his face subdued
To penetrative shame, whilst the wheeled seat
Of fortunate Caesar, drawn before him, branded
His baseness that ensued?          90

EROS                         I would not see 't.

ANTONY
Come, then, for with a wound I must be cured.
Draw that thy honest sword, which thou hast worn
Most useful for thy country.

EROS                         O, sir, pardon me!          95

ANTONY
When I did make thee free, swor'st thou not then
To do this when I bade thee? Do it at once,
Or thy precedent services are all
But accidents unpurposed. Draw, and come.

EROS
Turn from me then that noble countenance          100
Wherein the worship of the whole world lies.

ANTONY   Lo thee!                         ⌜*He turns away.*⌝

117. **I should:** i.e., I should do; **couldst not:** i.e., could not do for me

118–19. **got . . . record:** i.e., outdone me in gaining a noble place in history (**Record** is accented on the second syllable.)

121. **As:** i.e., as if

122. **scholar:** student, pupil

123. **of:** i.e., from

130. **his period:** i.e., its end

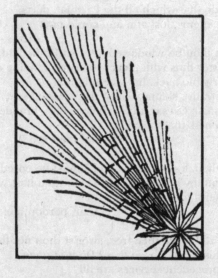

"The star is fall'n." (4.14.129)
From Hartmann Schedel, *Liber chronicorum*, [1493].

EROS
  My sword is drawn.
ANTONY                  Then let it do at once
  The thing why thou hast drawn it.                              105
EROS                              My dear master,
  My captain, and my emperor, let me say,
  Before I strike this bloody stroke, farewell.
ANTONY   'Tis said, man, and farewell.
EROS
  Farewell, great chief. Shall I strike now?                     110
ANTONY                              Now, Eros.
EROS
  Why, there, then.               ⌜*Stabs*⌝ *himself*.
              Thus I do escape the sorrow
  Of Antony's death.                        ⌜*Dies.*⌝
ANTONY                  Thrice nobler than myself,                115
  Thou teachest me, O valiant Eros, what
  I should and thou couldst not. My queen and Eros
  Have by their brave instruction got upon me
  A nobleness in record. But I will be
  A bridegroom in my death and run into 't                       120
  As to a lover's bed. Come then, and, Eros,
  Thy master dies thy scholar. To do thus
  I learned of thee. ⌜*He stabs himself.*⌝ How, not dead?
    Not dead?
  The guard, ho! O, dispatch me!                                 125

  *Enter a* ⌜*company of the*⌝ *Guard,* ⌜*one of them named
              Dercetus.*⌝

FIRST GUARD   What's the noise?
ANTONY
  I have done my work ill, friends. O, make an end
  Of what I have begun!
SECOND GUARD             The star is fall'n.
FIRST GUARD
  And time is at his period.                                     130

137. **this tidings:** i.e., these **tidings**

138. **enter me with him:** i.e., assure me of admittance to his presence and to his service

152. **found:** i.e., **found** to be true

153. **disposed:** come to terms

153–54. **that your rage . . . purged:** that your insane anger would not be appeased (In then-current medical terminology, these words could also mean "that the excess of the humor of choler in you would not be cleansed by a purgative medicine.")

156. **how it might work:** i.e., the effect that such news might produce

"Dido and her Aeneas." (4.14.63)
From [Guillaume Rouillé,] . . . *Prima pars promptuarii iconum* . . . (1553).

ALL                           Alas, and woe!
ANTONY   Let him that loves me strike me dead.
FIRST GUARD   Not I.
SECOND GUARD   Nor I.
THIRD GUARD   Nor anyone.                                    135
                    ⌐*All but Antony and Dercetus*⌐ *exit.*

DERCETUS
   Thy death and fortunes bid thy followers fly.
                          ⌐*He takes Antony's sword.*⌐
   This sword but shown to Caesar with this tidings
   Shall enter me with him.

                    *Enter Diomedes.*

DIOMEDES   Where's Antony?
DERCETUS   There, Diomed, there.                             140
DIOMEDES   Lives he? Wilt thou not answer, man?
                                  ⌐*Dercetus exits.*⌐

ANTONY
   Art thou there, Diomed? Draw thy sword, and give me
   Sufficing strokes for death.
DIOMEDES                 Most absolute lord,
   My mistress Cleopatra sent me to thee.                    145
ANTONY
   When did she send thee?
DIOMEDES                 Now, my lord.
ANTONY                                    Where is she?
DIOMEDES
   Locked in her monument. She had a prophesying
     fear                                                    150
   Of what hath come to pass. For when she saw—
   Which never shall be found—you did suspect
   She had disposed with Caesar, and that your rage
   Would not be purged, she sent you word she was
     dead;                                                   155
   But fearing since how it might work, hath sent

162. **bides:** (1) resides; (2) waits

164–65. **live . . . out:** i.e., outlive those who loyally serve you

166. **heavy:** sorrowful

168. **To grace:** i.e., by honoring or gratifying

**4.15** Antony is pulled up into the monument, where he dies.

---

Me to proclaim the truth, and I am come,
I dread, too late.

ANTONY
Too late, good Diomed. Call my guard, I prithee.

DIOMEDES
What ho! The Emperor's guard! The guard, what ho!  160
Come, your lord calls.

*Enter four or five of the Guard of Antony.*

ANTONY
Bear me, good friends, where Cleopatra bides.
'Tis the last service that I shall command you.

FIRST GUARD
Woe, woe are we, sir, you may not live to wear
All your true followers out.  165

ALL                                    Most heavy day!

ANTONY
Nay, good my fellows, do not please sharp fate
To grace it with your sorrows. Bid that welcome
Which comes to punish us, and we punish it,
Seeming to bear it lightly. Take me up.  170
I have led you oft; carry me now, good friends,
And have my thanks for all.

⌜They⌝ *exit bearing Antony* ⌜*and the body of Eros.*⌝

⌜Scene 15⌝
*Enter Cleopatra and her maids aloft, with*
*Charmian and Iras.*

CLEOPATRA
O Charmian, I will never go from hence.

CHARMIAN
Be comforted, dear madam.

CLEOPATRA                          No, I will not.
All strange and terrible events are welcome,

5. **Our . . . sorrow:** i.e., the **size** of **our sorrow**

7. **that . . . it:** i.e., Antony, for whom we grieve

13. **sphere:** See longer note to 2.7.16, pages 281–82.

14. **varying . . . world:** This figure of speech compares the alternation of day and night (light and darkness) to the ebb and flow of the tide that causes the shoreline to vary.

23. **importune death:** petition **death** (i.e., to delay)

28. **imperious show:** i.e., imperial triumph

30. **brooched:** adorned (as if with a brooch)

30–31. **if knife . . . operation:** i.e., if knives have edges, **drugs** have **operation,** or **serpents** have stings

32. **modest:** scrupulously chaste

Fortune turning her wheel. (4.15.51)
From [John Lydgate,] *The hystorye sege and dystruccyon of Troye* [1513].

But comforts we despise. Our size of sorrow,                    5
Proportioned to our cause, must be as great
As that which makes it.

*Enter Diomedes ⌈below.⌉*

                    How now? Is he dead?

DIOMEDES
His death's upon him, but not dead.
Look out o' th' other side your monument.                       10
His guard have brought him thither.

*Enter Antony ⌈below,⌉ and the Guard ⌈bearing him.⌉*

CLEOPATRA    O sun,
Burn the great sphere thou mov'st in. Darkling stand
The varying shore o' th' world! O Antony, Antony,
Antony! Help, Charmian! Help, Iras, help!                       15
Help, friends below! Let's draw him hither.
ANTONY                                          Peace!
Not Caesar's valor hath o'erthrown Antony,
But Antony's hath triumphed on itself.
CLEOPATRA
So it should be that none but Antony                            20
Should conquer Antony, but woe 'tis so!
ANTONY
I am dying, Egypt, dying. Only
I here importune death awhile until
Of many thousand kisses the poor last
I lay upon thy lips.                                            25
CLEOPATRA              I dare not, dear,
Dear my lord, pardon, I dare not,
Lest I be taken. Not th' imperious show
Of the full-fortuned Caesar ever shall
Be brooched with me; if knife, drugs, serpents have             30
Edge, sting, or operation, I am safe.
Your wife Octavia, with her modest eyes

33. **still conclusion:** silent judgment
34. **Demuring:** looking demurely
39. **heaviness:** (1) weight; (2) sorrow
41. **strong-winged Mercury:** In mythology **Mercury,** the messenger of the gods, was often pictured with wings at his heels and on his helmet. (See below.)
45. **Quicken:** revive
47. **heavy:** sorrowful
50. **high:** loudly
51. **huswife . . . wheel:** The goddess **Fortune,** who turns the **wheel** on which people's fortunes rise and fall, is here compared to a **huswife** at a spinning wheel. (See longer note, page 284, and picture, page 228.)
52. **offense:** offensiveness
56. **Gentle:** i.e., noble one
61. **Lament nor:** i.e., do not **lament** or

"Strong-winged Mercury." (4.15.41)
From Innocenzio Ringhieri, *Cento giuochi liberali . . .* (1580).

And still conclusion, shall acquire no honor
Demuring upon me. But come, come, Antony.—
Help me, my women!—We must draw thee up.—        35
Assist, good friends.        ⌜*They begin lifting him.*⌝
ANTONY                    O, quick, or I am gone.
CLEOPATRA
Here's sport indeed. How heavy weighs my lord!
Our strength is all gone into heaviness;
That makes the weight. Had I great Juno's power,        40
The strong-winged Mercury should fetch thee up
And set thee by Jove's side. Yet come a little.
Wishers were ever fools. O, come, come, come!
            *They heave Antony aloft to Cleopatra.*
And welcome, welcome! Die when thou hast lived;
Quicken with kissing. Had my lips that power,        45
Thus would I wear them out.        ⌜*She kisses him.*⌝
ALL    A heavy sight!
ANTONY    I am dying, Egypt, dying.
Give me some wine, and let me speak a little.
CLEOPATRA
No, let me speak, and let me rail so high        50
That the false huswife Fortune break her wheel,
Provoked by my offense.
ANTONY                    One word, sweet queen:
Of Caesar seek your honor with your safety—O!
CLEOPATRA
They do not go together.        55
ANTONY                    Gentle, hear me.
None about Caesar trust but Proculeius.
CLEOPATRA
My resolution and my hands I'll trust,
None about Caesar.
ANTONY
The miserable change now at my end        60
Lament nor sorrow at, but please your thoughts

69. **woo't:** i.e., wilt thou

74–75. **the garland . . . fall'n:** See longer note, page 284.

76. **odds:** difference

86. **No more . . . woman:** i.e., only **a woman** (and not an **Empress** [line 84])

88. **chares:** household work, chores; **were:** i.e., would be appropriate

89. **injurious gods:** gods who willfully inflict injury or wrong

92. **sottish:** foolish

" . . . the maid that milks . . . " (4.15.87)

From Pietro de Crescenzi, [*Ruralia commoda*, 1561].

In feeding them with those my former fortunes
Wherein I lived the greatest prince o' th' world,
The noblest, and do now not basely die,
Not cowardly put off my helmet to                      65
My countryman—a Roman by a Roman
Valiantly vanquished. Now my spirit is going;
I can no more.
CLEOPATRA          Noblest of men, woo't die?
Hast thou no care of me? Shall I abide                  70
In this dull world, which in thy absence is
No better than a sty? O see, my women,
The crown o' th' earth doth melt.—My lord!
⌐*Antony dies.*⌐

O, withered is the garland of the war;
The soldier's pole is fall'n; young boys and girls      75
Are level now with men. The odds is gone,
And there is nothing left remarkable
Beneath the visiting moon.
CHARMIAN                    O, quietness, lady!
⌐*Cleopatra swoons.*⌐
IRAS   She's dead, too, our sovereign.                  80
CHARMIAN   Lady!
IRAS   Madam!
CHARMIAN   O madam, madam, madam!
IRAS   Royal Egypt! Empress!     ⌐*Cleopatra stirs.*⌐
CHARMIAN   Peace, peace, Iras!                          85
CLEOPATRA
No more but e'en a woman, and commanded
By such poor passion as the maid that milks
And does the meanest chares. It were for me
To throw my scepter at the injurious gods,
To tell them that this world did equal theirs          90
Till they had stolen our jewel. All's but naught.
Patience is sottish, and impatience does
Become a dog that's mad. Then is it sin

98. **sirs:** sometimes applied to women, as here

99. **brave:** splendid; courageous

101. **high Roman fashion:** The early Romans saw suicide as heroic and as a proper response to affliction or to a fall from power. In *Hamlet* 5.2, Horatio announces his intention to take his own life with the words "I am more an antique **Roman** than a Dane."

105. **briefest:** most expeditious, hastiest

A "house of death" or charnel house. (4.15.94)
From *Todten-Tantz . . .* (1696).

To rush into the secret house of death
Ere death dare come to us? How do you, women?    95
What, what, good cheer! Why, how now, Charmian?
My noble girls! Ah, women, women! Look,
Our lamp is spent; it's out. Good sirs, take heart.
We'll bury him; and then, what's brave, what's
    noble,                                     100
Let's do 't after the high Roman fashion
And make death proud to take us. Come, away.
This case of that huge spirit now is cold.
Ah women, women! Come, we have no friend
But resolution and the briefest end.              105

               *They exit, bearing off Antony's body.*

# ANTONY

### AND

# CLEOPATRA

ACT 5

**5.1**   Caesar expresses grief for Antony's death. Fearing that Cleopatra will kill herself and thus prevent his displaying her in his triumphal march, he sends Proculeius to tell her that she has nothing to fear from Caesar.

---

2–3. **Being so . . . makes:** i.e., **tell him** that, being in such a hopeless state, he looks ridiculous in hesitating (to surrender)
5. **Wherefore:** for what purpose; **what:** who
6. **thus:** i.e., with a blood-stained sword in hand

# ⌜ACT 5⌝

⌜Scene 1⌝

*Enter Caesar ⌜with⌝ Agrippa, Dolabella, ⌜Maecenas,*
*Gallus, and Proculeius,⌝ his council of war.*

CAESAR, ⌜*aside to Dolabella*⌝
Go to him, Dolabella, bid him yield.
Being so frustrate, tell him, he mocks
The pauses that he makes.

DOLABELLA                    Caesar, I shall.

⌜*Dolabella exits.*⌝

*Enter Dercetus with the sword of Antony.*

CAESAR
Wherefore is that? And what art thou that dar'st                5
Appear thus to us?

DERCETUS               I am called Dercetus.
Mark Antony I served, who best was worthy
Best to be served. Whilst he stood up and spoke,
He was my master, and I wore my life                          10
To spend upon his haters. If thou please
To take me to thee, as I was to him
I'll be to Caesar; if thou pleasest not,
I yield thee up my life.

CAESAR                    What is 't thou say'st?             15

DERCETUS
I say, O Caesar, Antony is dead.

239

17. **breaking:** destruction

18. **crack:** thunderclap (as in the "crack of doom" on the Day of the Last Judgment)

19. **civil:** i.e., city

20. **their:** i.e., the lions'

21. **doom:** death

25. **self:** same

36. **Our most persisted deeds:** i.e., the outcomes we have worked most persistently to effect

38. **Waged . . . him:** i.e., contended with each other on even terms within him

40. **humanity:** i.e., a human being; **will give us:** have determined to **give** us humans

45. **followed thee:** pursued you like an enemy

48. **stall together:** tolerate the presence of each other; dwell **together**

CAESAR
  The breaking of so great a thing should make
  A greater crack. The round world
  Should have shook lions into civil streets
  And citizens to their dens. The death of Antony    20
  Is not a single doom; in the name lay
  A moiety of the world.

DERCETUS               He is dead, Caesar,
  Not by a public minister of justice,
  Nor by a hirèd knife, but that self hand    25
  Which writ his honor in the acts it did
  Hath, with the courage which the heart did lend it,
  Splitted the heart. This is his sword.
  I robbed his wound of it. Behold it stained
  With his most noble blood.    30

CAESAR             Look you sad, friends?
  The gods rebuke me, but it is tidings
  To wash the eyes of kings.

⌜AGRIPPA⌝          And strange it is
  That nature must compel us to lament    35
  Our most persisted deeds.

MAECENAS          His taints and honors
  Waged equal with him.

⌜AGRIPPA⌝       A rarer spirit never
  Did steer humanity, but you gods will give us    40
  Some faults to make us men. Caesar is touched.

MAECENAS
  When such a spacious mirror's set before him,
  He needs must see himself.

CAESAR           O Antony,
  I have followed thee to this, but we do lance    45
  Diseases in our bodies. I must perforce
  Have shown to thee such a declining day
  Or look on thine. We could not stall together
  In the whole world. But yet let me lament
  With tears as sovereign as the blood of hearts    50

51. **competitor:** partner; rival

52. **top . . . design:** i.e., the greatest of all undertakings

53. **front of war:** perhaps, line of battle

55. **mine . . . kindle:** i.e., my **heart** did **kindle** its **thoughts** (presumably its thoughts of courage, whose seat is the **heart**)

56. **Unreconciliable:** unreconcilable

56–57. **should . . . this:** i.e., should have broken apart our equal partnership with such a consequence (as Antony's death)

58. **meeter season:** more appropriate time

59. **The business . . . him:** i.e., the pressing nature of this man's **business** appears in his manner and expression

64. **preparèdly . . . herself:** may prepare to conform

67. **of us:** i.e., from me (the royal "we"); **ours:** i.e., my followers

68. **honorable:** i.e., honorably

74. **quality:** nature

76–77. **her life . . . triumph:** i.e., her presence alive in my triumphal procession **in Rome** would make it remembered forever

78. **with your speediest:** i.e., as rapidly as you can

79. **how . . . her:** i.e., what you discover about her

That thou my brother, my competitor
In top of all design, my mate in empire,
Friend and companion in the front of war,
The arm of mine own body, and the heart
Where mine his thoughts did kindle—that our stars          55
Unreconciliable should divide
Our equalness to this. Hear me, good friends—

*Enter an Egyptian.*

But I will tell you at some meeter season.
The business of this man looks out of him.
We'll hear him what he says.—Whence are you?          60

EGYPTIAN
A poor Egyptian yet, the Queen my mistress,
Confined in all she has, her monument,
Of thy intents desires instruction,
That she preparèdly may frame herself
To th' way she's forced to.          65

CAESAR                    Bid her have good heart.
She soon shall know of us, by some of ours,
How honorable and how kindly we
Determine for her. For Caesar cannot ⌜live⌝
To be ungentle.          70

EGYPTIAN          So the gods preserve thee.    *He exits.*

CAESAR
Come hither, Proculeius. Go and say
We purpose her no shame. Give her what comforts
The quality of her passion shall require,
Lest, in her greatness, by some mortal stroke          75
She do defeat us, for her life in Rome
Would be eternal in our triumph. Go,
And with your speediest bring us what she says
And how you find of her.

PROCULEIUS               Caesar, I shall.          80
               *Proculeius exits.*

88. **How hardly:** with what difficulty (i.e., how unwillingly)

89. **still:** always

90. **writings:** i.e., letters to Antony (See longer note, page 284.)

**5.2** While Proculeius is delivering Caesar's message of comfort to Cleopatra, other of Caesar's soldiers surprise and capture her. Dolabella enters and admits to her that Caesar means to lead her in triumph. Caesar enters and Cleopatra gives him a record of her possessions; her treasurer says that she has reported only a fraction of her worth. Caesar assures her of his goodwill and leaves. A countryman enters bringing asps in a basket of figs. Cleopatra dresses in her finest regalia and applies asps to her breast and arm. Iras falls dead, then Cleopatra dies. As the guards enter, Charmian applies an asp to herself and dies. Caesar promises to bury Cleopatra by Antony.

---

3. **knave:** servant

6. **accidents:** i.e., the operation of chance

7. **Which sleeps . . . dung:** i.e., which makes me sleep and nevermore taste the **dung** (See longer note, page 285.)

10. **fair demands:** legitimate requests

CAESAR
  Gallus, go you along.                    ⌜*Gallus exits.*⌝
                        Where's Dolabella,
  To second Proculeius?
ALL                    Dolabella!
CAESAR
  Let him alone, for I remember now                    85
  How he's employed. He shall in time be ready.
  Go with me to my tent, where you shall see
  How hardly I was drawn into this war,
  How calm and gentle I proceeded still
  In all my writings. Go with me and see                    90
  What I can show in this.
                                    *They exit.*


                    ⌜Scene 2⌝
        *Enter Cleopatra, Charmian,* ⌜*and*⌝ *Iras.*

CLEOPATRA
  My desolation does begin to make
  A better life. 'Tis paltry to be Caesar;
  Not being Fortune, he's but Fortune's knave,
  A minister of her will. And it is great
  To do that thing that ends all other deeds,                    5
  Which shackles accidents and bolts up change,
  Which sleeps and never palates more the dung,
  The beggar's nurse, and Caesar's.

                    *Enter Proculeius.*

PROCULEIUS
  Caesar sends greeting to the Queen of Egypt,
  And bids thee study on what fair demands                    10
  Thou mean'st to have him grant thee.
CLEOPATRA                        What's thy name?
PROCULEIUS
  My name is Proculeius.

19. **to keep decorum:** to do what is appropriate (for **a queen**)

22. **as:** i.e., that

26. **Make . . . reference:** i.e., refer your entire situation

30. **pray in aid:** beg your assistance (a legal term); **for kindness:** i.e., in devising kindnesses he may extend to you

33–34. **I send . . . got:** (1) I address him in terms of the **greatness** that is his by virtue of his conquests; (2) I send him the **greatness** that was once mine but now is his because he has conquered me.

35. **doctrine:** lesson

39. **Of him:** i.e., by him

40. **surprised:** captured

A nightingale. (4.8.23)
From Konrad Gesner, . . . *Historiae animalium* . . . (1585–1604).

CLEOPATRA                    Antony
　Did tell me of you, bade me trust you, but                                    15
　I do not greatly care to be deceived
　That have no use for trusting. If your master
　Would have a queen his beggar, you must tell him
　That majesty, to keep decorum, must
　No less beg than a kingdom. If he please                                      20
　To give me conquered Egypt for my son,
　He gives me so much of mine own as I
　Will kneel to him with thanks.
PROCULEIUS                          Be of good cheer.
　You're fall'n into a princely hand; fear nothing.                             25
　Make your full reference freely to my lord,
　Who is so full of grace that it flows over
　On all that need. Let me report to him
　Your sweet dependency, and you shall find
　A conqueror that will pray in aid for kindness                                30
　Where he for grace is kneeled to.
CLEOPATRA                              Pray you tell him
　I am his fortune's vassal and I send him
　The greatness he has got. I hourly learn
　A doctrine of obedience, and would gladly                                     35
　Look him i' th' face.
PROCULEIUS              This I'll report, dear lady.
　Have comfort, for I know your plight is pitied
　Of him that caused it.

　⌈*Gallus and Soldiers enter and seize Cleopatra.*⌉

⌈GALLUS⌉
　You see how easily she may be surprised.                                      40
　Guard her till Caesar come.
IRAS                          Royal queen!
CHARMIAN
　O, Cleopatra, thou art taken, queen!
CLEOPATRA, ⌈*drawing a dagger*⌉
　Quick, quick, good hands!

47. **Relieved:** rescued

48. **of death:** (1) i.e., **relieved** of (or released from) death; (2) i.e., **betrayed** of the chance to die

49. **languish:** suffering with disease

52. **undoing:** destruction

53. **acted:** performed

59. **meat:** food

63. **wait:** attend (as a slave or servant)

64. **chastised:** accent on the first syllable

66. **varletry:** varlets, attendants, menials

70. **Blow . . . abhorring:** i.e., lay their eggs in me until I am bloated and abhorrent to look at

71. **pyramides:** a four-syllable form of "pyramids" (See page 106.)

Death. (5.2.55)
From August Casimir Redel,
*Apophtegmata symbolica* . . . [n.d.].

PROCULEIUS, ⌜*seizing the dagger*⌝

       Hold, worthy lady, hold!  45
 Do not yourself such wrong, who are in this
 Relieved, but not betrayed.

CLEOPATRA       What, of death, too,
 That rids our dogs of languish?

PROCULEIUS       Cleopatra,  50
 Do not abuse my master's bounty by
 Th' undoing of yourself. Let the world see
 His nobleness well acted, which your death
 Will never let come forth.

CLEOPATRA      Where art thou, Death?  55
 Come hither, come! Come, come, and take a queen
 Worth many babes and beggars.

PROCULEIUS      O, temperance, lady!

CLEOPATRA
 Sir, I will eat no meat; I'll not drink, sir.
 If idle talk will once be necessary—  60
 I'll not sleep neither. This mortal house I'll ruin,
 Do Caesar what he can. Know, sir, that I
 Will not wait pinioned at your master's court,
 Nor once be chastised with the sober eye
 Of dull Octavia. Shall they hoist me up  65
 And show me to the shouting varletry
 Of censuring Rome? Rather a ditch in Egypt
 Be gentle grave unto me; rather on Nilus' mud
 Lay me stark naked, and let the waterflies
 Blow me into abhorring; rather make  70
 My country's high pyramides my gibbet
 And hang me up in chains!

PROCULEIUS     You do extend
 These thoughts of horror further than you shall
 Find cause in Caesar.  75

*Enter Dolabella.*

DOLABELLA     Proculeius,
 What thou hast done thy master Caesar knows,

78. **For:** i.e., as for

79. **to my:** i.e., under my

82. **what:** i.e., whatever

84. **employ me:** i.e., use me as your messenger

102. **His legs . . . ocean:** Antony is here compared to the Colossus, a gigantic bronze statue whose legs, according to legend, spanned the harbor at Rhodes.

103. **Crested the world:** surmounted the world as a crest

103–4. **propertied . . . spheres:** i.e., had the quality of the music of the spheres (the harmony, not heard by mortals, believed to be produced by the rotation of huge spheres moving the sun, moon, planets, and stars around the earth)

105. **quail:** cause to quail, daunt; **orb:** i.e., earth

The Colossus of Rhodes. (5.2.102)
From André Thevet, *Cosmographie de Leuant . . .* (1554).

And he hath sent for thee. For the Queen,
I'll take her to my guard.

PROCULEIUS                    So, Dolabella,                    80
It shall content me best. Be gentle to her.
⌈*To Cleopatra.*⌉ To Caesar I will speak what you
   shall please,
If you'll employ me to him.

CLEOPATRA                    Say I would die.                  85
                              *Proculeius exits.*

DOLABELLA
Most noble empress, you have heard of me.

CLEOPATRA
I cannot tell.

DOLABELLA          Assuredly you know me.

CLEOPATRA
No matter, sir, what I have heard or known.
You laugh when boys or women tell their dreams;   90
Is 't not your trick?

DOLABELLA          I understand not, madam.

CLEOPATRA
I dreamt there was an emperor Antony.
O, such another sleep, that I might see
But such another man.                                95

DOLABELLA                    If it might please you—

CLEOPATRA
His face was as the heavens, and therein stuck
A sun and moon, which kept their course and
   lighted
The little O, the earth.                             100

DOLABELLA                    Most sovereign creature—

CLEOPATRA
His legs bestrid the ocean, his reared arm
Crested the world. His voice was propertied
As all the tunèd spheres, and that to friends;
But when he meant to quail and shake the orb,       105

106. **For:** i.e., as for

108. **grew . . . reaping:** i.e., yielded an inexhaustible store of produce

110. **In his livery:** among his dependents

111. **crownets:** coronets

113. **plates:** coins

115. **might:** could

119. **nor ever:** i.e., or never

120. **It's past the size:** i.e., my image of such a man exceeds the bounds; **wants stuff:** lacks material

121. **vie . . . fancy:** compete with imagination in the production of marvelous shapes

122. **piece 'gainst fancy:** i.e., masterpiece in its competition with imagination

123. **Condemning shadows quite:** utterly discrediting imagination's ephemeral images

126. **As answering:** in a way that corresponds; **weight:** (1) burden; (2) importance

126–27. **Would . . . feel:** i.e., may I **never** achieve **success** if I do not **feel**

128. **rebound of yours:** i.e., recoil of your grief

He was as rattling thunder. For his bounty,
There was no winter in 't; an ⌈autumn 'twas⌉
That grew the more by reaping. His delights
Were dolphin-like; they showed his back above
The element they lived in. In his livery                    110
Walked crowns and crownets; realms and islands
    were
As plates dropped from his pocket.

DOLABELLA                                Cleopatra—

CLEOPATRA
Think you there was, or might be, such a man          115
As this I dreamt of?

DOLABELLA              Gentle madam, no.

CLEOPATRA
You lie up to the hearing of the gods!
But if there be nor ever were one such,
It's past the size of dreaming. Nature wants stuff    120
To vie strange forms with fancy, yet t' imagine
An Antony were nature's piece 'gainst fancy,
Condemning shadows quite.

DOLABELLA                        Hear me, good madam.
Your loss is as yourself, great; and you bear it        125
As answering to the weight. Would I might never
O'ertake pursued success but I do feel,
By the rebound of yours, a grief that ⌈smites⌉
My very heart at root.

CLEOPATRA                  I thank you, sir.                  130
Know you what Caesar means to do with me?

DOLABELLA
I am loath to tell you what I would you knew.

CLEOPATRA
Nay, pray you, sir.

DOLABELLA              Though he be honorable—

CLEOPATRA    He'll lead me, then, in triumph.           135

DOLABELLA    Madam, he will. I know 't.

145. **hard thoughts:** i.e., harsh **thoughts** (about me)

149. **sir:** lord

150. **project:** set forth; **cause:** case

151. **clear:** plain; free of blame, innocent

152. **like frailties:** i.e., **frailties** like those

155. **enforce:** emphasize (what you have done)

156. **apply yourself:** conform

159. **lay on me a cruelty:** i.e., make me appear cruel

163. **thereon:** i.e., on **my good purposes** (line 161); **I'll . . . leave:** a conventional farewell

164. **And may:** i.e., and you **may take leave** (Cleopatra plays on a second meaning of the phrase, where **leave** means permission to do something, and says, in effect, you may do as you please.)

165. **scutcheons:** the shields (emblazoned with coats of arms) of conquered enemies hung up as trophies

*Flourish. Enter Caesar, Proculeius, Gallus, Maecenas, and others of his train.*

ALL  Make way there! Caesar!
CAESAR  Which is the Queen of Egypt?
DOLABELLA  It is the Emperor, madam.

⌜*Cleopatra kneels.*⌝

CAESAR  Arise. You shall not kneel.                    140
  I pray you, rise. Rise, Egypt.
CLEOPATRA                    Sir, the gods
  Will have it thus. My master and my lord
  I must obey.                    ⌜*She stands.*⌝
CAESAR          Take to you no hard thoughts.          145
  The record of what injuries you did us,
  Though written in our flesh, we shall remember
  As things but done by chance.
CLEOPATRA                    Sole sir o' th' world,
  I cannot project mine own cause so well            150
  To make it clear, but do confess I have
  Been laden with like frailties which before
  Have often shamed our sex.
CAESAR                    Cleopatra, know
  We will extenuate rather than enforce.             155
  If you apply yourself to our intents,
  Which towards you are most gentle, you shall find
  A benefit in this change; but if you seek
  To lay on me a cruelty by taking
  Antony's course, you shall bereave yourself         160
  Of my good purposes, and put your children
  To that destruction which I'll guard them from
  If thereon you rely. I'll take my leave.
CLEOPATRA
  And may through all the world. 'Tis yours, and we,
  Your scutcheons and your signs of conquest, shall   165
  Hang in what place you please. Here, my good lord.
                    ⌜*She holds out a paper.*⌝

170. **Not . . . admitted:** excluding trivial items
175. **seel:** sew shut (See note to 3.13.141.)
183. **shift estates:** i.e., change places

T E M P E R A N Z A.

An allegorical depiction of Temperance. (5.2.58)
From Cesare Ripa, *Noua iconologia . . .* (1618).

CAESAR
  You shall advise me in all for Cleopatra.

CLEOPATRA
  This is the brief of money, plate, and jewels
  I am possessed of. 'Tis exactly valued,
  Not petty things admitted.—Where's Seleucus?     170

⌜*Enter Seleucus.*⌝

SELEUCUS   Here, madam.
CLEOPATRA
  This is my treasurer. Let him speak, my lord,
  Upon his peril, that I have reserved
  To myself nothing.—Speak the truth, Seleucus.

SELEUCUS     175
  Madam, I had rather seel my lips
  Than to my peril speak that which is not.

CLEOPATRA   What have I kept back?

SELEUCUS
  Enough to purchase what you have made known.

CAESAR
  Nay, blush not, Cleopatra. I approve
  Your wisdom in the deed.     180

CLEOPATRA         See, Caesar, O, behold
  How pomp is followed! Mine will now be yours,
  And should we shift estates, yours would be mine.
  The ingratitude of this Seleucus does
  Even make me wild.—O slave, of no more trust     185
  Than love that's hired! What, goest thou back? Thou
    shalt
  Go back, I warrant thee! But I'll catch thine eyes
  Though they had wings. Slave, soulless villain, dog!
  O rarely base!     190

CAESAR         Good queen, let us entreat you—

CLEOPATRA
  O Caesar, what a wounding shame is this,
  That thou vouchsafing here to visit me,

**196–97. Parcel . . . envy:** Editors have never satisfactorily explained the word **parcel** as it is used here, where Seleucus, by adding his malice, somehow affects the **sum** of Cleopatra's disgraces.

**198. lady trifles:** trinkets appropriate for a lady

**199. Immoment toys:** small articles of no moment; **dignity:** worth

**200. modern:** ordinary; **withal:** with

**202. Livia:** Octavius Caesar's wife

**203. unfolded:** displayed (i.e., exposed, betrayed)

**204. With:** i.e., by; **bred:** brought up, educated

**208. chance:** (ruined) fortune

**210. Forbear:** leave us

**211. misthought:** thought ill of

**213. answer others' merits:** are responsible for the wrong others do  **merits:** that which is deserved, whether good or evil

**217. roll of conquest:** inventory of the spoils of victory

**219. make prize:** i.e., haggle (The usual meaning of **make prize** is "seize as plunder.")

**224. dispose you:** make arrangements for you

Doing the honor of thy lordliness
To one so meek, that mine own servant should          195
Parcel the sum of my disgraces by
Addition of his envy! Say, good Caesar,
That I some lady trifles have reserved,
Immoment toys, things of such dignity
As we greet modern friends withal, and say          200
Some nobler token I have kept apart
For Livia and Octavia, to induce
Their mediation, must I be unfolded
With one that I have bred? The gods! It smites me
Beneath the fall I have. ⌈*To Seleucus.*⌉ Prithee, go          205
   hence,
Or I shall show the cinders of my spirits
Through th' ashes of my chance. Wert thou a man,
Thou wouldst have mercy on me.

CAESAR                              Forbear, Seleucus.          210
                              ⌈*Seleucus exits.*⌉

CLEOPATRA
Be it known that we, the greatest, are misthought
For things that others do; and when we fall,
We answer others' merits in our name—
Are therefore to be pitied.

CAESAR                         Cleopatra,          215
Not what you have reserved nor what acknowledged
Put we i' th' roll of conquest. Still be 't yours!
Bestow it at your pleasure, and believe
Caesar's no merchant to make prize with you
Of things that merchants sold. Therefore be          220
   cheered.
Make not your thoughts your prisons. No, dear
   queen,
For we intend so to dispose you as
Yourself shall give us counsel. Feed and sleep.          225
Our care and pity is so much upon you
That we remain your friend. And so adieu.

230. **words me:** plies me with **words**
235. **spoke:** i.e., given instructions

Roman lictors. (5.2.261)
From Onofrio Panvinio, . . . *De lvdis circensibvs, libri II. De trivmphis liber vnvs* . . . (1642).

CLEOPATRA
  My master and my lord!
CAESAR                    Not so. Adieu.
                *Flourish. Caesar and his train exit.*

CLEOPATRA
  He words me, girls, he words me, that I should not     230
  Be noble to myself. But hark thee, Charmian.
                ⌜*She whispers to Charmian.*⌝

IRAS
  Finish, good lady. The bright day is done,
  And we are for the dark.
CLEOPATRA, ⌜*to Charmian*⌝   Hie thee again.
  I have spoke already, and it is provided.     235
  Go put it to the haste.
CHARMIAN              Madam, I will.

                *Enter Dolabella.*

DOLABELLA
  Where's the Queen?
CHARMIAN              Behold, sir.          ⌜*She exits.*⌝
CLEOPATRA                    Dolabella.     240
DOLABELLA
  Madam, as thereto sworn by your command,
  Which my love makes religion to obey,
  I tell you this: Caesar through Syria
  Intends his journey, and within three days
  You with your children will he send before.     245
  Make your best use of this. I have performed
  Your pleasure and my promise.
CLEOPATRA                    Dolabella,
  I shall remain your debtor.
DOLABELLA                    I your servant.     250
  Adieu, good queen. I must attend on Caesar.
CLEOPATRA
  Farewell, and thanks.              *He exits.*
                Now, Iras, what think'st thou?

254. **Thou . . . shown:** Here and in the following lines Cleopatra imagines that part of Octavius Caesar's triumphal procession will be like a pageant in which she and her court are mocked.

255. **Mechanic:** vulgar, base

257. **Uplift us:** lift us up

258. **of:** i.e., because **of**

259. **drink:** draw in, inhale

261. **Saucy:** insolent; **lictors:** Roman officers who attended the magistrate and executed judgment on offenders (See page 260.)

262. **like:** as if we were; **scald:** contemptible (literally, "scabby")

263. **Ballad us:** i.e., sing ballads about us; **quick:** quick-witted, inventive

267. **Some . . . greatness:** i.e., a boy actor parody my majesty in a squeaking voice (On Shakespeare's stage, Cleopatra herself was, of course, played by a boy actor.)

268. **posture:** attitude, demeanor

274. **fool:** frustrate

278. **Cydnus:** See Enobarbus' description of Cleopatra on the River **Cydnus** at 2.2.226–56.

279. **Sirrah:** a term of address normally used to male servants or social inferiors, but occasionally used to address a woman

281. **chare:** task, chore

284. **Wherefore's:** i.e., what is

Thou an Egyptian puppet shall be shown
In Rome as well as I. Mechanic slaves                         255
With greasy aprons, rules, and hammers shall
Uplift us to the view. In their thick breaths,
Rank of gross diet, shall we be enclouded
And forced to drink their vapor.

IRAS                          The gods forbid!           260

CLEOPATRA
Nay, 'tis most certain, Iras. Saucy lictors
Will catch at us like strumpets, and scald rhymers
⌜Ballad⌝ us out o' tune. The quick comedians
Extemporally will stage us and present
Our Alexandrian revels. Antony                              265
Shall be brought drunken forth, and I shall see
Some squeaking Cleopatra boy my greatness
I' th' posture of a whore.

IRAS                          O the good gods!

CLEOPATRA    Nay, that's certain.                        270

IRAS
I'll never see 't! For I am sure mine nails
Are stronger than mine eyes.

CLEOPATRA                          Why, that's the way
To fool their preparation and to conquer
Their most absurd intents.                                  275

*Enter Charmian.*

                          Now, Charmian!
Show me, my women, like a queen. Go fetch
My best attires. I am again for Cydnus
To meet Mark Antony. Sirrah Iras, go.—
Now, noble Charmian, we'll dispatch indeed,               280
And when thou hast done this chare, I'll give thee
    leave
To play till Doomsday.—Bring our crown and all.
                          ⌜*Iras exits.*⌝ *A noise within.*
Wherefore's this noise?

289. **What:** i.e., how

291. **placed:** fixed

294 SD. **Countryman:** See longer note, page 285.

297. **worm:** serpent (See page 266.)

299. **him:** i.e., it

301. **immortal:** his mistake for "mortal" (i.e., deadly)

303. **on 't:** i.e., of it

305. **of one:** i.e., from one; **longer:** i.e., longer ago

306. **honest:** truthful (with wordplay on the sense "chaste" in the lines that follow); **something given:** somewhat inclined; **lie:** the first of a number of possible sexual puns that continue with **died** (had an orgasm) and, perhaps, with **worm**

310–11. **believe . . . do:** a comic allusion to theological differences between Protestants, with their doctrine of salvation by faith, and Catholics, with their doctrine of salvation by works

312. **falliable:** his mistake for "infallible"

*Enter a Guardsman.*

GUARDSMAN                    Here is a rural fellow          285
 That will not be denied your Highness' presence.
 He brings you figs.

CLEOPATRA
 Let him come in.              *Guardsman exits.*
              What poor an instrument
 May do a noble deed! He brings me liberty.          290
 My resolution's placed, and I have nothing
 Of woman in me. Now from head to foot
 I am marble-constant. Now the fleeting moon
 No planet is of mine.

*Enter Guardsman and ⌜Countryman, with a basket.⌝*

GUARDSMAN              This is the man.          295
CLEOPATRA  Avoid, and leave him.    *Guardsman exits.*
 Hast thou the pretty worm of Nilus there
 That kills and pains not?
⌜COUNTRYMAN⌝  Truly I have him, but I would not be
  the party that should desire you to touch him, for  300
  his biting is immortal. Those that do die of it do
  seldom or never recover.
CLEOPATRA  Remember'st thou any that have died on 't?
⌜COUNTRYMAN⌝  Very many, men and women too. I
  heard of one of them no longer than yesterday—a  305
  very honest woman, but something given to lie, as a
  woman should not do but in the way of honesty—
  how she died of the biting of it, what pain she felt.
  Truly, she makes a very good report o' th' worm.
  But he that will believe all that they say shall never  310
  be saved by half that they do. But this is most
  falliable, the worm's an odd worm.
CLEOPATRA  Get thee hence. Farewell.
⌜COUNTRYMAN⌝  I wish you all joy of the worm.
                    ⌜*He sets down the basket.*⌝

316. **look you:** a phrase used to get someone's attention

317. **do his kind:** i.e., act according to its nature

322. **Take . . . care:** i.e., do not worry

329. **dress her:** season or cook (the **dish**); **whore-son:** vile

331. **they make:** i.e., the gods create (Proverbial: "**make** or **mar.**")

333. **forsooth:** truly

337. **moist:** moisten

338. **Yare:** deftly; **Methinks:** it seems to me that

342. **their after wrath:** i.e., the **wrath** that the **gods** will surely visit on those whom they have earlier favored with such marvelous **luck**

343. **my title:** i.e., wife (to her **husband** Antony)

344. **other elements:** i.e., earth and water (See note to 4.10.4.)

"The pretty worm of Nilus," or asp. (5.2.297)
From Edward Topsell, *The historie of serpents . . .* (1608).

CLEOPATRA  Farewell.                                      315

⌐COUNTRYMAN⌐  You must think this, look you, that the
  worm will do his kind.

CLEOPATRA  Ay, ay, farewell.

⌐COUNTRYMAN⌐  Look you, the worm is not to be trusted
  but in the keeping of wise people, for indeed there  320
  is no goodness in the worm.

CLEOPATRA  Take thou no care; it shall be heeded.

⌐COUNTRYMAN⌐  Very good. Give it nothing, I pray you,
  for it is not worth the feeding.

CLEOPATRA  Will it eat me?                                325

⌐COUNTRYMAN⌐  You must not think I am so simple but
  I know the devil himself will not eat a woman. I
  know that a woman is a dish for the gods if the devil
  dress her not. But truly these same whoreson devils
  do the gods great harm in their women, for in every  330
  ten that they make, the devils mar five.

CLEOPATRA  Well, get thee gone. Farewell.

⌐COUNTRYMAN⌐  Yes, forsooth. I wish you joy o' th'
  worm.                                      *He exits.*

     ⌐*Enter Iras bearing Cleopatra's royal regalia.*⌐

CLEOPATRA
  Give me my robe. Put on my crown. I have            335
  Immortal longings in me. Now no more
  The juice of Egypt's grape shall moist this lip.
         ⌐*Charmian and Iras begin to dress her.*⌐
  Yare, yare, good Iras, quick. Methinks I hear
  Antony call. I see him rouse himself
  To praise my noble act. I hear him mock             340
  The luck of Caesar, which the gods give men
  To excuse their after wrath.—Husband, I come!
  Now to that name my courage prove my title.
  I am fire and air; my other elements
  I give to baser life.—So, have you done?            345

348. **aspic:** asp
353. **leave-taking:** saying farewell
356. **This:** i.e., Iras' dying first
359. **mortal:** deadly
361. **intrinsicate:** intricate
362. **fool:** here a term of endearment (like **wretch** in line 360)
365. **Unpolicied:** without political sagacity
366. **eastern star:** Venus, the morning **star**

A sixteenth-century image of Cleopatra's
death scene. (5.2.360 SD)
From Theodor de Bry, *Emblemata nobilitati* . . . (1592).

Come then, and take the last warmth of my lips.
Farewell, kind Charmian.—Iras, long farewell.
⌜*She kisses them. Iras falls and dies.*⌝
Have I the aspic in my lips? Dost fall?
If thou and nature can so gently part,
The stroke of death is as a lover's pinch,                    350
Which hurts and is desired. Dost thou lie still?
If thus thou vanishest, thou tell'st the world
It is not worth leave-taking.

CHARMIAN
  Dissolve, thick cloud, and rain, that I may say
  The gods themselves do weep!                              355

CLEOPATRA                       This proves me base.
  If she first meet the curlèd Antony,
  He'll make demand of her, and spend that kiss
  Which is my heaven to have.—Come, thou mortal
    wretch,      ⌜*She places an asp on her breast.*⌝   360
  With thy sharp teeth this knot intrinsicate
  Of life at once untie. Poor venomous fool,
  Be angry and dispatch. O, couldst thou speak,
  That I might hear thee call great Caesar ass
  Unpolicied!                                               365

CHARMIAN     O eastern star!

CLEOPATRA                       Peace, peace!
  Dost thou not see my baby at my breast,
  That sucks the nurse asleep?

CHARMIAN               O, break! O, break!        370

CLEOPATRA
  As sweet as balm, as soft as air, as gentle—
  O Antony!—Nay, I will take thee too.
              ⌜*She places an asp on her arm.*⌝
  What should I stay—                           *Dies.*

CHARMIAN   In this wild world? So, fare thee well.
  Now boast thee, Death, in thy possession lies     375
  A lass unparalleled. Downy windows, close,
              ⌜*She closes Cleopatra's eyes.*⌝

377. **Phoebus:** i.e., sun (Phoebus Apollo was the Roman god of the sun.)

378. **Of eyes:** i.e., by eyes

379 SD. **rustling:** moving rapidly and noisily

389. **Descended of:** i.e., **descended** from

394. **Touch their effects:** attain their fulfillment

And golden Phoebus, never be beheld
Of eyes again so royal. Your crown's ⌜awry.⌝
I'll mend it, and then play—

*Enter the Guard rustling in.*

FIRST GUARD
Where's the Queen?                                          380
CHARMIAN                    Speak softly. Wake her not.
FIRST GUARD
Caesar hath sent—
CHARMIAN                    Too slow a messenger.
                                      ⌜*She takes out an asp.*⌝
O, come apace, dispatch! I partly feel thee.
FIRST GUARD
Approach, ho! All's not well. Caesar's beguiled.          385
SECOND GUARD
There's Dolabella sent from Caesar. Call him.
                                      ⌜*A Guardsman exits.*⌝
FIRST GUARD
What work is here, Charmian? Is this well done?
CHARMIAN
It is well done, and fitting for a princess
Descended of so many royal kings.
Ah, soldier!                              *Charmian dies.* 390

*Enter Dolabella.*

DOLABELLA
How goes it here?
SECOND GUARD        All dead.
DOLABELLA                    Caesar, thy thoughts
Touch their effects in this. Thyself art coming
To see performed the dreaded act which thou             395
So sought'st to hinder.

*Enter Caesar and all his train, marching.*

ALL   A way there, a way for Caesar!

398. **augurer:** augur, seer, prophet
399. **That:** i.e., that which
400. **Bravest:** (1) finest; (2) most courageous
401. **leveled:** aimed (i.e., guessed)
410. **trimming up:** putting right
415. **like sleep:** i.e., as if asleep
416. **As:** i.e., as if
417. **toil:** net, snare; **grace:** charm, beauty
419. **vent:** discharge; **blown:** swollen
421. **aspic's:** asp's
426. **pursued conclusions infinite:** conducted innumerable experiments

DOLABELLA
  O sir, you are too sure an augurer:
  That you did fear is done.
CAESAR   Bravest at the last,                  400
  She leveled at our purposes and, being royal,
  Took her own way. The manner of their deaths?
  I do not see them bleed.
DOLABELLA               Who was last with them?
FIRST GUARD
  A simple countryman that brought her figs.      405
  This was his basket.
CAESAR           Poisoned, then.
FIRST GUARD              O Caesar,
  This Charmian lived but now; she stood and spake.
  I found her trimming up the diadem
  On her dead mistress; tremblingly she stood,     410
  And on the sudden dropped.
CAESAR              O, noble weakness!
  If they had swallowed poison, 'twould appear
  By external swelling; but she looks like sleep,     415
  As she would catch another Antony
  In her strong toil of grace.
DOLABELLA          Here on her breast
  There is a vent of blood, and something blown.
  The like is on her arm.                  420
FIRST GUARD
  This is an aspic's trail, and these fig leaves
  Have slime upon them, such as th' aspic leaves
  Upon the caves of Nile.
CAESAR           Most probable
  That so she died, for her physician tells me     425
  She hath pursued conclusions infinite
  Of easy ways to die. Take up her bed,
  And bear her women from the monument.
  She shall be buried by her Antony.

430. **clip:** embrace

432. **Strike:** i.e., shock, upset, disturb; **make them:** i.e., **make them** happen

432–33. **is . . . which:** i.e., is to be pitied to the same extent that it brings **glory** to the one who

437. **solemnity:** ceremonial occasion

No grave upon the earth shall clip in it                           430
A pair so famous. High events as these
Strike those that make them; and their story is
No less in pity than his glory which
Brought them to be lamented. Our army shall
In solemn show attend this funeral,                                435
And then to Rome. Come, Dolabella, see
High order in this great solemnity.

*They all exit, ⌜the Guards*
*bearing the dead bodies.⌝*

# Longer Notes

**1.1.6. tawny:** Philo's reference to Cleopatra's skin color as **tawny** or brown is at odds with Cleopatra's self-description at 1.5.32–33: "Think on me / That am with Phoebus' amorous pinches black." The play may thus insist that we see Cleopatra as dark-skinned, though whether brown-skinned or black-skinned is not clear. The issue of Cleopatra's skin color only becomes more complicated when one compares the uses of **tawny** and **black** in this play to their uses in other Shakespeare plays. In *A Midsummer Night's Dream*, the Athenian Hermia is called a "tawny Tartar [i.e., Gypsy]" (3.2.274); and Rosaline, a lady in the French Princess' retinue in *Love's Labor's Lost*, is once called a "whitely [i.e., pale] wanton" (3.1.206) and once said to be as "black as ebony" (4.3.267).

**1.2.29–30. Herod of Jewry:** Editors have suggested that Charmian's wish to have **Herod . . . do homage** to her child may recall Herod's refusal to worship Christ, whose life Herod sought in the Slaughter of the Innocents. Pageants still performed during Shakespeare's youth depicted the Slaughter, and gave Herod the role of a raging tyrant.

**1.2.69. hear me:** Shakespeare here gives Charmian and then Iras (in the first sentence of the next speech) language that might well have been heard by his audience as mockery of phrasing in the Church of England's official prayer book, *The Book of Common Prayer*, which reads: "O Lord hear our prayer . . . And let our cry come unto you."

**1.2.107 Labienus:** Quintus Labienus, a general who supported Brutus and Cassius against Antony and Octavius Caesar, defected to Rome's enemy, the Parthians (inhabitants of today's Iraq and Iran), after his allies' defeat at Philippi. (For Shakespeare's earlier treatment of the battle of Philippi, see act 5 of his play *Julius Caesar*.)

**1.3.25–26. What, says . . . to come:** These lines seem to echo Ovid's *Heroides* 7.139, where Ovid imagines Queen Dido writing to her lover Aeneas, who has told her he must leave her: "'Sed jubet ire deus.' Vellem vetuisset adire" ["'But,' you say, 'the god orders you to go.' Ah, I wish he had forbidden you to come"]. (See Th. Zielinski, "Marginalien," *Philologus* 64 (1905): 1–26.) Shakespeare's audience would have known well the story of Dido and Aeneas, and those who recognized the lines might well have been amused at Cleopatra's representing herself as a later version of the tragic Dido and at her replacing Aeneas' gods with Antony's wife Fulvia.

**1.3.35. shake the thronèd gods:** Here Cleopatra uses hyperbole to compare Antony to Jove, who, in Roman mythology, shook Mount Olympus (at the top of which he was enthroned) to its foundation whenever he swore an oath.

**1.3.65. purge:** In this passage, "quietness" or "rest" (what we call "peace") is represented as a body that has grown ill and in need of cleansing through violent action. According to the medical theory of the time, the sick body would be understood to contain too much of one or more of the bodily humors or fluids called black bile, yellow bile, blood, and phlegm. For the body to heal, it must be purged of the excess through frequent evacuation of the bowels, through vomiting, or through medicinal blood-letting.

**1.3.100. target:** By adding to Antony's conventional oath "by my sword" the words "And target," Cleopatra mocks Antony by associating him with a style of weaponry that was quite old-fashioned in London by the time this play was performed. At that date, nobles and their followers, as well as fashionable gentlemen, used rapiers (and daggers); only the lower classes or the old-fashioned would fight with sword and **target** (i.e., buckler).

**1.3.102. Herculean:** Antony's family claimed to descend from Hercules, and the historical Antony strove to emphasize in the way he dressed the physical resemblance he bore to representations of Hercules. The play contains a pattern of association of Antony with Hercules.

Here, however, Cleopatra's use of **Herculean**, like the rest of this speech, probably mocks Antony. In complimenting him on his success in acting the part of an enraged man, she associates him with the figure of *Hercules furens*, or Hercules in a fury. As Shakespeare implies in *A Midsummer Night's Dream*, the role of this Hercules, though immensely tragic in Greek drama, may have been famous in Shakespeare's day as an extravagant, ranting part. According to *Dream's* Bottom: "I could play Ercles rarely, or a part to tear a cat in, to make all split: *The raging rocks / And shivering shocks / Shall break the locks / Of prison gates. . . .*" (1.2.27–32).

**1.3.109. oblivion:** Cleopatra's enigmatic metaphor "O, my oblivion is a very Antony" has been explained in a variety of ways. Among the proposed explanations are the following: (1) in my forgetfulness, I am as negligent as Antony is in leaving me; (2) I am altogether forgotten by Antony, who, in neglecting me, is entirely himself; (3) I am forgetful because I am so consumed by Antony that I can think of nothing else.

1.4.50. **feared:** This word is usually changed to "deared" by editors, who explain "deared" to mean "loved." "Deared" is used once in this sense by Sir John Davies in his 1603 work *Microcosmos*. Nonetheless, the usual editorial change is questionable on two grounds. First, "deared" is not recorded elsewhere in Shakespeare. Second, "deared" had other meanings that are inappropriate to the context and that previous editors seem not to have known. One such meaning is "galled" (i.e., annoyed, made sore), the sense of the word employed by Arthur Hall in his 1581 translation of ten books of Homer's *Iliad* (10.90). This additional meaning would have made "deared" just as hard for a seventeenth-century audience to construe as the Folio's reading **feared.**

1.5.28. **arm:** Although this word has been interpreted by many editors to mean "armor" or "weapon," these meanings seem to have been acquired by **arm** only some time after Shakespeare wrote. It seems more likely that **arm** means "that which one relies upon for support." This is the sense of **arm** in Jeremiah 17.5: "Cursed be the man that trusteth in man, and maketh flesh his arm, and withdraweth his heart from the Lord." Thus, when Cleopatra speaks of Antony as "the arm / And burgonet of men," she presents Antony as the one upon whom men depend (**arm**) and the one who protects men (**burgonet**).

2.1.26. **wanned:** In the Folio this word is spelled "wand." This spelling has been interpreted by some editors, including us, to be equivalent to the modern word "wanned" and by others as "waned," meaning "withered, aging." Since Plutarch (in Shakespeare's principal source, Thomas North's translation of Plutarch's *Life of Marcus Antonius*) stresses that Cleopatra meets Antony when she is "at the age when a woman's beauty is at the prime," the adjective "waned" seems to us unlikely.

**2.2.64–65. If . . . with:** Editors have suggested that these lines are particularly difficult to read because Antony is both denying that Caesar's stated grievance has any substance and yet acknowledging that Caesar may have different and better grounds (**matter whole**) for lodging a grievance against Antony. Later in the scene (lines 108–17), Antony will explicitly apologize to Caesar for neglecting to **lend** him **arms and aid when** Caesar **required them** (line 106).

**2.6.32. Thou . . . house:** Plutarch's *Life of Marcus Antonius* observes that when the house of Pompey the Great, confiscated by the state, "was put to open sale, Antonius bought it: but when they asked him money for it, he made it very strange, and was offended with them. . . . [Antony] was yet much more hated in respect of the house he dwelt in, the which was the house of Pompey the great: a man famous for his temperance, modesty and civil life. . . . For it grieved [the Romans] . . . that the house . . . was full of tumblers, antic dancers, jugglers, players, jesters, and drunkards."

**2.7.16. disaster:** The use of this word by the First Servant may complete some astronomical wordplay that begins with his use of **huge sphere** and **move**. According to the Ptolemaic cosmology still current in Shakespeare's day, the planets (as well as the sun and the moon) circled the earth in huge crystalline spheres. In this speech, Lepidus may be compared to a planet in such a sphere, a planet absurdly unable to **move in 't.** The embarrassment of his predicament then is compared to the embarrassment of having empty eye sockets, themselves somewhat spherical in shape. These bring **disaster** upon the cheeks; the word **disaster** also means a calamity inflicted upon the earth by the stars (another name for the planets in this period).

3.7.75 SD **Soldier:** Leeds Barroll ("Scarrus and the Scarred Soldier," *Huntington Library Quarterly* 22 [1958]: 31–39) makes a strong case that the **Soldier** who appears under this generic designation for the first time in this scene is the same character who later appears under the specific designation "Scarrus." Among his evidence, Barroll notes that the ranks of the two characters are the same and that both characters call attention to the wounds they have sustained in battle. While we find Barroll's argument persuasive, it is not generally the policy of this edition as a whole to construct composite characters from multiple designations in the early printed texts; thus we do not call this **Soldier** "Scarrus."

3.10.13. **ribaudred:** Proposed emendations of **ribaudred** include "ribauld" (ribald, or offensively abusive, scurrilous, wantonly irreverent or impious), "ribald-rid" (common to every ribald knave), and "ribauded" (an obsolete variant form of "ribalded"). Whatever the word may be, it seems certainly to have been severely derogatory.

4.2.0 SD. **others:** Among those listed in the 1623 Folio as entering at this point is the character Alexas. We have not included him in this stage direction for two reasons.

First, he has no role in this scene; second, and more important, his presence in this scene would be confusingly at odds with the dialogue of 4.6. There Enobarbus notes that "Alexas did revolt and went to Jewry [i.e., Judea] . . . there did dissuade / Great Herod to incline himself to Caesar / And leave his master Antony. For this pains, / Caesar hath hanged him" (lines 14–18). The present scene, 4.2, is set on the eve of the second battle between Antony and Octavius; 4.6 is set on the morning of the battle. That Alexas could be in Antony's camp the night before the battle and then, during the night, have revolted, gone to Judea, persuaded Herod to desert Antony, and been hanged by Caesar is simply impossible. We have thus cut Alexas' name from this entrance stage direction.

**4.12.45–47. better 'twere . . . many:** Editors have been divided on the question of which deaths could have been **prevented** by Antony's killing Cleopatra in his **fury.** Some have thought that Antony's words hearken back to earlier moments in the action when he was wildly angry with Cleopatra: if he had killed her then, he could have prevented the many deaths his army has suffered in subsequent wars and perhaps even his own death, which he now begins to contemplate. Others have suggested that his words refer to the encounter with Cleopatra that has just concluded: if he had killed her before she left, he would have saved her from the fears of death that will now overtake her because of Antony's threats against her. Compare "Cowards die many times before their deaths" (*Julius Caesar* 2.2.34).

**4.12.48–53. The shirt . . . self:** Hercules mortally wounded the centaur **Nessus** with a poisoned arrow. The dying **Nessus,** in revenge, deceived Hercules' wife

Deianira into the belief that the **shirt** soaked with his poisoned blood would act as a love charm upon Hercules, binding him to her. She therefore had Hercules' servant **Lichas** take the **shirt of Nessus** to Hercules. Driven mad by the pain brought on by the poisoned shirt, Hercules threw **Lichas** so far into the air that he fell into the sea. Hercules then sought his own death by fire. See Ovid's *Metamorphoses*, book 9.

4.15.51. **huswife ... wheel:** The word **huswife** meant "housewife," but also had a negative meaning similar to the later word "hussy." There is wordplay on these two meanings in this reference to the goddess **Fortune,** who is said to grant favors to all but to be true to none.

4.15.74–75. **the garland ... fall'n:** The garland of the war may refer to the wreath that was used to crown the victor in a war. However, the proximity of **garland** to **pole** and to **boys and girls** (line 75) has suggested to critics that the image of the **soldier's pole** may (also or instead) refer to a village festivity in which a **pole** decked with garlands of flowers is the center of the games played by **boys and girls,** who run around the **pole** holding the garlands. If the image is not of such a festivity, then perhaps **soldier's pole** may refer to a "standard" or other rallying point for soldiers in battle, or perhaps even to the polestar, by which soldiers might orient themselves.

5.1.90. **writings:** According to Plutarch's *Life of Marcus Antonius,* Caesar "called for all his friends and showed them the letters *Antonius* had written to him, and his answers also sent him again, during their quarrel and strife: and how fiercely and proudly the other answered him to all just and reasonable matters he wrote unto him."

5.2.7. **Which sleeps . . . dung:** Many editors have resisted the unpleasant idea produced by taking literally Cleopatra's words **palates . . . the dung** (i.e., tastes the manure). Some have emended the line to read "dug" for **dung.** Many of those who have not made this emendation have explained the line's meaning by interpreting **dung** as the "dungy earth" of 1.1.40. Still others have represented the line as an example of metonymy in which **dung** is used to stand in place of the food that is grown by means of fertilizing the earth with **dung.**

5.2.294 SD. **Countryman:** The Folio text designates this character as "Clowne." This designation is often taken to mean no more than that the role was played by the company's comic character-actor. We change the name to "Countryman," first, because the character is introduced as a "rural fellow" at line 285 and referred to as "a simple countryman" at line 405; second, because that designation comes closer to defining him than does "comic character-actor"; and, third, because one meaning of the word "clown" was **countryman.**

# Textual Notes

The reading of the present text appears to the left of the square bracket. Unless otherwise noted, the reading to the left of the bracket is from **F**, the First Folio text (upon which this edition is based). The earliest sources of readings not in **F** are indicated as follows: **F2** is the Second Folio of 1632; **F3** is the Third Folio of 1663–64; **F4** is the Fourth Folio of 1685; **Ed.** is an earlier editor of Shakespeare, beginning with Rowe in 1709. No sources are given for emendations of punctuation or for corrections of obvious typographical errors, like turned letters that produce no known word. **SD** means stage direction; **SP** means speech prefix; ***uncorr.*** means the first or uncorrected state of the First Folio; ***corr.*** means the second or corrected state of the First Folio; ~ stands in place of a word already quoted before the square bracket; ∧ indicates the omission of a punctuation mark.

| | |
|---|---|
| **1.1** | 1. general's] F (Generals) |
| | 4. Mars,] ~: F |
| | 44. On] F (One) |
| | 58. whose] F2; who F |
| **1.2** | 0. SD *Eunuch, Alexas*] Ed.; *Eunuch, and Alexas* F |
| | 4. charge] Ed.; change F |
| | 12. banquet] F (Banket) |
| | 41. fertile] Ed.; fore-tell F |
| | 64. Alexas] Ed.; *Alexas* (as SP) F |
| | 82. SD *2 lines earlier in* F |
| | 83. Saw] F2; Saue F |
| | 121. awhile] awhlle F |
| | 124. SP SECOND MESSENGER] Ed.; I. *Mes.* F |

125. SP ANTONY] Ed.; *omit* F
136. me.] ~∧ F
140. lowering] F (lowring)
145. SD *1/2 line earlier in* F
149. them.] ~, F
152. occasion] Ed.; an occasion F
185. and] aud F
195. leave] Ed.; loue F
200. Hath] F2; Haue F
210. hair] F (heire)
212. place is . . . requires] F2; places . . .
     require F

**1.3**   3. who's] F (Whose)
31. first] fitst F
35. thronèd] F (Throaned)
54. services] Seruicles F
76. vials] F (Violles)
97. blood.] ~∧ F
99. my] F2; *omit* F

**1.4**   3. Our] Ed.; One F
8. Vouchsafed] Ed.; vouchsafe F
10. abstract] F2; abstracts F
13. enough] F (enow)
34. chid∧] ~: F
52. lackeying] Ed.; lacking F
65. wassails] Ed.; Vassailes F
76. browsèd] Ed.; brows'd F
86. we] F2; me F

**1.5**   3. mandragora] *Mandragoru* F
5. time∧ ] ~: F
39. SD *Antony*] Ed.; *Caesar* F
45. queen] Qu ene F
58. dumbed] Ed.; dumbe F
60. th' extremes] F (yᵉ extremes)

**2.1** 3, 7, 20, 23, 46. SP MENAS] Ed.; *Mene.* F
26. wanned] F (wand)

32. Lethe'd] F (Lethied)
49. warred] F2; wan'd F
52–53. greater. . . . all,] ∼, . . . ∼: F
60–63. you. . . . cause?] ∼, . . . ∼. F
83. Shrewdness] F (Shrodenesse)
84. disquiet. . . . must∧] ∼, . . . ∼, F
84. you must] F *corr.*; youm ust F *uncorr.*
85. it.] F *corr.*; ∼? F *uncorr.*
86–87. you . . . Alexandria;] ∼, . . . ∼∧ F
110. knowledge.] ∼, F
116. as befits] F *corr.*; as b efits F *uncorr.*
121. remember∧ . . . need∧] ∼: . . . ∼, F
128. soldier∧ only.] ∼, ∼∧ F
137–39. staunch, . . . world∧] ∼∧ . . . ∼: F
139. O' th'] F (Ath')
145. so,] Ed.; say∧ F
146. reproof] Ed.; proofe F
199. Haste] F (Hast)
206. SD *All . . . exit.*] Ed.; *Exit omnes. Manet Enobarbus, Agrippa, Mecenas.* F
212. digested] F (disgested)
228. Burned] F (Burnt)
230. lovesick with them.] ∼. ∼ ∼∧ F
237. Venus] Venns F
241. glow] Ed.; gloue F
244. gentlewomen] F2; Gentlewoman F
260–61. guest, . . . entreated.] ∼: . . . ∼, F
262. heard] F (hard)

**2.3**

4. prayers] ptayers F
12. SD *exit.*] F (*Exit.*)
26. afeard,] Ed.; a feare: F
29. thee; . . . but∧ . . . thee.] ∼∧ . . . ∼: . . . ∼, F
35. away] Ed.; alway F

38. Parthia.] ~, F
41. chance.] ~, F
44. inhooped] F (in hoopt)
46. SD *1/2 line later in* F

**2.4**   8. the Mount] F2; Mount F
**2.5**   12–13. river. . . . off,] ~∧ . . . ~. F
14. Tawny-finned] Ed.; Tawny fine F
27. SD *1/2 line later in* F
34. him,] ~. F
36. lipped] F *corr.* (lipt); 1 pt F *uncorr.*
44. face—] ~∧ F
51. is] Ed.; 'tis F
104. SD *1/2 line later in* F
117. didst,] ~: F
120. face, to me∧] ~∧ ~ ~, F

**2.6**   0. SD *Flourish . . . marching.*]   Ed.;
*Flourish. Enter Pompey, at one
doore with Drum and Trumpet: at
another Caesar, Lepidus, Anthony,
Enobarbus, Mecenas, Agrippa,
Menas with Souldiers Marching.* F
12. gods:] ~. F
18. Made the] F2; Made F
22. is] F2; his F
32. father's] Fatherrs F
36. present—how you take∧] ~∧ ~ ~ ~ ~)
F
54. telling,] ~. F
69. Fortune] Fotune F
74. composition] composion F
85. meanings] Ed.; meaning F
89. of] F3; omit F
108. SD *They . . . Menas.*] Ed.; *Exeunt.
Manet Enob. & Menas* F

**2.7**   1. o' their] F2; o' th' their F
4. colored] Conlord F

9. greater] greatet F
40. SD *2 lines later in* F
43. What] Whar F
94. SP MENAS] F *corr.* (Men.); Mən. F
    *uncorr.*
107. then, is] Ed.; then he is F
116. grows] F2; grow F
136. vats] F (*Fattes*)
142. off.] of∧ F
146. Splits] F (*Spleet's*)
146. speaks] F *corr.* (speakes); speakest F
    *uncorr.*
152. father's] F2; Father F
154–55. not. . . . Menas,] ~∧ ~: F
156. SP MENAS] Ed.; *omit* F
158. hear] F *corr.* (heare); heare a F *un-*
    *corr.*
161. SP ENOBARBUS] *Enor.* F
162. Hoo!] F *corr.* (Hoa,); Hoa∧ F *uncorr.*
162. SD *They exit.*] F *corr.* (*Exeunt.*);
    *Exenut.* F *uncorr.*

**3.1**  0. SD *before*] F *corr.*; *before* F *uncorr.*
1. struck] F (stroke)
6, 30, 39. SP SILIUS] Ed.; *Romaine, Rom.* F
6. Ventidius] F *corr.*; *Ventidus* F *uncorr.*
9. whither] F (whether)
17. too] F *corr.*; to F *uncorr.*
22. by th'] F *corr.* (by' th'); by, th' F
    *uncorr.*
29. Should] F *corr.*; hould F *uncorr.*
42. there] F *corr.*; their F *uncorr.*

**3.2**  1. are] F *corr.*; art F *uncorr.*
11. SP AGRIPPA] Ed.; *Ant.* F
18. figures] Ed.; Figure F
24–25. beetle. . . . So,] ~, ~: F
31. bond] F (band)

43. least] F (lest)

45. serve] F *corr.* (serue); seure F *un-corr.*

49. Fare thee] F *corr.* (fare thee); farethee F *uncorr.*

59. the full of tide] F *corr.*; the of full tide F *uncorr.*

63. that∧ . . . horse;] F *corr.* (~∧ . . . ~,); ~, . . . ~∧ F *uncorr.*

71. wept] Ed.; weepe F

77. I∧ let you] F *corr.*; I, let ʌou F *uncorr.*

**3.3**   6. pleased] F *corr.* (pleas'd); plaes'd F *uncorr.*

21. speak. . . . voiced] F *corr.* (speake, . . . voic'd); speake∧ . . . voic'c F *uncorr.*

27. looked'st] Ed.; look'st F

**3.4**   6. me;] ~, F

7. honor,] ~: F

8. them] Ed.; then F

8. measure∧ . . . me;] ~: . . . ~, F

9. him,] ~: F

9. took 't] Ed.; look't F

26. yours] F2; your F

33. Your] F2; You F

35. solder] F (soader)

41. has] F2; he's F

**3.5**   14. world, thou hast] Ed.; would thou hadst F

14. chaps, no more,] chapsn o more, F

16. grind the one] Ed.; grinde F

**3.6**   14. he there] Ed.; hither F

14. kings] Ed.; King F

18. habiliments] F (abiliments)

20. reported,] ~∧ F

31. triumvirate] F (Triumpherate)

32. being, that∧] ~∧ ~, F
45. lord] F (L.)

**3.7**    6. Is 't not∧] Ed.; If not, F
46. muleteers] F (Militers)
65. Actium] F (Action)
71. impossible;] ~∧ F
86. led] F (leade)
90. SP CANIDIUS] Ed.; *Ven.* F
101. in] Ed.; with F

**3.10**    0. SD *Enobarbus*] Ed.; *Enobarbus and Scarus* F
17. June] F2; Inne F
25. height] F (heighth)
33. he] F2; his F

**3.11**   20. that] Ed.; them F
37. struck] F (strooke)
45. unqualitied] vnqualited F
48. seize] F (cease)
62. tow] Ed.; stowe F
64. Thy] Ed.; The F
70. played] F (plaid)

**3.12**   16. lessens] F2; Lessons F
17. breathe] F (breath)

**3.13**   32. caparisons] Ed.; Comparisons F
40. alike.] ~, F
60. us, you know∧] ~∧ ~ ~, F
65. Caesar] F2; *Cæsars* F
79. SD *Enobarbus exits.*] Ed.; *Exit Enob.* F
91. deputation] Ed.; disputation F
113. me. Of late∧] ~∧ ~ ~. F
116. SD *Servants*] Ed.; *a Seruant* F, *1/2 line later*
130. This] Ed.; the F
131. errand] F (arrant)
141–42. eyes, . . . filth∧] ~∧ . . . ~, F

|       | 162. SD *1/2 line later in* F |
|-------|-------------------------------|
|       | 170. whipped∧ . . . him.] ∼. . . . ∼, F |
|       | 186. SD *Thidias exits.*] Ed.; *Exit Thid.* F |
|       | 199. smite] Ed.; smile F |
|       | 202. discandying] F (discandering) |
|       | 206. sits] Ed.; sets F |
|       | 235. SD *All . . . exit.*] Ed.; *Exeunt.* F |
|       | 240. on] Ed.; in F |
|       | 242. SD *He exits.*] Ed.; *Exeunt.* F |
| **4.1** | 4. combat,] ∼. F |
| **4.2** | 0. SD *Iras, with*] Ed.; *Iras, Alexas, with* F |
|       | 12. SD *1/2 line later in* F |
| **4.3** | 8. SP THIRD] Ed.; 1 F |
| **4.4** | 7. too] Ed.; too, *Anthony* F |
|       | 9. SP ANTONY Ah] Ed.; Ah F |
|       | 11. SP CLEOPATRA Sooth] Ed.; Sooth F |
|       | 19. daff 't] F (daft) |
|       | 32. SP CAPTAIN] Ed.; *Alex.* F |
|       | 42. thee∧] ∼. F |
| **4.5** | 1, 4, 9. SP SOLDIER] Ed.; *Eros* F |
|       | 8. Who's] F (Whose) |
|       | 25. Dispatch.] ∼∧ F |
|       | 25. SD *They exit.*] Ed.; *Exit* F |
| **4.6** | 13. SD *All . . . exit.*] Ed.; *Exeunt.* F |
|       | 14. Jewry] *Iewrij* F |
|       | 21. sorely] F (forely) |
|       | 22. more] F2; mote F |
|       | 39. heart.] ∼, F |
|       | 40. not,] ∼: F |
|       | 41. feel.] ∼∧ F |
| **4.7** | 3. *They exit.*] Ed.; *Exit.* F |
|       | 9. SD *Sound . . . off.*] Ed.; *Far off.* F, *after line 6* |
| **4.8** | 2. gests] Ed.; guests F |
| **4.11** | 0. SD *Caesar*] *Cæsvr* F |
| **4.12** | 1. yond] F (yon'd) |

3. 'tis] 'ris F
3. SD *Alarum . . . fight.*] *3 lines earlier
      in F, preceding "Enter Antony and
      Scarus."*
5. augurs] Ed.; Auguries F
23. spanieled] Ed.; pannelled F

**4.13**     13. death.] ~∧ F
**4.14**     5. towered] Ed.; toward F
13. dislimns] F (dislimes)
23. Caesar] Ed.; Caesars F
112. SD *Stabs*] Ed.; *Killes* F, *1 line earlier*
117. not.] ~, F
135. SD *All . . . exit.*] Ed.; *exeunt* F
172. SD *They exit.*] F (*Exit*)

**4.15**     28. Lest] F (Least)
30. me;] ~, F
31. operation,] ~. F
53. queen:] ~∧) F
63. lived∧] ~. F
75. soldier's] F (Souldiers)
86. e'en] F (in)
105. SD *off*] F (*of*)

**5.1**     0. SD *Enter . . . war.*] Ed.; *Enter Caesar,
      Agrippa, Dolabella, Menas, with his
      Counsell of Warre.* F
13. thou] F (yᵘ)
34, 39. SP AGRIPPA] Ed.; *Dol., Dola.* F
45. lance] F (launch)
57. SD *3 lines later in* F
62. all∧ she has,] ~, ~ ~∧ F
63. intents∧ desires∧] ~, ~, F
69. live] Ed.; leaue F
75. Lest] F (Least)

**5.2**     0. SD *Enter . . . Iras.*] Ed.; *Enter Cleo-
      patra, Charmian, Iras, and Mar-
      dian.* F

15. bade] F (bad)
18. queen] Queece F
29. dependency] dependacie F
40. SP GALLUS] Ed.; *Pro.* F
66. varletry] F (Varlotarie)
67. Egypt∧] ~. F
85. SD *1 line earlier in* F
100. little O, the] F (little o'th')
107. autumn 'twas] Ed.; *Anthony* it was F
127. success∧] ~: F
128. smites] Ed.; suites F
136. SD *Caesar, Proculeius*] Ed.;
       *Proculeius, Caesar* F
137. there!] ~∧ F
139. SD *Cleopatra*] F (*Cleo.*)
168–69. brief∧ . . . of.] ~: . . . ~, F
186–87. Thou shalt] F (y^u shalt)
189. soulless∧] Soule-lesse, F
213. merits∧ . . . name—] ~, . . . ~∧ F
234. thee] th e F
252. *He exits.*] F (*Exit*), *1 line earlier*
263. Ballad] F2; Ballads F
263. o'] F (a)
294. SD *Countryman*] this ed.; *Clowne* F
299 *and hereafter.* SP COUNTRYMAN] this
       ed.; *Clow.* F
378. awry] Ed.; away F
379. SD *Enter . . . in.*] Ed.; *Enter . . . in,
       and Dolabella.* F
410–11. diadem∧ . . . mistress;] ~; . . . ~∧ F
437. solemnity] Solmemnity F

# *Antony and Cleopatra:*
# A Modern Perspective

## Cynthia Marshall

Near the end of *Antony and Cleopatra,* the captive Cleopatra muses about her dead lover: "I dreamt there was an emperor Antony. / O, such another sleep, that I might see / But such another man" (5.2.93–95). Disregarding repeated attempts by Caesar's follower Dolabella to interrupt her rapturous description, Cleopatra finally asks him, "Think you there was, or might be, such a man / As this I dreamt of?" to which he replies, "Gentle madam, no" (5.2.115–17). In a realistic sense, Dolabella's answer is correct: Cleopatra has spoken of Antony as a Herculean figure who strides the seas scattering islands like coins, a figure of mythic proportion. Yet the force of Cleopatra's imaginative act, the vivid quality of her dream, suggests a limitation in Dolabella's technical accuracy. This exchange, testing both the status of heroes and the visionary capacity of lovers, is indicative of the play's preoccupations as well as its method of considering them. By repeatedly featuring conflicts between different points of view, *Antony and Cleopatra* functions not simply as tragedy, history, or *Liebestod* (a story of a couple dying for love) but as an inquiry into the historical, political, philosophical, and aesthetic grounds on which *any* story might be staged in the theater.

Because ancient Rome served as a model for Shakespeare's English culture, *Antony and Cleopatra* presumes an audience with some prior knowledge of Roman history. It dramatizes events from 40 BCE, when Rome was ruled by the uneasy triumvirate of Mark

Antony, Octavius Caesar, and Lepidus (established after the assassination of Julius Caesar), to 30 BCE, when the civil war that culminated in Octavius Caesar's defeat of Mark Antony at Actium destroyed the triumvirate. But if *Antony and Cleopatra* continues in a chronological sense from where *Julius Caesar* left off, it exhibits a strikingly different attitude toward its historical material. While the earlier play focuses on disputes internal to Roman rule, the later one is concerned with the politics of a vast empire spanning the Mediterranean. The arguments in *Julius Caesar* center on questions of political philosophy and civic duty, but in *Antony and Cleopatra* these issues are complicated by attention to spheres of erotic experience and family life that we now think of as private. A telling example of this transformation of attitude between the two plays is Cleopatra's reference to Antony's "sword Philippan" (2.5.27); previously used at the battle of Philippi, which concludes *Julius Caesar*, it is here employed by Cleopatra in erotic play with an Antony dressed in her "tires and mantles" (2.5.26). *Antony and Cleopatra* was written much later in Shakespeare's career than *Julius Caesar*, and in *Antony and Cleopatra* Shakespeare goes much further in probing beneath the surface of historical narrative and in questioning the terms on which heroic reputations were based than he had in earlier English or Roman history plays. Accordingly, the play has posed problems of generic classification and of response, for *Antony and Cleopatra* defies much of what we have come to associate with either a history play or a heroic tragedy: Antony shares the spotlight with Cleopatra, the point of view is uncertain, and heroic virtue is in scant supply. Even the play's structure, with its profusion of short scenes, its elimination of staged battles, and its extension for an entire act after the hero's death, challenges traditional notions of dramatic tragedy.

Like most of the characters in *Antony and Cleopatra*, Shakespeare uses the past to measure the significance of present events. Yet in this play he suggests that access to history is compromised not only by the viewer's belatedness but also by limitation of perspective and by the reliability of sources: witness Cleopatra's success in compelling from the messenger a personally flattering account of Octavia (3.3). Moreover, Shakespeare seems peculiarly aware of the extent to which historical narratives are shaped by myths and legends. Much as Plutarch, whose *Life of Marcus Antonius* served as the main source for *Antony and Cleopatra*, attempted to differentiate between myth and history while including both in his treatment of *Noble Grecians and Romans,* so Shakespeare offers mythic invocation alongside a chastening skepticism. Octavius Caesar nostalgically invokes the warrior Antony of bygone days who could "drink / The stale of horses" and feed on "strange flesh" (1.4.70–71, 77). Philo, in the speech that opens the play, compares Antony as a "triple pillar of the world" to "plated Mars" (1.1.13, 4). For Octavius and Philo, as for the other Romans in the play, Antony's descent from his former glory to the embarrassing spectacle of his passion for Cleopatra plays out another myth, that of sexual temptation and its destructive results, familiar from the tale of Hercules and Omphale. Antony himself frequently subscribes to this myth, lamenting his temptation to "lose [him]self in dotage" and resolving to break free from the clutches of his "enchanting queen" (1.2.129, 143). But a comparison between Antony's moments of despondency and his equally strong exhilaration in happy moments with Cleopatra—"Let Rome in Tiber melt and the wide arch / Of the ranged empire fall. Here is my space" (1.1.38–39)—especially as his passion is echoed and continued in her words, suggests that the romantic myth of transcendent love may be the strongest one the play has to offer. Nevertheless, if Shakespeare can be said to endorse the legendary love of Antony and Cleopatra, his method of doing so is distinctly odd: the love affair plays against a chorus of doubtful voices intent on puncturing the stability or accuracy of any enshrined romance.

This contrast of viewpoints is built on the play's central structural principle, a binary opposition between Rome and Egypt. The play's Rome, on the one hand, is a predominantly male social order encouraging individual discipline, valor, and devotion to the state. Egypt, on the other hand, is a looser society valuing sensual and emotional pleasure. By juxtaposing these two settings, Shakespeare highlights the cultural contrast. He also uses the opposition to create complicated patterns of judgment by positioning some of his characters as commentator figures. Philo and Demetrius in 1.1, or Scarus and Canidius in 3.10, offer Roman value judgments on Antony's Egyptian escapades; yet Enobarbus appreciates Cleopatra and Egyptian life and thus becomes a challenging conveyor of culture for the other Romans. Early in the play, another commentator, the Soothsayer, advises Antony that he will never thrive near Octavius. As Janet Adelman points out, questioning and judgment are central to the play's structure.[1]

As critics have responded to the play, Rome has traditionally been the winner in the implicit contest between Roman and Egyptian values. Bernard Beckerman notes how the audience is initially "invited to see events with Roman eyes, eyes that rarely see anything but the imperfections of Egypt."[2] Looking through Roman eyes has in fact led some readers to scorn the play altogether; for instance, George Bernard Shaw objected to giving "sexual infatuation" a tragic treatment it scarcely warranted.[3] Many have judged Cleopatra a manipulative, self-serving temptress or femme fatale; some have endorsed the enraged Antony's charge that she is a whore (4.12.15). But recent critical paradigms have made it possible to view the play through more or less Egyptian eyes, celebrating the feminine values exemplified by Cleopatra and the realm in which she reigns. Hélène Cixous, for instance, praises the "ardor" and "passion" of "she who is incomprehensible."[4] Although Cixous' praise is definitely for Cleopatra as a woman, the positive valuation she gives to incomprehensibility signals a breakdown of the opposition between Rome and Egypt. Cixous and other contemporary thinkers show that the either/or logic of binarism is itself a typically "Roman" pattern. Or to put their argument another way, Cleopatra's "infinite variety" (2.2.277) deconstructs an oppositional logic. Her femininity is not the logical opposite of Antony's masculinity but a disruptive counterpart that throws gender norms into question. Understood in these terms, Egypt does not so much contrast with Rome as reveal the limitations of Roman rule. Thus Shakespeare's portrayal of the relationship between Cleopatra and Antony, and of that between Egypt and Rome, illustrates what Jacques Derrida calls *différance*, the logic through which two terms are caught in irresolvable dependency on one another.

As a great encounter between West and East as well as a great love story, *Antony and Cleopatra* enacts a basic pattern of colonialism. Shakespeare draws on a network of stereotypes when he shows orderly, ambitious Roman conquerors confronting exotically decadent, emotional Egyptian subjects. Given the enormous indebtedness of Shakespeare's culture to the Roman world—Rome offered models for English politics, mythology, literature, architecture—one might expect the play firmly to endorse the Western system of values. That this does not quite happen is partly the result of the reiterated ironies against "the boy Caesar" (3.13.21), dismissed by Cleopatra as "paltry" in his pursuit of dominion, since "Not being Fortune, he's but Fortune's knave" (5.2.2–3). The play largely supports Cleopatra's assessment: Octavius is rigidly militaristic and chillingly manipulative. (Although the Romans regularly used marriage to foster political alliances, Octavius' bartering of his sister is disconcertingly set against the passion between Antony and Cleopatra.) In marked contrast to the title characters, Octavius not only lacks a personal dimension but appears simple-minded in his understanding of human affairs. He admits only a single aspect of Antony, measuring him as a heroic soldier fallen from honor to become "th' abstract of all faults," "not more manlike / Than Cleopatra" (1.4.10, 5–6). That Antony *has* lost his former heroism is as true, of course, as Dolabella's denial that Cleopatra's dream man ever existed. Yet few who read or see the play sympathetically would want to limit their assessments to the ones these Romans voice. Reassuringly familiar as the terms of Octavius' moral opprobrium and Dolabella's realism may be, the play offers pleasures beyond them. Neither love nor imagination will square with Roman virtue, and in pursuing these two themes Shakespeare subverts a victory of Roman over Egyptian values. Perhaps he was appealing to an English audience aware that their country was once a colonial "other" to Rome.

As a character, Antony embodies the opposition between Roman and Egyptian value systems; his story enacts the collapse of that opposition. He spans the worlds of West and East geographically, appearing in numerous settings in the course of the play's action, and he is torn between competing loyalties. After temporarily securing his political alliance with Octavius through marriage to Octavia, Antony abandons her, saying "though I make this marriage for my peace, / I' th' East my pleasure lies" (2.3.45–46). Officially representing a dominating Rome in Egypt, Antony has (to the dismay of his Roman partners) "gone native," adopting the mores of his conquered territory. As Dympna Callaghan points out, a tendency to become the other is part of Antony's character.[5] Fighting against barbarians, he reportedly endured "more / Than savages could suffer" (1.4.69–70); governing a luxuriously decadent territory, he immerses himself in sensuality. Cleopatra delights in Antony's complexity, praising his "well-divided disposition" (1.5.62), his "heavenly mingle" (69). For her, appreciating his value is a matter of perspective: "Though he be painted one way like a Gorgon, / The other way 's a Mars" (2.5.144–45). For Antony himself, however, the internalization of antithetical values becomes disturbingly disintegrative. He is repeatedly "robbed" of his sword (4.14.28, 5.1.29), first by Cleopatra, later by Dercetus—an emblem of his loss of masculinity. Masculine identity, by Roman standards, requires a coherency and stability that Antony's passion for Cleopatra dissolves, and as a result he shames himself, most memorably by following Cleopatra's ships at the battle of Actium. Caught between the rival demands to maintain Roman authority and to pursue his ardor for Cleopatra, he feels torn apart and compares himself to a shape in the clouds, feeling he "cannot hold this visible shape" (4.14.18). Even the heroic suicide that would offer a final image of cohesion eludes him; he falls on his sword like a "bridegroom" running into "a lover's bed" (4.14.120–21), and survives to utter the dismaying question "Not dead?" (4.14.124). Although he claims to

die "a Roman by a Roman / Valiantly vanquished"
(4.15.66–67), we are given the image of a lover's rather
than a hero's death.

Antony's decline clearly can be understood in moral
terms as a fall away from Roman grace, but Shakespeare
complicates this interpretation. Antony, more than Cleopatra, is the play's central object of interest and desire:
his Roman partners as well as his Egyptian lover yearn
for his presence and attentions. In Antony, Shakespeare
illustrates Plutarch's remark that "the soul of a lover
lived in another body, and not in his own."[6] Antony's
melancholic recognition that he does not own or control his existence undermines the oppositional morality
that produces heroic paradigms. It also deconstructs
the logic of colonialism, whereby a conquering power
eclipses another culture and/or set of values. Antony
instead becomes uncomfortably aware of the interpene-
tration of self and other in the various spheres of love,
politics, and ethics.

Watching the play or thinking about it as drama, one
realizes that theater too is able to break down established differences by encouraging emotional and imaginative connections. The complex interplay of voices and
viewpoints in *Antony and Cleopatra* requires us to do
something more difficult than merely choosing sides in
a moral debate. We are asked to participate in shifting
judgments—to follow Enobarbus, for instance, when he
is compelled by his disenchantment to abandon Antony,
only to be devastated by his captain's generous response
to his betrayal. "Be a child o' th' time" (2.7.117) Antony
advises the fastidious Octavius Caesar, and the play
likewise solicits our imaginative involvement. Yet the
spectacles to which we attend are riddled with comments that puncture the presented illusion. Cleopatra's
reference to the actor who will "boy [her] greatness"

(5.2.267) famously complicates her final defiance of Caesar. Similarly, her remark on lifting Antony's body to her monument—"Here's sport indeed. How heavy weighs my lord!" (4.15.38)—bizarrely compounds the meanings of *sport* and *heaviness*, calling a theater audience's attention to the sheer physical challenges of the scene being staged. A queen who can win admiration while hopping through the street clearly understands the seductive power of surprising mixtures of tone. Like a modern film star intent on maintaining her fans' fascination, Cleopatra defies an analysis measuring truth and sincerity, but she is anything but shallow. In her most profound moments, she reminds us of how devotion and delight can merge with sheer playfulness. Rather than asking viewers to suspend their disbelief, *Antony and Cleopatra* features characters who disbelieve their own presentations of experience and who somehow are all the more compelling for it. Shakespeare scours received myths with skepticism, and then audaciously presents them for his audience's admiring participation.

In acknowledging the flux of temporality, Antony's advice to "be a child o' th' time" implicitly points to the difficulty of representing historical events in a world of change. Shakespeare leaves unanswered questions about motivations and meaning instead of offering his version of the illustrious love affair as definitive. Moreover, the play effectively counters received history: even though Octavius Caesar was the acknowledged victor of the story, defeating Antony to become emperor of Rome, the play's final act presents not his triumph but Cleopatra's. With superb poise she stages her own death, collapsing time to become again the queen who first met Antony at Cydnus and merging death into new life ("Dost thou not see my baby at my breast, / That sucks the nurse asleep?" [5.2.368–69]). She achieves a magnificence that leaves Caesar looking like an "ass / Unpolicied" (5.2.364–65). In their final moments, both Antony and Cleopatra refer to an afterlife—"Where souls do couch on flowers, we'll hand in hand" (4.14.61); "Husband, I come!" (5.2.342)—although the play presents no sustained belief system to support these images of reunion. Instead, it offers theatrical apotheosis as the "new heaven, new earth" (1.1.18–19) necessary to demonstrate Antony's and Cleopatra's love.

Shakespeare returns in this play to a theme of *A Midsummer Night's Dream*, the capacity of erotic imagination to transform ordinary experience. But where the lovers of the earlier play were in the directive power of love juices, the mature lovers Antony and Cleopatra are fully conscious of devoting themselves to eros and of altering the course of history with their actions. Antony and Cleopatra make a claim for love as a force that dissolves established barriers, even established identities. Staging their story, Shakespeare makes a similar claim for theater.

---

1. Janet Adelman, *The Common Liar: An Essay on "Antony and Cleopatra"* (New Haven: Yale University Press, 1973), p. 14.

2. Bernard Beckerman, "Past the Size of Dreaming," in *Twentieth Century Interpretations of "Antony and Cleopatra,"* ed. Mark Rose (Englewood Cliffs, N.J.: Prentice-Hall, 1977), p. 102.

3. George Bernard Shaw, "Three Plays for Puritans," in *The Complete Prefaces of Bernard Shaw* (London: Paul Hamlyn, 1965), p. 749.

4. Hélène Cixous, *The Newly Born Woman*, trans. Betsy Wing (Minneapolis: University of Minnesota Press, 1986), p. 126.

5. Dympna Callaghan, "Representing Cleopatra in the Post-colonial Moment," in *Antony and Cleopatra*, ed. Nigel Wood, Theory in Practice (Buckingham, [Bucks.]: Open University Press, 1996), pp. 58–59.

6. Plutarch, *The Life of Marcus Antonius*, in *Narrative and Dramatic Sources of Shakespeare*, ed. Geoffrey Bullough (London: Routledge and Kegan Paul, 1964), 5:301.

# Further Reading

*Antony and Cleopatra*

Adelman, Janet. *The Common Liar: An Essay on "Antony and Cleopatra."* New Haven: Yale University Press, 1973.

In this influential book-length study of the play, Adelman argues that *Antony and Cleopatra* engages its readers and audiences in a constant struggle to achieve "right judgment," a dilemma both complicated and enriched by the play's many "moments of framed commentary." Most of these moments yield contradictions between the stage action of the protagonists and the glorious poetry used to describe them (e.g., the fissure between Cleopatra's elaborate dream of Antony in act 5 and his poor military decisions and bungled suicide enacted earlier). Almost every major action (such as why Antony marries Octavia when he plans to return to Cleopatra) is to some degree inexplicable, and nothing goes unquestioned. Further contributing to the "uncertainty that is an essential feature" of the play is the repeated use of hyperbole and paradox—two devices that are especially appropriate because they "gain our credence by appealing to our doubt." Adelman gives considerable attention to the Venus-Mars and Dido-Aeneas analogues, which Shakespeare drew on in fashioning the multiple identities of his protagonists. While most of the play insists on audience skepticism, the final scene invites assent through a secular leap of faith as we are asked to view the lovers as "semi-divine creatures" whose love transcends the temporal and spatial bonds of mortality. In *Antony and Cleopatra* Shakespeare suggests that "occasionally truth can be told only in lies."

Barroll, J. Leeds. *Shakespearean Tragedy: Genre, Tradition, and Change in "Antony and Cleopatra."* Washington, D.C.: Folger Books, 1984.

In the hope of deducing "something about the nature of all Shakespearean tragedy," Barroll makes *Antony and Cleopatra* the cornerstone of this study of the literary, historical, and philosophical backgrounds of Shakespeare's tragic dramaturgy. The volume consists of three parts: (1) "The Nature of Tragic Drama," which addresses the aesthetic arrangement of suffering and the dramatic challenge inherent in representing the human figure on stage without the aid of an all-knowing narrative voice whose commentary sheds light on character and event; (2) "The Tragic Person," which specifically focuses on Antony and Cleopatra as flawed characters deluded by their self-images as, respectively, the consummate soldier and "the most beautiful woman on earth"; and (3) "The Tragic Ethic," which takes up the issue of empire and conquest and the view from outside Rome. While the tragic protagonists are directly responsible for their failures, in the end we find "the comedy of triumph rather than the tragedy of failure" because what is underscored is "their mighty efforts to stay whole," not "their disintegration." Shakespeare's protagonists cannot tell us how to judge the events in which they are intimately involved; for that we must turn to the evaluative commentary of the "minor" characters who surround them. Consequently, the tragedy of a character like Antony "becomes the tragedy of his world too."

Barton, Anne. "'Nature's Piece 'Gainst Fancy': The Divided Catastrophe in *Antony and Cleopatra*" (1974 lecture). In *Essays, Mainly Shakespearean*, pp. 113–35. Cambridge: Cambridge University Press, 1994.
    Barton's focus in this essay is Shakespeare's use of the "divided catastrophe," a structural device that allows for a further development of the tragic action following

the death of the protagonist through an extended treatment of another character. In *Antony and Cleopatra*, by assigning Antony's suicide to the end of act 4 and devoting the entire fifth act to Cleopatra and her delayed death—a structure found in no other Renaissance dramatic treatment of the story—Shakespeare elicits and gratifies an unconventional longing in the audience for the death of a character who has not been villainous: we want Cleopatra to die because we want her to prove faithful to Antony. The love story of Antony and Cleopatra "has fluctuated continually between the sublime and the ridiculous. . . . Only if Cleopatra keeps faith with Antony now and dies can the flux of the play be stilled, and their love claim value."

Charnes, Linda. "Spies and Whispers: Exceeding Reputation in *Antony and Cleopatra*." In *Notorious Identity: Materializing the Subject in Shakespeare*, pp. 103–47. Cambridge, Mass.: Harvard University Press, 1993.
   In her study of the ideological foundations of "notorious identity" (the pathological form of fame) in *Richard III*, *Troilus and Cressida*, and *Antony and Cleopatra*, Charnes observes that Shakespeare is less interested in "reproducing cultural mythography" than in demonstrating what is involved in the experience of being repeated, that process through which each "notorious" figure confronts the determinant power of an infamous name as he or she fashions a new identity. Unique in the canon for its great number of messengers, *Antony and Cleopatra* is the Shakespeare text that most emphatically explores the "relationship between staging spectacle and 'controlling the press.'" Of all the legendary figures Shakespeare depicted, Antony and Cleopatra "achieve the highest degree of alterity to their prescribed roles." To reduce *Antony and Cleopatra* to a love story is to view

it only in terms of the protagonists' self-representation and Caesar's final tribute; the "central issue must be regarded not as what the love story is apart from the play's other discourses but, rather, what it does in relation to them."

Doran, Madeleine. "'High Events as These': The Language of Hyperbole in *Antony and Cleopatra*." In *Shakespeare's Dramatic Language*, pp. 154–81. Madison: University of Wisconsin Press, 1976.

Doran locates "the distinctive and controlling feature" of *Antony and Cleopatra* in the trope and mode of thought known as hyperbole, which informs the characterization, imagery, spatial dynamic, and key issue of the play: namely, "the world for love." She is particularly interested in the way Shakespeare juxtaposes "the golden threads" of a heightened style and "the plain, tough fibers" of direct speech so as to enrich and complicate rather than reduce images of greatness. Enobarbus' famous encomium to Cleopatra (2.2.226–81) best illustrates the playwright's "management of the hyperbolic and the actual so that the value of neither is destroyed." Shakespeare's favoring of hyperbole reflects the Renaissance pressure toward "the ideal, the excellent, the distinguished, the quintessential" in society, poetry, and history.

Drakakis, John, ed. *Antony and Cleopatra*. New Casebooks. Basingstoke: Macmillan, 1994.

Drakakis' collection of twelve commentaries (eleven reprints and one previously unpublished essay) is part of a new series designed to "reveal some of the ways in which contemporary criticism has changed our understanding of commonly studied texts and writers and . . . of the nature of criticism itself." The volume comprises the following essays: John F. Danby's *"Antony and Cleopatra:* A Shakespearean Adjustment" (from *Elizabethan and Jacobean Poets*), Janet Adelman's "Nature's Piece 'gainst Fancy: Poetry and the Structure of Belief in *Antony and Cleopatra"* (from *The Common Liar*), Phyllis Rackin's "Shakespeare's Boy Cleopatra, the Decorum of Nature, and the Golden World of Poetry," Terence Hawkes' *"King Lear* and *Antony and Cleopatra:* The Language of Love" (from *Shakespeare's Talking Animals: Language and Drama in Society*), H. Neville Davies' "Jacobean *Antony and Cleopatra,"* Margot Heinemann's "'Let Rome in Tiber melt': Order and Disorder in *Antony and Cleopatra,"* Linda T. Fitz's "Egyptian Queens and Male Reviewers: Sexist Attitudes in *Antony and Cleopatra* Criticism," Barbara C. Vincent's "Shakespeare's *Antony and Cleopatra* and the Rise of Comedy," Jonathan Dollimore's *"Antony and Cleopatra* (c. 1607): *Virtus* under Erasure" (from *Radical Tragedy: Religion, Ideology, and Power in the Drama of Shakespeare and His Contemporaries*), Marilyn French's *"Antony and Cleopatra"* (from *Shakespeare's Division of Experience*), Ania Loomba's "'Traveling Thoughts': Theatre and the Space of the Other" (from *Gender, Race, Renaissance Drama*), and Jyotsyna Singh's "Renaissance Anti-theatricality, Anti-feminism, and Shakespeare's *Antony and Cleopatra."* The essays either anticipate or exhibit the postmodern recognition of the instability of the playtext and the consequent refusal to impose a single, monolithic reading that tries to resolve all questions and contradictions. Drakakis observes that *"Antony and Cleopatra* is a text that submits itself to a variety of theoretically-informed approaches, partly because of its obviously dialectical structure, but also because it traverses a range of issues which have direct relevance to current questions of history, theatre, genre, race, gender, and politics."

Dusinberre, Juliet. "Squeaking Cleopatras: Gender and Performance in *Antony and Cleopatra*." In *Shakespeare, Theory, and Performance,* edited by James C. Bulman, pp. 46–67. London: Routledge, 1996.

In this performance study of *Antony and Cleopatra,* Dusinberre brings a feminist interest in power relations and gender transference to the study of the play's reception, focusing specifically on the implications for audience response inherent in the shift from a boy actor playing the role of Cleopatra to an actress in the part. From the Restoration onward the confusion of actress and role has been central to reactions to the play in performance: "A woman acting Cleopatra can never be simply a medium as the boy in Shakespeare's theatre arguably was. She is always a representative of her society's views on sensuality, and these views color her own interpretation . . . and the reactions of the audience." In Shakespeare's time the theatrical or performative energy informing the boy actor's capacity to upstage the male "stars" of the company (especially in the final act) eclipsed the medium of his male body. Consequently, there was no need to be preoccupied (as male reviewers since the Victorian era have been) with the figure playing Cleopatra as "the principal signifier of the anxieties and obsessions, pleasurable and less pleasurable, which dominate the audience who watches her." The actresses discussed by Dusinberre include Sarah Siddons, Ellen Terry, Isabella Glyn, Vivian Leigh, Peggy Ashcroft, Judi Dench, and Glenda Jackson.

James, Heather. "To Earn a Place in the Story: Resisting the *Aeneid* in *Antony and Cleopatra*." In *Shakespeare's Troy: Drama, Politics, and the Translation of Empire,* pp. 119–50. New York: Cambridge University Press, 1997.

James investigates the ways in which Shakespeare's dramatic translations of the Troy legend in *Titus Andronicus, Troilus and Cressida, Antony and Cleopatra, Cymbeline,* and *The Tempest* served to legitimate the cultural place of the theater in late Elizabethan and early Stuart London. The author contends that in *Antony and Cleopatra* the protagonists are acutely aware of an obligation "to promote or disrupt the stories in which their meanings will be recorded." "Seizing the Vergilian conventions through which they are recognizable as the legendary Antony and Cleopatra, the pair resist the characterological exhaustion planned by Caesar." Nowhere is this resistance more pronounced for Antony than in the five lines anticipating a blissful afterlife for himself and Cleopatra in which they will supersede "Dido, and her Aeneas" (4.14.60–64); here, Antony "defends his value of erotic love and protects his heroic exemplarity" by directly countering the derisive depiction of his choices found in the *Aeneid.* For Cleopatra, the ultimate resistance comes in her elaborately performed suicide in which she constructs her own myth of selfhood and in her "dream" of Antony in which she recomposes his heroic image. "Engrossed by the notion of playing to a court that is itself increasingly mimicking the theater," Shakespeare in *Antony and Cleopatra* invites his audiences "to join him in *imagining* the theater rather than merely attending it—to join in inventing the theater's cultural place."

Kinney, Clare. "The Queen's Two Bodies and the Divided Emperor: Some Problems of Identity in *Antony and Cleopatra.*" In *The Renaissance Englishwoman in Print: Counterbalancing the Canon,* edited by Anne M. Haselkorn and Betty S. Travitsky, pp. 177–86. Amherst: University of Massachusetts Press, 1990.

Kinney distinguishes between the gender-bound identifications of Cleopatra with the mutability and variety of Egypt, and of Antony and Caesar with the rigid and exclusive divisions of Rome. While Cleopatra answers to many names in the play, the one that captures her identity most fully is the name *Egypt*, which triggers in the hearer's mind "a kind of referential oscillation between the woman and the nation." In Cleopatra the monarch's two bodies—her private self as a woman and her public self as a queen—fuse in her embrace of "all possible versions of womankind, and the male principle too." Antony and Caesar, in contrast, never "embody Rome. . . . They are merely Roman"; and to be Roman is to exist only in a public capacity that leads to a fragmented and limited sense of self. Where others see a diminishment of Cleopatra in her death, opting as she does to die "after the high Roman fashion" (4.15.101), Kinney sees the continuation of the Egyptian self of complementarity, for the Serpent of the Nile chooses as her instrument of death another serpent of the Nile.

Levine, Laura. "Strange Flesh: *Antony and Cleopatra* and the story of the dissolving warrior." In *Men in Women's Clothing: Anti-theatricality and Effeminization, 1579–1642*, pp. 44–72. New York: Cambridge University Press, 1994.

Levine relates the New Historicist concern with the theatricalization of power to the issue of gender to argue that in *Antony and Cleopatra* "masculinity itself is presented as a theatrical construct[,] . . . a role that must be performed in order to exist." In Shakespeare's story of the "dissolving warrior," the performance of masculinity, however, proves malleable rather than fixed, always in danger of being transformed into the feminine. As a result, performance of the male self leads not to power but to a sense of powerlessness. The play exhibits the anxiety and fear informing the anti-theatrical tracts written at the end of the sixteenth and beginning of the seventeenth centuries: the anxiety that the convention of dressing boy actors in female attire would lead to a constitutive change in gender, and the fear that actions on the stage could lead audiences to engage in destructive behavior. Cleopatra's memory of dressing Antony in her "tires and mantles" and wearing his sword (2.5.26–27) illustrates the former, her scripted "mock" death (4.13.9–14) that drives Antony to his suicide (4.14) the latter. In Caesar, the mouthpiece of anti-theatricality who paradoxically longs for what he criticizes, Shakespeare offers a critique of the anti-theatrical position. The criterion that mediates the two sides of this dialectic is found in the last act as Caesar and Cleopatra compete to see who will "get the final performance, who will get the prerogative to stage her." In staging her own death, thereby defeating Caesar, Cleopatra performs and thus creates "a self." Theatrical expression, then, is required to allay anti-theatrical anxieties.

Loomba, Ania. *Gender, Race, Renaissance Drama*. Manchester: Manchester University Press, 1989, esp. pp. 75–79, 124–30.

Central to this feminist analysis of the sexual politics of gender and race in Renaissance drama is the idea that gender as a product of cultural conditioning determines the place of women in their society, with race functioning as a further qualifier of that position. Observing how *Antony and Cleopatra*'s many spatial shifts and geographic metaphors compress "issues of imperial expansion, political power, and sexual domination," Loomba considers the tensions between Rome as masculine and imperial and Egypt as its threatening "other," an alien territory with which and to which Cleopatra is geographically defined and confined. The Egyptian queen's "gender renders her politically unacceptable, her political status [as a female ruler] problematises her femininity, and her racial otherness [her blackness] troubles, doubly, both power and sexuality." Cleopatra's final subversion of the patriarchal construction imposed on her as "the white man's ultimate 'other'" comes in the fifth act when, recognizing that shared political power with Antony is no longer possible, she opts for "a politics of sublimation, rather than a transcendence of politics."

Mack, Maynard. *"Antony and Cleopatra:* The Stillness and the Dance." In *Shakespeare's Art: Seven Essays,* edited by Milton Crane, pp. 79–113. Chicago: University of Chicago Press, 1973.

   In this frequently cited essay, Mack describes the "unique metabolism" of *Antony and Cleopatra* as a "defiant pluralism" that results from Shakespeare's deliberate structuring of polarities (Rome/Egypt, nature/art, war/love, indulgence/austerity, etc.) in ways that resist neat schematization. A principle of "mutability and mobility" permeates every aspect of the play: the spatial and geographic shifts, the frequent change of scene, the iteration of farewells and reunions, the imagery (e.g., the ebb and flow of the tide and the rising and setting of the sun, moon, and stars), and numerous emotional reversals. Ambiguity and flux are essential to the characterization of the protagonists, neither of whom can be reduced to any one of the many names or categories assigned to them. Even the language resists logical expectations with its proliferation of oxymorons and paradoxes and its favoring of the optative mood, which grammatically expresses a world in motion (e.g., "Let Rome in Tiber melt"). Shakespeare countered all the flux and impermanence by imaginatively extending the love affair into the realm of allegory and myth through analogies to the Venus-Mars and Dido-Aeneas stories and through evocations of themes and conventions associated with the sonnet tradition.

Marshall, Cynthia. "Man of Steel Done Got the Blues: Melancholic Subversion of Presence in *Antony and Cleopatra*." *Shakespeare Quarterly* 44 (1993): 385–422.

Hank Williams, Jr., could have dedicated the song quoted in the title of this article to Antony since the play "dramatizes a version of the blues." Marshall draws on the psychoanalytic theories and constructs of identity and melancholy found in the work of Sigmund Freud, Jacques Lacan, Judith Butler, and Julia Kristeva to probe the relationship between Antony's melancholy (the blues) and his awareness of his dissolving identity as a "man of steel" (4.4.43). She argues that in the figure of Antony "the blues expresses the loss of control with which love threatens (but ultimately . . . enlarges) masculine identity." Central to the author's reading is an understanding of gender as performative and a questioning of "theater's complicity in producing the illusion of coherent subjects." The exchange between Antony and Eros in 4.14.1–14 "declares identity—both physical and psychological—to depend upon a spectator, thus suggesting the text's parallel between subject formation and theatrical process." Antony may be fascinated by Cleopatra's fluid identity, but it threatens "his need for an Other against whom he can solidify a self." Rejecting the traditional binarisms that posit Egypt as feminine and Rome as masculine, Marshall demonstrates how both Antony and Cleopatra display masculine and feminine characteristics. She further observes that "more clearly in *Antony and Cleopatra* than in most of Shakespeare's plays, the emphasis on gender is not secretly limited to the feminine."

Plutarch. *The Life of Marcus Antonius*. From *Lives of the Noble Grecians and Romanes*, translated by Sir Thomas North (1579). In *Narrative and Dramatic Sources of Shakespeare*, edited by Geoffrey Bullough, vol. 5, pp. 254–321. 1964. Rpt., London: Routledge and Kegan Paul; New York: Columbia University Press, 1975. [The entire section on the play's sources and analogues occupies pp. 215–449.]

Plutarch's life of Antony as found in North's translation is considered the primary source for Shakespeare's play. The dramatist borrowed extensively from Plutarch for his incidents, and on occasion from North for his phrasing (one of the most notable verbal parallels being Enobarbus' famous description of Cleopatra's mesmerizing appearance on the Cydnus). Shakespeare compresses the ten years that pass in Plutarch's narrative, making only veiled references to some important events (e.g., the difficult Parthian campaigns), omitting mention of others (the eight years' duration of Antony's marriage to Octavia and the children they had), and taking liberties with chronology (having, for example, the deaths of his protagonists occur on the same day). Characters like Iras and Charmian are developed from hints in Plutarch, but Enobarbus, who is merely a name in the source, is entirely Shakespeare's creation. Abandoning Plutarch's moralistic tone, Shakespeare makes his version of the story more than the fall of a great man, and his Cleopatra more than the instrument of that downfall. While suggestions of a dual attitude toward Antony and Cleopatra are present in Plutarch, it remained for Shakespeare to magnify the complexity of the lovers, imbuing them from beginning to end with paradox and ambiguity. Shakespeare supplemented his major source with material (which Bullough either reprints or excerpts) from Plutarch's *Life of Octavius Caesar Augustus* (North's 1603 edition), Samuel Daniel's *Tragedy of Cleopatra* (1599 edition), and *The Civil Wars* by Appian of Alexandria, translated by W.B. (1578).

Rackin, Phyllis. "Shakespeare's Boy Cleopatra, the Decorum of Nature, and the Golden World of Poetry." *PMLA* 87 (1972): 201–12.

Cleopatra's prescient awareness that, if taken to Rome by Caesar, she would be forced to see "Some squeaking Cleopatra boy [her] greatness / I' th' posture of a whore" (5.2.267–68) is central to Rackin's argument that *Antony and Cleopatra* dramatizes the clash between two views of poetry prevalent in the Renaissance—namely, that poetry imitates nature (and is thus subject to the dictates of decorum and verisimilitude) and that poetry (in the words of Sidney's famous *Defense*) creates a "golden" world beyond nature's "brazen" one. The interplay between these two notions of poetry and poetic truth are given voice and space in the Roman rationalistic reliance on measurement that discounts romantic rhetoric and spectacle, and in the Egyptian celebration of theatrical show and rejection "of a merely quantitative, reckoning standard." The "recklessness" inherent in the passage—i.e., precisely at the moment when she is about to stage her greatest show, beguile all, and "establish [her and Antony's] tragic worth," Cleopatra calls attention to the disparity between dramatic illusion and the reality of the theatrical convention in which a boy actor played the part—is the "keynote" of *Antony and Cleopatra* as a whole: the most obvious examples are its extensive violation of the unities of time and space, its episodic structure, and its tragic protagonists who are often rendered in a comic light.

Rose, Mark, ed. *Twentieth Century Interpretations of "Antony and Cleopatra."* Englewood Cliffs, N.J.: Prentice-Hall, 1977.

    This collection of important pre-1980 scholarship on the play reprints the following essays: Maurice Charney's "Style in the Roman Plays" (from *Shakespeare's Roman Plays: The Function of Imagery in the Drama*), Julian Markels' "The Pillar of the World: *Antony and Cleopatra* in Shakespeare's Development" (from the book of the same title), Reuben A. Brower's "*Antony and Cleopatra:* The Heroic Context" (from *Hero and Saint: Shakespeare and the Graeco-Roman Heroic Tradition*), John F. Danby's "*Antony and Cleopatra:* A Shakespearian Adjustment" (from *Elizabethan and Jacobean Poets*), John Holloway's "*Antony and Cleopatra*" (from *The Story of the Night: Studies in Shakespeare's Major Tragedies*), and Robert Ornstein's "The Ethic of the Imagination: Love and Art in *Antony and Cleopatra*" (from *Later Shakespeare,* Stratford-upon-Avon Studies 8). Also included are excerpts from *Prefaces by Bernard Shaw,* Northrop Frye's *Fools of Time: Studies in Shakespearean Tragedy,* Janet Adelman's *Common Liar,* and Maynard Mack's "*Antony and Cleopatra:* The Stillness and the Dance." Printed for the first time is Bernard Beckerman's essay "Past the Size of Dreaming," in which the author, using the first scene as a microcosm of the whole, finds the heart of the play not in its "sprawling spectacle" and epic sweep of political and military events but rather in the more intimate "subtle motions of thought and feeling passing between" the two protagonists. In the introduction to the anthology, Rose addresses the "rather special position" *Antony and*

*Cleopatra* occupies in the Shakespeare canon as the dramatist begins to move away from the tone, mood, and structure distinguishing his major tragedies and toward the defining characteristics of the late romances "in which love at last triumphs and things lost are miraculously recovered."

Scott, Michael. *Antony and Cleopatra*. Text and Performance Series. London: Macmillan; Atlantic Highlands, N.J.: Humanities Press, 1983.
   The first part of the volume examines the language, imagery, characterization, and dramatic action of the play under the following headings: the Queen of Love (despite all her inconsistencies, Cleopatra is "first and foremost" a queen), the divided self (i.e., Antony, who is torn between Venus/Eros and Hercules/Mars), the paradox of experience (to see the play's contrasts solely in terms of "moral polarities" is to misread the text), and Cleopatra's death (a scene "crucial in bringing together the theme, purpose and theatricality that have pervaded the work"). The second part of the book provides an overview of the play's performance history from the seventeenth century to 1982, with special attention to the Antonys and Cleopatras of Laurence Olivier and Vivian Leigh (the Michael Benthall/Olivier 1951 London and New York revival), Richard Johnson and Janet Suzman (Trevor Nunn's 1972 Royal Shakespeare Company [RSC] staging), Alan Howard and Glenda Jackson (Peter Brook's 1978 RSC production), and Colin Blakely and Jane Lapotaire (Jonathan Miller's 1980 BBC version). A postscript deals with Adrian Noble's 1982 RSC production at The Other Place with Helen Mirren and Michael Gambon.

Simmons, J. L. "*Antony and Cleopatra:* New Heaven, New Earth." In *Shakespeare's Pagan World: The Roman Tragedies,* pp. 109–63. Charlottesville: University Press of Virginia, 1973.

In an attempt to reconcile the idealistic poetry of *Antony and Cleopatra* with the realistic action that often undercuts it, Simmons posits a tragedy embedded in a comic structure. Drawing on the work of Northrop Frye and C. L. Barber, the author sees Egypt as a green world of liberation and Saturnalian festival that releases its inhabitants from the pressures of time and the rigid conventions and laws of Roman society. The worlds of Egypt and Rome thus find their analogues in the Belmont and Venice of *The Merchant of Venice*, the forest and court of *A Midsummer Night's Dream* and *As You Like It*, and the tavern and court of the *Henry IV* plays. What makes *Antony and Cleopatra* a "delightful tragedy" is Cleopatra's triumphant death, but even in the final scene the play's conflict between love's idealistic aspirations ("new heaven, new earth") and imperfect reality ("the dungy earth") continues. In the mingling of the tragic and comic, it is appropriate that a clown should bring on the means of death. Reminiscent of the heroines of Shakespeare's romantic comedies, Cleopatra steps forward at the end "like the queen of comedy, arranging the happy ending of marriage and winning the admiration and approval of the Roman world's highest moral sense." Love and honor are reconciled and the lovers are granted the immortality that comes with "the height of fame."

Wofford, Susanne, ed. *Shakespeare's Late Tragedies: A Collection of Critical Essays*. Englewood Cliffs, N.J.: Prentice-Hall, 1996.

This anthology of new perspectives on *Macbeth, Coriolanus,* and *Antony and Cleopatra* includes five post-1980 critical studies of *Antony* that relate the play to its early-seventeenth-century and twentieth-century cultural and political contexts: Jonathan Dollimore's "*Antony and*

*Cleopatra* (c. 1607): *Virtus* under Erasure" (from *Radical Tragedy: Religion, Ideology, and Power in the Drama of Shakespeare and His Contemporaries*), Heather James' "The Politics of Display and the Anamorphic Subjects of *Antony and Cleopatra*" (the basis for the chapter from her book *Shakespeare's Troy: Drama, Politics, and the Translation of Empire* cited above), Ania Loomba's "Theatre and the Space of the Other in *Antony and Cleopatra*" (from *Gender, Race, Renaissance Drama*), Michael Goldman's "*Antony and Cleopatra*: Action as Imaginative Command" (from *Acting and Action in Shakespearean Tragedy*), and Barbara Hodgdon's " 'Doing the Egyptian': Critical/Theatrical Performances, Oxford and London, 1906" (from *Restaging Shakespeare's Cultural Capital: Women, Queens, Spectatorship*). In her introductory essay, Wofford explores dismemberment as "the principal political and figurative action" of the late tragedies: "If [*Macbeth* and *Coriolanus*] show why the tragic protagonist might need to escape suffocating or destructive totalities even at the risk of complete loss of self, *Antony and Cleopatra* can be read as a play that re-members and re-collects the dissevered tragic body in part by reimagining tragic dismemberment and the scattering of the self as bounty."

Wood, Nigel, ed. *Antony and Cleopatra*. Theory in Practice. Buckingham, [Bucks.]: Open University Press, 1996.

  As part of a series intended to bridge the gap between theory and practice, the four essays in this volume offer distinct readings of *Antony and Cleopatra* derived from particular schools of contemporary literary criticism: Barbara J. Baines employs René Girard's theory of mimesis in "Girard's Doubles and *Antony and Cleopatra*"; Dympna Callaghan applies Gayatri Chakravorty

Spivak's interweaving of issues of race, class, and gender in "Representing Cleopatra in the Post-colonial Moment"; Mary Hamer draws on Luce Irigaray's study of feminist otherness in "Reading *Antony and Cleopatra* through Irigaray's Speculum"; and Robert Wilcher takes up the complex question of genre (specifically citing the work of Ferdinand de Saussure, Jonathan Culler, Alastair Fowler, E. D. Hirsch, Jr., and Northrop Frye) in "*Antony and Cleopatra* and Genre Criticism."

Worthen, W. B. "The Weight of Antony: Staging 'Character' in *Antony and Cleopatra.*" *Studies in English Literature 1500–1900* 26 (1986): 295–308.

Worthen uses the monument scene (4.15) to focus his argument that throughout *Antony and Cleopatra* Shakespeare forces audience attention "to the means of theater . . . as part of our attention to the drama itself." Antony in this scene and Cleopatra in her elaborately staged suicide compel our engagement in the complex dynamic between the materiality of the individual actor and his style of acting, the role itself (i.e., the sequence of actions performed), and the "character" (i.e., the fictive identity described in the narrative text, which is often at odds with the role in performance). In the physical act of hoisting a full-grown man ten or twelve feet in the air (if indeed this was the manner of staging), Antony is "momentarily suspended between legendary greatness and its tragic acting, his body resisting the Roman gesture and its lofty rhetoric while it gains an affecting weight of its own." Throughout the play Shakespeare seems to italicize the tension between text (the "narrative character" retrospectively reconstructed) and performance ("the actor's histrionic characterization"): i.e., the likelihood that the "performed character" of the actor will be inadequate to the "markedly ideal or ironic 'character'" established in the narrative text. In *Antony and Cleopatra,* Shakespeare "invites us to weigh both the story and its acting, and to find in the case of these huge spirits the specific gravity of the stage."

## Shakespeare's Language

Abbott, E. A. *A Shakespearian Grammar.* New York: Haskell House, 1972.

This compact reference book, first published in 1870, helps with many difficulties in Shakespeare's language. It systematically accounts for a host of differences between Shakespeare's usage and sentence structure and our own.

Blake, Norman. *Shakespeare's Language: An Introduction.* New York: St. Martin's Press, 1983.

This general introduction to Elizabethan English discusses various aspects of the language of Shakespeare and his contemporaries, offering possible meanings for hundreds of ambiguous constructions.

Dobson, E. J. *English Pronunciation, 1500–1700.* 2 vols. Oxford: Clarendon Press, 1968.

This long and technical work includes chapters on spelling (and its reformation), phonetics, stressed vowels, and consonants in early modern English.

Houston, John. *Shakespearean Sentences: A Study in Style and Syntax.* Baton Rouge: Louisiana State University Press, 1988.

Houston studies Shakespeare's stylistic choices, considering matters such as sentence length and the relative positions of subject, verb, and direct object.

Examining plays throughout the canon in a roughly chronological, developmental order, he analyzes how sentence structure is used in setting tone, in characterization, and for other dramatic purposes.

Onions, C. T. *A Shakespeare Glossary*. Oxford: Clarendon Press, 1986.

This revised edition updates Onions' standard, selective glossary of words and phrases in Shakespeare's plays that are now obsolete, archaic, or obscure.

Robinson, Randal. *Unlocking Shakespeare's Language: Help for the Teacher and Student*. Urbana, Ill.: National Council of Teachers of English and the ERIC Clearinghouse on Reading and Communication Skills, 1989.

Specifically designed for the high-school and undergraduate college teacher and student, Robinson's book addresses the problems that most often hinder present-day readers of Shakespeare. Through work with his own students, Robinson found that many readers today are particularly puzzled by such stylistic devices as subject-verb inversion, interrupted structures, and compression. He shows how our own colloquial language contains comparable structures, and thus helps students recognize such structures when they find them in Shakespeare's plays. This book supplies worksheets— with examples from major plays—to illuminate and remedy such problems as unusual sequences of words and the separation of related parts of sentences.

Williams, Gordon. *A Dictionary of Sexual Language and Imagery in Shakespearean and Stuart Literature*. 3 vols. London: Athlone Press, 1994.

Williams provides a comprehensive list of the words to which Shakespeare, his contemporaries, and later Stuart writers gave sexual meanings. He supports his identification of these meanings by extensive quotations.

## Shakespeare's Life

Baldwin, T. W. *William Shakspere's Petty School*. Urbana: University of Illinois Press, 1943.

Baldwin here investigates the theory and practice of the petty school, the first level of education in Elizabethan England. He focuses on that educational system primarily as it is reflected in Shakespeare's art.

Baldwin, T. W. *William Shakspere's Small Latine and Lesse Greeke*. 2 vols. Urbana: University of Illinois Press, 1944.

Baldwin attacks the view that Shakespeare was an uneducated genius—a view that had been dominant among Shakespeareans since the eighteenth century. Instead, Baldwin shows, the educational system of Shakespeare's time would have given the playwright a strong background in the classics, and there is much in the plays that shows how Shakespeare benefited from such an education.

Beier, A. L., and Roger Finlay, eds. *London 1500–1700: The Making of the Metropolis*. New York: Longman, 1986.

Focusing on the economic and social history of early modern London, these collected essays probe aspects of metropolitan life, including "Population and Disease," "Commerce and Manufacture," and "Society and Change."

Bentley, G. E. *Shakespeare's Life: A Biographical Handbook*. New Haven: Yale University Press, 1961.

This "just-the-facts" account presents the surviving

documents of Shakespeare's life against an Elizabethan background.

Chambers, E. K. *William Shakespeare: A Study of Facts and Problems*. 2 vols. Oxford: Clarendon Press, 1930.

Analyzing in great detail the scant historical data, Chambers' complex, scholarly study considers the nature of the texts in which Shakespeare's work is preserved.

Cressy, David. *Education in Tudor and Stuart England*. London: Edward Arnold, 1975.

This volume collects sixteenth-, seventeenth-, and early-eighteenth-century documents detailing aspects of formal education in England, such as the curriculum, the control and organization of education, and the education of women.

De Grazia, Margreta. *Shakespeare Verbatim: The Reproduction of Authenticity and the 1790 Apparatus*. Oxford: Clarendon Press, 1991.

De Grazia traces and discusses the development of such editorial criteria as authenticity, historical periodization, factual biography, chronological development, and close reading, locating as the point of origin Edmond Malone's 1790 edition of Shakespeare's works. There are interesting chapters on the First Folio and on the "legendary" versus the "documented" Shakespeare.

Dutton, Richard. *William Shakespeare: A Literary Life*. New York: St. Martin's Press, 1989.

Not a biography in the traditional sense, Dutton's very readable work nevertheless "follows the contours of Shakespeare's life" as he examines Shakespeare's career as playwright and poet, with consideration of his patrons, theatrical associations, and audience.

Fraser, Russell. *Young Shakespeare*. New York: Columbia University Press, 1988.

Fraser focuses on Shakespeare's first thirty years, paying attention simultaneously to his life and art.

Schoenbaum, S. *William Shakespeare: A Compact Documentary Life*. New York: Oxford University Press, 1977.

This standard biography economically presents the essential documents from Shakespeare's time in an accessible narrative account of the playwright's life.

## Shakespeare's Theater

Bentley, G. E. *The Profession of Player in Shakespeare's Time, 1590–1642*. Princeton: Princeton University Press, 1984.

Bentley readably sets forth a wealth of evidence about performance in Shakespeare's time, with special attention to the relations between player and company, and the business of casting, managing, and touring.

Berry, Herbert. *Shakespeare's Playhouses*. New York: AMS Press, 1987.

Berry's six essays collected here discuss (with illustrations) varying aspects of the four playhouses in which Shakespeare had a financial stake: the Theatre in Shoreditch, the Blackfriars, and the first and second Globe.

Cook, Ann Jennalie. *The Privileged Playgoers of Shakespeare's London*. Princeton: Princeton University Press, 1981.

Cook's work argues, on the basis of sociological, economic, and documentary evidence, that Shakespeare's audience—and the audience for English Renaissance drama generally—consisted mainly of the "privileged."

Greg, W. W. *Dramatic Documents from the Elizabethan Playhouses.* 2 vols. Oxford: Clarendon Press, 1931.
    Greg itemizes and briefly describes many of the play manuscripts that survive from the period 1590 to around 1660, including, among other things, players' parts. His second volume offers facsimiles of selected manuscripts.

Gurr, Andrew. *Playgoing in Shakespeare's London.* Cambridge: Cambridge University Press, 1987.
    Gurr charts how the theatrical enterprise developed from its modest beginnings in the late 1560s to become a thriving institution in the 1600s. He argues that there were important changes over the period 1567–1644 in the playhouses, the audience, and the plays.

Harbage, Alfred. *Shakespeare's Audience.* New York: Columbia University Press, 1941.
    Harbage investigates the fragmentary surviving evidence to interpret the size, composition, and behavior of Shakespeare's audience.

Hattaway, Michael. *Elizabethan Popular Theatre: Plays in Performance.* London: Routledge & Kegan Paul, 1982.
    Beginning with a study of the popular drama of the late Elizabethan age—a description of the stages, performance conditions, and acting of the period—this volume concludes with an analysis of five well-known plays of the 1590s, one of them (*Titus Andronicus*) by Shakespeare.

Shapiro, Michael. *Children of the Revels: The Boy Companies of Shakespeare's Time and Their Plays.* New York: Columbia University Press, 1977.

Shapiro chronicles the history of the amateur and quasi-professional child companies that flourished in London at the end of Elizabeth's reign and the beginning of James'.

## The Publication of Shakespeare's Plays

Blayney, Peter. *The First Folio of Shakespeare*. Hanover, Md.: Folger, 1991.

Blayney's accessible account of the printing and later life of the First Folio—an amply illustrated catalog to a 1991 Folger Shakespeare Library exhibition—analyzes the mechanical production of the First Folio, describing how the Folio was made, by whom and for whom, how much it cost, and its ups and downs (or, rather, downs and ups) since its printing in 1623.

Hinman, Charlton. *The Norton Facsimile: The First Folio of Shakespeare*. 2nd ed. New York: W. W. Norton, 1996.

This facsimile presents a photographic reproduction of an "ideal" copy of the First Folio of Shakespeare; Hinman attempts to represent each page in its most fully corrected state. The second edition includes an important new introduction by Peter Blayney.

Hinman, Charlton. *The Printing and Proof-Reading of the First Folio of Shakespeare*. 2 vols. Oxford: Clarendon Press, 1963.

In the most arduous study of a single book ever undertaken, Hinman attempts to reconstruct how the Shakespeare First Folio of 1623 was set into type and run off the press, sheet by sheet. He also provides almost all the known variations in readings from copy to copy.

# Key to
# Famous Lines and Phrases

There's beggary in the love that can be reckoned.
[Antony—1.1.16]

Let Rome in Tiber melt and the wide arch
Of the ranged empire fall. Here is my space.
[Antony—1.1.38–39]

Who tells me true, though in his tale lie death,
I hear him as he flattered.    [Antony—1.2.105–6]

Eternity was in our lips and eyes,
Bliss in our brows' bent.    [Cleopatra—1.3.44–45]

     My salad days,
When I was green in judgment, cold in blood.
[Cleopatra—1.5.88–89]

The barge she sat in like a burnished throne
Burned on the water. . . .    [Enobarbus—2.2.227 ff.]

Age cannot wither her, nor custom stale
Her infinite variety.    [Enobarbus—2.2.276–77]

Her tongue will not obey her heart, nor can
Her heart inform her tongue—the swan's-down
  feather
That stands upon the swell at the full of tide
And neither way inclines.    [Antony—3.2.56–60]

We have kissed away
Kingdoms and provinces.

[*Scarus*—3.10.9–10]

O, this false soul of Egypt! This grave charm, . . .
Like a right gypsy hath at fast and loose
Beguiled me to the very heart of loss.—

[*Antony*—4.12.27–32]

Unarm, Eros. The long day's task is done,
And we must sleep.    [*Antony*—4.14.44–45]

We'll bury him; and then, what's brave, what's
   noble,
Let's do 't after the high Roman fashion
And make death proud to take us.

[*Cleopatra*—4.15.99–102]

Finish, good lady. The bright day is done,
And we are for the dark.    [*Iras*—5.2.232–33]

Give me my robe. Put on my crown. I have
Immortal longings in me.    [*Cleopatra*—5.2.335–36]

      . . . she looks like sleep,
As she would catch another Antony
In her strong toil of grace.    [*Caesar*—5.2.415–17]